# *Floorwork,*
# *Basic Acrobatics*

# ADVANCED LABANOTATION SERIES

## EDITOR
### Ann Hutchinson Guest
Director, Language of Dance® Centre, London, UK

### Vol. 1, 1:
*Canon Forms*
by Ann Hutchinson Guest
and Rob van Haarst

### Vol. 1, 2:
*Shape, Design, Trace Patterns*
by Ann Hutchinson Guest
and Rob van Haarst

### Vol. 1, 3:
*Kneeling, Sitting, Lying*
by Ann Hutchinson Guest
and Rob van Haarst

### Issue 4:
*Sequential Movements*
by Ann Hutchinson Guest
and Joukje Kolff

### Issue 5:
*Hands, Fingers*
by Ann Hutchinson Guest
and Joukje Kolff

### Issue 6:
*Floorwork, Basic Acrobatics*
by Ann Hutchinson Guest
and Joukje Kolff

### Issue 7:
*Center of Weight*
by Ann Hutchinson Guest
and Joukje Kolff

### Issue 8:
*Handling of Objects, Props*
by Ann Hutchinson Guest
and Joukje Kolff

### Issue 9:
*Spatial Variations*
by Ann Hutchinson Guest,
and Joukje Kolff

# *Floorwork,*
# *Basic Acrobatics*

BY

**ANN HUTCHINSON GUEST**

AND

**JOUKJE KOLFF**

DANCE
BOOKS

Dance Books Ltd,
4 Lenten Street, Alton, Hampshire GU34 1HG

Printed in the United Kingdom by H. Charlesworth & Co.,
Huddersfield

ISBN: 1 85273 093 5

This book was written and produced at the Language of Dance® Centre:
    The Language of Dance® Centre
    17 Holland Park
    London W11 3TD
    United Kingdom
    T: +44 (0)20 7229 3780
    F: +44 (0)20 7792 1794
    web: http://www.lodc.org
    e-mail: info@lodc.org

Ann Hutchinson Guest

Joukje Kolff

# Contents

Introduction to the Series   xiii

Preface   xv

Acknowledgements   xvii

I   SUPPORTING ON THE HANDS, ELBOWS, SHOULDERS AND HEAD   2

1   Supporting on the Hands   2
    Walking on the Hands   4
    Handstands - Level   8
    Supporting on the Fingers   8

2   Turning on the Hands   10

3   Supporting on the Elbows, Shoulders and Head   14
    Elbow Stands   14
    Elbow Stands - Level   14
    Shoulder Stands   16
    Headstands   16

II   'ON ALL FOURS' AND RELATED SITUATIONS   18

4   Mixed Support Situations   18
    Method A: Central 'Place'   20
    Method B: Isolated Body Part Signs in Support Columns   20
    Method C: Direction of Limbs to Clarify Supports   22
    Method D: Direction-from-Body-Part Indications (DBP)   22
    Method E: Split Body System   24

5   Method A: Central 'Place'   26
    Distance   26
    Relative Distance   26
    Exact Distance   28
    Disadvantages of Method A   30

6      Method B: Isolated Body Part Signs in Support Columns    32

         Straight Path    32

         Validity    34

         Circular Path    34

         Ad Libitum    36

         Circular Path Around a Focal Point    36

7      Method C: Direction of Limbs to Clarify Supports    38

8      Method D: Direction-from-Body-Part Indications (DBP)    42

         DBP - 'Place' Directions    42

         Distance    43

         DBP Examples    44

         Touching Gestures    44

         Point of Measurement    44

         Level    46

         DBP in Path Signs    46

         Order of Reference    48

         Rule 1    48

         Rule 2    48

         Writing a Position    48

         Writing Movement    50

         Previous Location    50

         Present Location    50

         Reference to a Static Support, *(i)*    50

         Previous Location of Same Body Part, *(ii)*    50

         Previous Location of a 'Lifted' Part, *(iii)*    52

         The Present (New) Location of Another Part, *(iv)*    52

         Divided Front    56

         Reference to Part off the Floor    56

9      Method E: Split Body (SB)    58

         Split Body Key    58

         Foot and Hand Positions    59

         Walking Patterns    60

         SB with Gesture Indications for the Arms    62

         Preferred Usage    62

10      Torso Directions - Inverted, Augmented, Sections    64

         Torso Directional Indication - Options    64

| | | |
|---|---|---|
| | Inverted Body Sections | 64 |
| | Clarification of Terminology: 'Crab' Versus 'Bridge' Position | 64 |
| | Augmented Body Sections | 66 |
| III | REVOLUTIONS OF THE BODY | 68 |
| 11 | Turning Around the Vertical or Spinal Axis | 68 |
| | Rule 1 | 68 |
| | Rule 2 | 68 |
| | Statement of Axis | 68 |
| | Turning on All Fours | 70 |
| | One-eighth Turn around the Vertical Line of Gravity | 71 |
| | One-eighth Turn around the Spinal Axis | 72 |
| | One-quarter Turn | 72 |
| | One-half Turn | 74 |
| | Change of Torso Direction | 74 |
| 12 | Somersaulting | 78 |
| | Somersault - Analysis | 78 |
| | Somersault Rolls | 78 |
| | Front | 80 |
| | Indication of Degree of Somersault | 80 |
| | Somersaulting in the Air | 82 |
| | Indication of Trampoline | 84 |
| | Traveling | 84 |
| | Somersault Written with Direction Symbols | 88 |
| 13 | Cartwheeling | 90 |
| | Cartwheel - Analysis | 90 |
| | Front | 90 |
| | 'Blind Turns' (Non-Swivel Turns) on the Hands | 92 |
| | Basic Notation | 92 |
| | Indication of Degree of Cartwheel | 94 |
| | Cartwheeling with Different Step Directions | 96 |
| | 'Diagonal Cartwheel' | 96 |
| | 'Forward Cartwheel' | 98 |
| | Cartwheeling in Sitting and Lying | 98 |
| | Cartwheeling in the Air | 100 |
| 14 | Somersault and Cartwheel Paths | 102 |

|  | Distance | 108 |
|---|---|---|
| 15 | Combined Revolutions of the Body | 110 |
|  | Analysis | 112 |
|  | Spatial Retention for Revolution or Path | 114 |
|  | Turn With Somersault | 116 |
|  | Overlap of Actions | 118 |
|  | Turn and Cartwheel | 118 |
| 16 | Other Axes of Rotation | 120 |
|  | Diagonal Axes | 120 |
|  | Degree of Rotation | 122 |
|  | Indications for Body Orientation | 122 |
|  | Range of Pins for Axes | 122 |
|  | Body Part as Axis | 124 |
| IV | CLARIFICATIONS | 126 |
| 17 | Distance | 126 |
| 18 | Use of Black Pins for Tracks | 128 |
|  | Tracks - Feet | 128 |
|  | Black Pins for Sagittal Tracks | 130 |
|  | Black Pins for Lateral Tracks | 132 |
|  | Sagittal Tracks for Knees | 134 |
|  | Sagittal Tracks for Hands | 134 |
| 19 | The Use of Track Pins | 136 |
|  | Definition | 136 |
|  | Normal Track | 136 |
|  | The Sagittal Tracks | 136 |
|  | The Sagittal Track Pin Signs | 136 |
|  | The Sagittal Center Lines | 138 |
|  | Track Pins for Leg Gestures | 140 |
|  | Track Pins for Vertical Leg Gestures | 140 |
|  | Track Pins for Sagittal Leg Gestures | 140 |
|  | Track Pins for Supporting on the Hands | 142 |
|  | Track Pins for Supporting on the Feet | 142 |
|  | Lateral Steps | 144 |
|  | Track Pins for All Fours | 144 |

|  | Diagonal Steps on All Fours | 148 |
|  | Lateral Steps on All Fours | 148 |
| 20 | Use of Columns | 150 |
|  | Floorwork Staff | 152 |
|  | Indication of Timing | 152 |
|  | An Example of Floorwork Staff | 154 |
| 21 | Validity of Support Indications | 156 |
|  | Category 1.  Supporting on the Feet, Knees or Foot-knee | 156 |
|  | Category 2.  Supporting on Other Body Parts or on 'All Fours' | 156 |
|  | Automatic Retention | 158 |
|  | Explicit Statement of Retention | 158 |
|  | Release by Indication of Gesture | 158 |
|  | Release by Indication of Action Strokes | 160 |
|  | Release by Indication of Release Signs | 160 |
|  | Weight Released, Contact Retained | 162 |
|  | 'Spot Hold' for Retention of Weight | 162 |
| 22 | Miscellaneous | 164 |
|  | Retention Signs and Pre-signs on Center Staff Line | 164 |
|  | Part of Foot Contacting in Mixed Support Situations | 164 |
|  | Layout | 166 |
|  | Carets | 170 |
|  | Same Spot Caret | 170 |
|  | Momentary Auxiliary Support | 172 |
| V | READING EXAMPLES | 174 |
| 23 | Supporting on the Hands and Shoulders | 174 |
|  | Supporting on the Hands | 174 |
|  | Supporting on the Shoulders and Other Body Parts | 176 |
| 24 | On 'All Fours' | 180 |
|  | Method A - Central 'Place' | 180 |
|  | Method B - Isolated Body Part Signs in Support Columns | 182 |
|  | Method C - Statement of Limb Direction | 185 |
|  | Method D - Direction-from-Body-Part | 186 |
| 25 | Turning | 190 |

| | | |
|---|---|---:|
| 26 | Somersaults, Log Rolling | 200 |
| 27 | Cartwheeling | 208 |
| | Cartwheel on Bar | 210 |
| | Cartwheel and Turn Combined | 210 |
| VI | APPENDICES | 212 |
| A | Track Pins | 212 |
| | Diagonal Tracks for the Arms | 212 |
| | Diagonal Center Line | 212 |
| | Lateral Tracks for the Arms | 214 |
| | Sagittal Tracks for Backward Arm Gestures | 216 |
| | Vertical Tracks for the Arms | 216 |
| | Further Subdivisions of Tracks for Arm Gestures | 216 |
| | Track Pins for Lateral Leg Gestures | 218 |
| | Track Pins for Diagonal Leg Gestures | 218 |
| | Track Pins for Diagonal Steps | 218 |
| B | Pins - when Black, when Track, when Tack? | 220 |
| | Black Pins | 220 |
| | Track Pins | 222 |
| | Flat Pins, Tacks | 222 |
| | Combining Black Pins and Tack Pins | 222 |
| | Pins for All Fours Situations | 224 |
| C | Table of Contents from *Kneeling, Sitting, Lying* | 226 |
| D | Historical Background on Labanotation Textbooks | 231 |
| Notes | | 234 |
| Bibliography | | 251 |
| Index | | 253 |
| Useful Contact Information | | 260 |

# Introduction to the Series

The <u>Advanced Labanotation</u> series provides a detailed exposition of the many topics introduced in the chapters of the 1970 textbook *Labanotation - The System of Analyzing and Recording Movement*. To make the material immediately accessible to the reader, each book in this series begins at a basic level, thus avoiding the need for immediate reference to other texts.

Within the series each topic is published independently as soon as it is completed in order to make the information immediately available. Topics for which there is at present a lack of information available, and those for which there is an immediate need, are being presented first.

Detailed theoretical exposition is supported by appropriate notated examples, and, where needed, figure illustrations of the movements and positions. A selection of reading materials from choreographic scores illustrates the different points, with the examples taken from various sources and styles of movement. Finally, a detailed index facilitates rapid access to required information and, for the researcher, extensive endnotes and a bibliography indicate background and sources.

# Preface

This issue aims to survey the ways of writing floorwork and basic acrobatics in Labanotation. The term 'floorwork' is a colloquial expression referring to any situation in which the body is supported on parts other than the feet or knees. Body positions and movements in floorwork often involve rolling of some kind, sometimes sliding, and changes of support, be it lying on parts of the torso, leaning on the elbows, etc.

The <u>Advanced Labanotation</u> issue *Kneeling, Sitting, Lying* discussed ways of lowering to the ground, body positions in which the body is supported on the feet and/or knees only, or on a part or parts of the torso (as in sitting or lying), and the transitions between these positions. The table of contents of *Kneeling, Sitting Lying* has been reproduced for the reader's information as Appendix C.

Floorwork sequences may use some form of 'all fours' (supporting on hands and feet or hands and knees) as transitions or for locomotion. Choices given for writing movement on 'all fours' reflect earlier theory as well as more recent analysis, the writer being given choices for particular needs. In each presentation of a form of movement, a simple, abbreviated form is provided as well as precise, detailed examples.

In addition to the main topics, both the present text and *Kneeling, Sitting, Lying* contain clarification sections on aspects of Labanotation that have a general scope but are particularly important for writing floorwork and basic acrobatics. In *Kneeling, Sitting, Lying* these sections dealt with *systems of reference, rolling and wheeling, timing, distance* among others. The present text has clarifications on *revolutions of the body using other axes, pins modifying direction symbols, the floorwork staff* and *validity of supports*.

# Acknowledgements

We are much indebted to the ground-breaking study on floorwork presented by Maria Szentpál in her Hungarian textbook (Szentpál 1969-76). In comparison to other areas of the system, Albrecht Knust (1979) is not particularly rich in floorwork examples but remains an authority on the fundamentals of the notation system.

For checking the drafts of this material and for actively taking part in discussions concerning issues and problems we gratefully acknowledge the help given by our consultants, Jacqueline Challet-Haas, Ilene Fox, János Fügedi, David Henshaw, Sheila Marion and Lucy Venable whose detailed and judicious comments contributed much to the correction and clarification of working drafts.

Our thanks go to Traute Molik-Riemer for contributing the many figure drawings and to Roma Dispirito for producing the Labanotation examples on *Calaban*. We are grateful to Helen Coxon for co-ordinating the compilation of the book and to Jane Dulieu who undertook the final review and proofreading with her keen eye for accuracy.

We are also grateful to the notators of the Reading Examples and to the choreographers for giving permission for use of these excerpts from their scores.

The many stages of production of these books would not have been possible without the generous support of the National Endowment for the Humanities, Washington, D.C., the Guggenheim Fellowship awarded to Ann Hutchinson Guest and a grant from the Arts and Humanities Research Board, London.

To conclude, we must also express appreciation to Andy Adamson who developed the *Calaban* software used to produce the Labanotation graphics.

# *Floorwork,*
# *Basic Acrobatics*

# I  SUPPORTING ON THE HANDS, ELBOWS, SHOULDERS AND HEAD

## 1  Supporting on the Hands

1.1.  In a handstand the body is supported on the hands only. This can be expressed very succinctly as in **1a**. No rotational state is given for the arms; the hands generally point forward when supporting with fingers spread. This is natural and practical for balancing. In writing a handstand the notation usually states explicitly the situation of the torso. Ex. **1b** shows that the torso is upside down. The same can be described in **1c** with an inverted torso sign, the context will usually dictate the choice. (For an explanation of inverted body sections see 10.3 or Hutchinson Guest 1970, p. 273.) To alert the reader to the inverted sign, the waist sign can be inserted, as in **1d**.

1.2.  In **1e** the inverted augmented body section from the wrists to the feet points toward the ceiling, illustrated in **1f**. Note that, when balancing in such a straight line, the natural curve in the spine is understood. The augmented body section is placed in the usual torso column as it includes the whole torso. (For augmented body sections see 10.9-13.)

1.3.  Ex. **1g** shows a general statement of direction for torso and legs in a handstand. In **1h** directions are more specific, the legs are not vertical but $^1/_3$ way *forward*. The arch in the back is a contraction of the torso over the *back surface*. Arching the back and bringing the feet forward from the hips (i.e. toward the direction into which the hands are pointing) is a familiar alignment used to maintain balance in handstands, as shown in **1i**.[1] In this 'upside down' situation, forward and backward are often easily confused. As shown in the illustration forward (F) is the direction in which the hands are pointing (and it is forward for orientation of Front, the main facing direction for the body-as-a-whole); the front surface of the torso faces backward (B).

1.4.  Ex. **1j** is a simple statement of moving into a handstand from standing. The torso leans forward as weight is taken forward on both hands, i.e. the hands 'step' forward (for level of such steps see 1.13). At the same time one leg begins to move backward and upward. The torso continues downward into the upside-down position as both legs move toward the ceiling. The end position for the torso can be written as chest-to-pelvis up (inverted torso) as in **1d**, but, as in the starting position of **1g**, the standard manner of getting into a handstand is easier to read. Another way to achieve balance in a handstand is to bring the pelvis in balance over the hands before extending the legs, **1k**, illustrated in **1l**.

## Supporting on the Hands

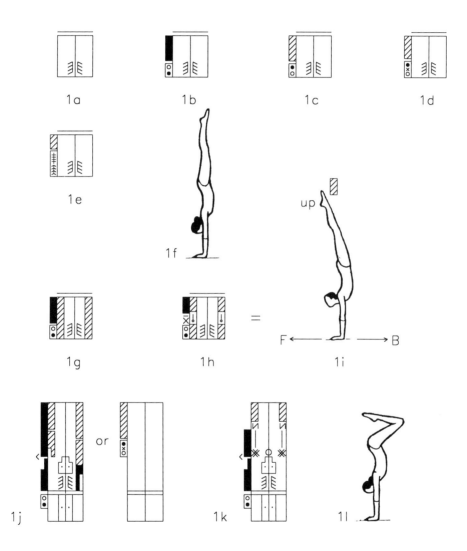

1.5. It is standard for the hands to be placed approximately below the shoulders, i.e. they are separated by the width of the shoulder area or may be slightly farther apart. For the hands the direction 'place' is under the shoulder. If another position of the hands is desired track pins or displacement pins (tacks) can be used to indicate intermediate locations. (For tracks and track pins see Sections 18, 19 and Appendices A, B.)

1.6. In a fourth position on the hands, as in **1m**, the right hand is more forward and the left hand more backward than in a standard handstand. Each hand is in its own track, as illustrated in **1n**. To be on line as if supporting on a pole, the center track pins must be added as in **1o**, illustrated in **1p**. Ex. **1q** is the alternate version, used before track pins were evolved.

1.7. **Walking on the Hands.** Ex. **1r** shows alternating support on the right and left hands while the body travels forward. This general way of writing forward walking on the hands is recommended whenever exact detail is not required. The traveling path shows the continuity. Since no distance is stated, a comfortable distance should be assumed. (For distance see Section 17.) Ex. **1s** is the same movement written using direction symbols. In each of these examples the weight ends on the left hand. Stepping on the hands 'in place' is shown in **1t**. Note the carets to indicate same part of the body. Each hand takes weight under its own shoulder, the weight shifts from hand to hand until count 5 when weight ends on both hands. For each of these shifts the balance in the body adjusts as need be. (For use of carets as in **1t** and **1v** see 22.14-18 and the <u>Advanced Labanotation</u> issue *Kneeling, Sitting, Lying* Section 38.16.)

1.8. In **1u** each hand is shown to release before it takes a step in place. Here the caret refers only to the same part of the body and does not indicate a shift.

1.9. In **1v** the right hand steps forward of where it was. On count 2 the left hand steps 'in place' under its shoulder; weight is now on both hands as in the starting position. The right hand then steps backward, the left 'joins' it, ending 'in place', weight on both hands. On the last count there is no change, no spring. This sequence is comparable to **1w** in which the same spatial pattern is performed on the feet (except that the hands step a shoulder width apart). In **1w** an additional hold sign is needed at the end to prevent springing from the feet, this is because of the basic rule that a gap after supporting on the feet means absence of support, go into the air. *This automatic springing rule for gaps in all support columns does not apply to supporting on the hands, thus in **1v** the weight remains on both hands.*

## Supporting on the Hands (continued)

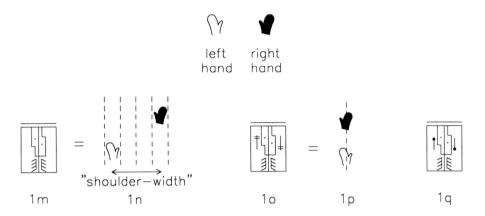

left    right
hand    hand

"shoulder—width"

1m          1n          1o          1p          1q

## Walking on the Hands

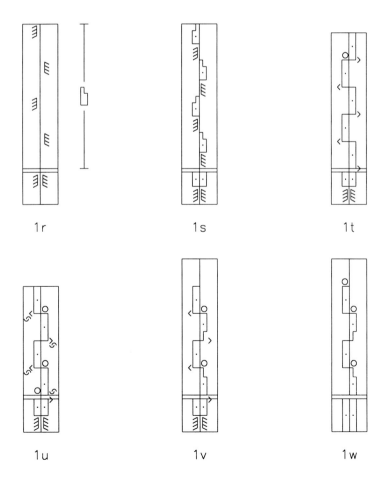

1r          1s          1t

1u          1v          1w

1.10.  The following examples are intended to clarify direction for hand supports in relation to the situation of 'place' (under the respective shoulder).  In the hand diagrams given below each example, the placement of the left hand (white) in relation to the right hand (black) is illustrated.  In the sequence of **1x** the right hand steps to the right (of its shoulder), the left steps into its new 'place' under the left shoulder.  This is then repeated, the hands end a shoulder-width apart.  Diagram **1y** below the notation shows the position reached on counts 2 and 4.

1.11.  A rocking movement occurs in **1z**.  The right hand steps to the side.  Instead of moving into place the left hand steps to the left bringing it more or less back to where it was before, i.e. where it started, causing this rocking to and fro.  This pattern is then repeated.  Diagram **1aa** shows the placement reached on counts 2 and 4.

1.12.  Ex. **1ab** is more specific, using Direction-from-Body-Part (DBP) indications (see Section 8) to show hand placement in walking sideward on the hands.  From a handstand only on the left hand the right hand steps sideward to the right of the left hand.  Note that this placement will be a comfortable distance sideward unless a longer or shorter distance is specified.  On count 2 the left hand steps exactly next to the right hand, as in a first position for the feet.  The sideward position sign (relationship pin) specifies the lateral placement leaving no gap between the hands.  The two steps are then repeated.  Illustration **1ac** shows the position reached on counts 2 and 4.  These step indications carry no information about level; the normally extended arm is understood.

## Walking on the Hands (continued)

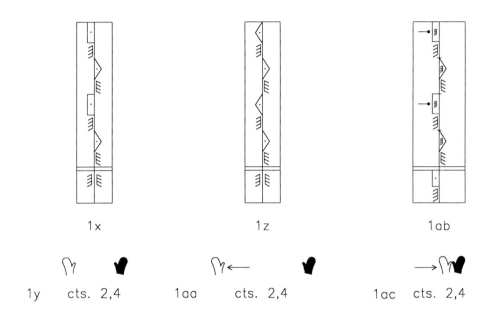

1x                              1z                              1ab

1y     cts. 2,4          1aa     cts. 2,4          1ac     cts. 2,4

1.13. **Handstands - Level.** When support on the hands is indicated without direction symbols, **1ad**, a handstand in middle level is understood, **1ae**. Indication of level in handstands is analogous to level in standing on the feet.

In *middle level* the hands are flat on the floor and the arms are usually extended (i.e. not in their normally relaxed, slightly curved state; straight arms help balance). This use of the hand is spelled out in **1af**[2], which specifies the whole of the hand surface being on the floor (indicated by the hooks used to show support on the whole foot). The hand flat on the floor is illustrated in **1ag**.

A *low level* handstand is written in **1ah**. The body is lowered through bending the arms (a slight arm bend provides more resilience), the hands are usually flat on the floor, this is spelled out in **1ai**. The degree of bend for the arm, comparable to the legs in standing, is indicated in the arm column. This position is illustrated in **1aj**.

In *high level* the arms are usually extended and the body is supported on the 'phalanges', the 'limbs' of the fingers, **1ak**. This is comparable to being on half toe on the foot and could be written as **1al**. The palm is lifted off the floor and the fingers may be slightly spread, as illustrated in **1am**.[3]

1.14. **Supporting on the Fingers.** Placing the signs for the fingers in the support column, **1an**, provides a general indication of supporting on the fingers.[4] It could, therefore, be performed as in **1am** or **1aq**. Because these finger signs can easily be misread for hand signs, use of statements such as **1ak** or **1al** can be more practical. Supporting specifically on the 'limbs' of the fingers is shown in **1ao**. Supporting on the pads of the fingers can be shown as in **1ap**, illustrated in **1aq**. This part of the finger(s) is commonly used when touching an object, as in checking wet paint. Supporting on the very tips of the fingers can be written as **1ar**, a counterpart to supporting on *pointe* on the feet, the hooks having the same meaning, i.e. on the tips. This can also be specified with the sign for the extremity of the fingers, that is, use of the four dots for each finger, as in **1as**. In the drawing, **1at**, the fingers are bent to achieve true finger tip contact. Supporting on one, two or three fingers could also be shown.

## Handstands - Level

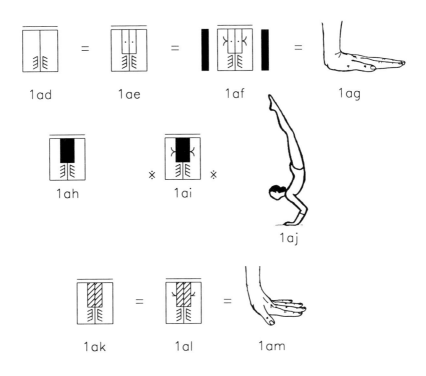

1ad = 1ae = 1af = 1ag

1ah 1ai 1aj

1ak = 1al = 1am

## Supporting on the Fingers

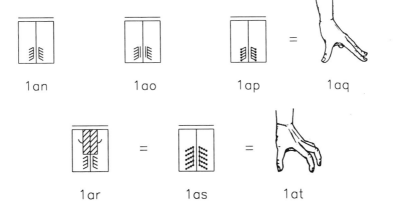

1an 1ao 1ap = 1aq

1ar = 1as = 1at

# 2   Turning on the Hands

2.1.  In the following examples a simple general statement of the handstand body position has been given.  All turns on the hands are assumed to be non-swivel ('blind') turns.[5]  When turning is anticipated, the hands are placed appropriately, i.e. with a preparatory inward or outward arm rotation, so that swiveling need not occur.  Unless gloves are worn, swiveling on the palms is usually uncomfortable.  This is comparable to placement of the feet when walking in a small circle with non-swivel steps.  Exs. **2a-j** illustrate turning, i.e. changing front while stepping (walking) on the hands.

2.2.  Ex. **2a** shows walking four steps forward on the hands on $^1/_4$ clockwise circular pathway.  This could also be written as **2b**.  In **2c** the same movement is executed on the spot, i.e. without traveling; no directions are given to indicate traveling.  In **2d** the steps are stated as being in place, hence again the performer remains over the same spot.[6]  To achieve this, s/he must step slightly backward on the right hand and slightly forward on the left, as illustrated in **2e**. The focal point around which one turns is the point between the two hands; any other focal point would need to be stated (see **6o-6q**).  Because support is on the hands, the turn sign placed outside the staff does not imply a swiveling action while turning.  Details of swivel or non-swivel must be added.

# Turning on the Hands

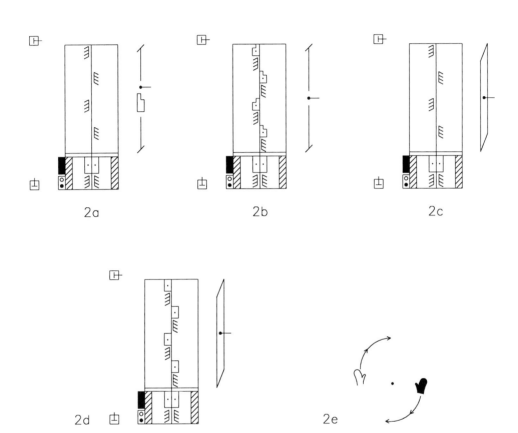

2.3.  In **2f** two steps on the hands are shown combined with a half-turn; the performer travels toward downstage with each step.  It is assumed here that turning is achieved as in a 'blind turn' by a preparatory rotation of the arm rather than by swiveling on the supporting hand.  Some overlap is indicated between the step and the turn of the body-as-a-whole.[7]

2.4.  Ex. **2g** spells out the understood performance of **2f**, except that in **2g** there is no overlap between the step and the turn of the body.  The preparatory $^1/_4$ outward arm rotation is shown here as well as the direction for the hand placement at the start of the step; both are not needed, one statement would suffice.  During the turning action the hand has a space hold and the arm rotation is cancelled.  For the left arm a $^1/_4$ inward rotation occurs which is then cancelled during the turning action.

2.5.  The traveling and turning of the previous two examples could be written more simply as **2h** (revolving on a straight path), for which, again, non-swiveling is assumed for the hands.

2.6.  Exs. **2i** and **2j** offer slightly different ways of performing **2h**.  In **2i**, $^1/_4$ rotation on the left hand occurs before the right hand steps, and another $^1/_4$ rotation on the right hand before the step backward on the left hand.  The non-swivel technique is spelled out here through placement of space holds for the hands next to the arm column.

2.7.  Ex. **2j**, which is similar to **2i**, shows **2h** performed with a $^1/_8$ blind turn on the left hand before the right hand steps, causing the step direction for the right hand to be diagonal.  Space holds have now been left out since blind turns are assumed.

2.8.  'Break' dancing occasionally includes swiveling on the hands.  As mentioned, for this it is convenient to wear gloves or to hold a pad of some kind.  (For Reading Examples see Sections 23-27.)

# Turning on the Hands (continued)

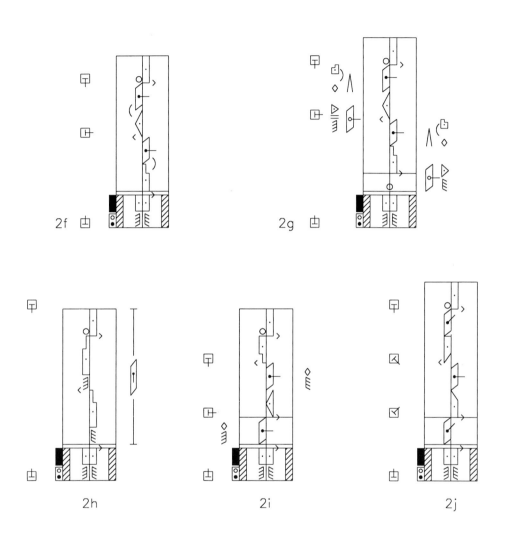

2f     2g

2h     2i     2j

# 3 Supporting on the Elbows, Shoulders and Head

3.1. **Elbow Stands.** In an elbow stand the notation convention is to show support on the elbows, even though in this position the lower arms and hands are understood to support the body and help balance. This is comparable to use of the lower legs and feet while kneeling.

3.2. An elbow stand can be written simply by placing the elbow signs in support columns, **3a**. It is understood that the body is up, in balance over the support, but it is usually desirable to give a general statement such as **3b** or **3c**. Note the use of inverted body section symbols in these examples.

3.3. As mentioned before, in 1.3, true verticality is less usual, since an arch in the torso helps maintain balance. The arch is spelled out in **3d**, illustrated in **3e**. Here the upright inverted torso is shown to be contracted over the back surface. The legs are balancing in what physically is a backward direction, but for the general orientation of the performer is in the forward high direction. Note the indications of F and B for forward and backward placed on the figure illustration for clarity.

3.4. **Elbow Stands - Level.** Levels for elbow stands follow the convention established for levels in kneeling. Usually an elbow stand is in *high level*, shown in **3d**, the upper arms being perpendicular to the floor (as in **3e**). In *middle level* the body is slightly lower because of a sharper angle at the elbow, **3f** illustrated in **3g**. In a *low level* support the shoulders are practically at floor level, **3h** illustrated in **3i**. In gymnastics low level elbow stands are known as 'chest stands'; although the chest may touch the floor, it does not support on the floor. In the examples the indication ' ≈ ', a sign used in mathematics, means 'equals approximately'; this sign can be viewed as a combination of the equal sign and the horizontal ad lib. sign.[8]

## Elbow Stands

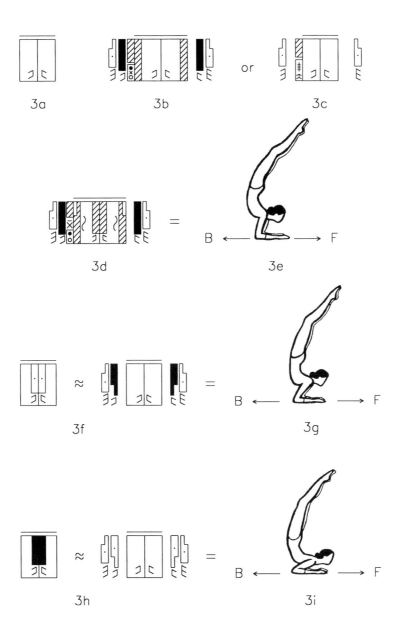

3a

3b

or

3c

3d = 3e

B ←——→ F

3f ≈ = 3g

B ←——→ F

3h ≈ = 3i

B ←——→ F

3.5. **Shoulder Stands.** A shoulder stand ('candle' position) is written in a simple version in **3j**, illustrated in **3k**. The more precise description for this support is given in **3l**. The arms are resting forward on the floor for balance. This arm contact with the floor is understood and need not be written. In this position the body is supported on the top upper part of the shoulder area, i.e., the shoulders and the area of the cervical vertebrae. Unlike handstands and elbow stands, in a shoulder stand the head is *backward* of the body rather than below it or forward. Consequently shoulder stands are closer to lying on the back, while hand and elbow stands are closer to lying on the front.

3.6. Ex. **3m** shows a transition from lying to a shoulder stand. The impetus is given first by the knees drawing up and then the legs swinging backward before extending toward the ceiling. At the end of the example the hands grasp the sides of the waist. The end position is easy to maintain because the trunk is kept in position by the hands. Also, in practice, the base of support is not strictly limited to the shoulder; as shown here, the backs of the upper arms may take some weight in helping to maintain balance. There is usually no need to write this.

3.7. **Headstands.** Supporting only on the head is very precarious. The hands are usually involved, if only for balance. In **3n**, illustrated in **3o**, most of the body weight is on the head; the hands help support. No specific placement of arms is stated here, but usually hands and head form a tripod.

3.8. Ex. **3p** shows a possible transition from standing, feet apart, to a position on hands and head.[9] The forehead is placed on the floor in front of the hands (this is understood, not written); the torso ends upside-down. Weight is then taken on the top of the head but also remains on the hands. *In supports on parts of the body other than on feet only, knees only and hands only, a new support does not cancel a previous support, a release should be indicated where needed.* Continuing with **3p**, the arms remain bent (low level support) as the legs reach their end position by describing an arc in the air. (See Section 21 for validity of support indications.)

## Shoulder Stands

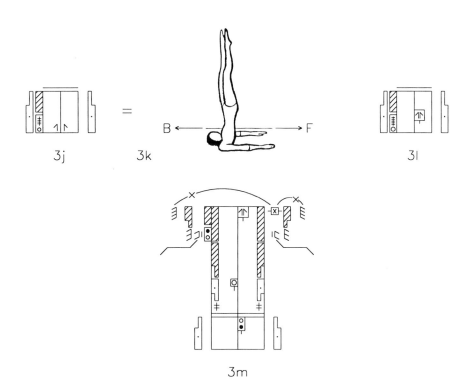

3j    3k    B ← → F    3l

3m

## Headstands

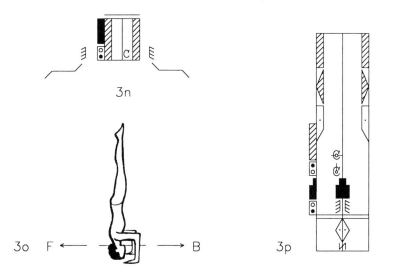

3n

3o   F ← → B   3p

# II  'ON ALL FOURS' AND RELATED SITUATIONS

The term 'on all fours' refers to the situation where the body is supported either on hands and feet, or hands and knees.  On occasion the elbows may be supporting instead of the hands.  From the point of view of Labanotation, these positions fall into the same general category as combinations such as standing on one hand and one foot, standing on the feet and one elbow, and many more similar situations, all termed for convenience 'mixed supports'.  Section 4 gives a definition of 'mixed supports' and a survey of different methods of description which can be applied.  Sections 5-8 investigate each of these methods more closely.  The methods are presented here in the chronological order in which they were evolved in the development of Labanotation, this does not suggest any order of preference.

# 4   Mixed Support Situations

4.1.  In the following explanations the term 'mixed support (situation)' is reserved for cases in which the body is supported

(1)   on one or two of the upper extremities (i.e. on hands or elbows) *and* on one or two of the lower extremities (i.e. on feet or knees).  Standing 'on all fours' on hands-and-feet, hands-and-knees, elbows-and-knees, etc. are examples of mixed supports.

OR

(2)   on part of the torso *and* on one or more of the extremities, as for instance in supporting on a shoulder (or the shoulder area) and the feet, or having weight on the head and the back of the pelvis.

The positions on the feet and/or on the knees alone, on the hands alone, on the elbows alone, or on the head alone (see Part I), are not termed 'mixed support' positions.

Note the term 'mixed kneeling' only refers to supporting on one knee and the other foot.  These positions are dealt with in the <u>Advanced Labanotation</u> issue *Kneeling, Sitting, Lying* (Section 4) and do not belong to the 'mixed support' category discussed here.

4.2. Ex. **4a** shows the familiar position on hands and knees. In such a position, 'place' (the point from where direction for support indications is established in Labanotation) is no longer below one supporting body part or exactly between two such parts as in standing, kneeling and sitting, but is located between three or four points of support. As a result, in all but simple, symmetrical positions, it can be difficult to determine exactly where 'place' is. In **4a**, an 'x' marks the appropriate place for the line of gravity, the vertical line through the center of weight, for the body as a whole (see the Advanced Labanotation issue on center of weight). The 'standard' way of determining direction is therefore not always the most suitable for mixed support situations.

4.3. Labanotation offers five methods of analysis, here identified as A-E. A is the 'Central Place' method established by Knust; for him it was the standard method. The need was felt for other approaches; these are given here as the alternatives B-E. The choice between these methods depends on what is best suited to the purpose of the notation, what kind of movement is involved, what produces the most direct and simple statements, and on whether there is a need for exactness of performance. The five methods are first presented briefly and then each is investigated more thoroughly.

### Mixed Support Situations

(hands shoulder –
width apart)

4a

4.4. **Method A: Central 'Place'** (Exs. **4b-4f** and Section 5). Positions on 'all fours' can be analyzed as open positions with two points of support situated on one side of 'place' and two on the other. Direction signs indicate the direction from 'place', therefore **4b** and **4c** describe the position of **4a** in which 'x' marks the location of 'place', the center point between the supports. Note use in **4c** of the expanded staff and the additional support columns. The Inner Subsidiary Columns (ISC) are identified as being support columns through use of the horizontal staples below the staff. (For use of columns see Section 20.)

Because direction is judged from 'place', in the illustration of **4a**, strictly the hands should be together, side by side. However, the established convention is that the hands support a shoulder-width apart unless something other is indicated. The knees are under the hips, usually slightly apart.

As supports change and weight is shifted, determining the exact location of 'place', and therefore the appropriate direction symbols for the supports, can be difficult.

Method A has the advantage of being based on fundamental principles used in other contexts (e.g. open positions when only on the feet). In practice it has proved cumbersome for writing many movement progressions and therefore is not generally recommended.

Distance between supports is shown in the starting position of **4d**, written in **4e**. The right hand is slightly more forward than the left and the left knee slightly more backward than the right. This same position is written with the broad staff in **4f**.

4.5. **Method B: Isolated Body Part Signs in Support Columns** (Ex. **4g** and Section 6). This method consists of placing the symbols for the supporting body parts in the support columns. While this way of writing only allows for general statements, it simplifies analysis when little detail is needed. It is particularly suited for writing alternating supports, e.g. for showing types of gait 'on all fours' (see **6a**) or for 'walking' on the feet around the supporting hand (see **6n**).

Ex. **4g** starts with standing on hands and knees. The performer then walks forward on the right hand, left knee, then left hand, and right knee. Traveling is shown by the path sign. As in all these examples, the hand supports do not cancel the knee/foot supports. (For validity of supports see Section 21.)

## Method A: Central 'Place'

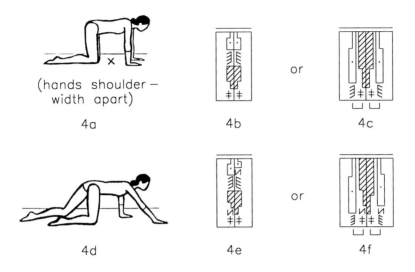

(hands shoulder —
width apart)

4a

or

4b

4c

4d

4e

4f

## Method B: Isolated Body Part Signs in Support Columns

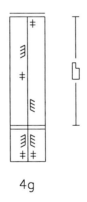

4g

4.6. **Method C: Direction of Limbs to Clarify Supports** (Exs. **4h-4j** and Section 7). This method is an augmentation of Method B in that directions in the arm and leg gesture columns are added. The gesture of an arm or leg is written in the usual way; only the parts supporting are written in the support column.[10] Ex. **4h** shows the position of **4a** (repeated here), while **4i** is the notation for **4d** (repeated here). In **4j**, as the torso tilts forward, the arms move to side low in preparation for taking weight on the hands, shown by the appropriate body part in the support column. In the position reached the hands will be quite far apart; as a result the torso will be forward horizontal. Note use of broad staff here to provide four support columns.

This method can be quite precise. It is practical for the occasional hand support when the body weight is on the feet, knees or torso most of the time; it is also suitable when the gesture is more important than the locomotion or weight placement. However, it should be noted that in **4j** the kneeling situation has been written in the standard way rather than through describing leg gestures. Such statement is usually preferable to that of **4h** and **4i**.

4.7. **Method D: Direction-from-Body-Part Indications (DBP)** (Ex. **4k** and Section 8). These indications allow for great precision in describing the exact placement of supporting parts on the floor in relation to each other. They are usually the best description for complex and detailed notation of mixed support situations.

Ex. **4k** shows the movement of getting into the position of **4a**. Passing from kneeling to supporting on hands and knees, the hands are shown to support forward of the knees, right hand forward of the right knee and left hand forward of the left knee, and the torso ending forward horizontal.

Note that **4b**, **4c**, **4h** and **4k** only serve as samples. The positions described are not exactly the same. In **4k**, for instance, the hands will be closer together than in the other examples because they are directly in front of the knees.

As mentioned before, in all these movement examples the hand supports do not cancel the knee supports. (For validity of support indications see Section 21.)

## Method C: Direction of Limbs to Clarify Supports

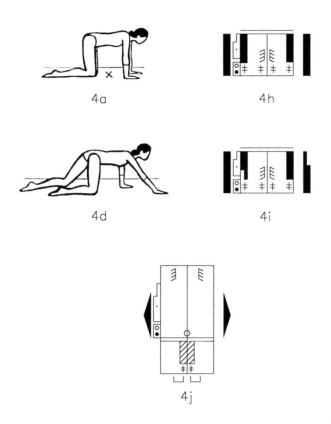

4a                    4h

4d                    4i

4j

## Method D: Direction-from-Body-Part Indications (DBP)

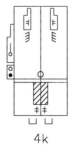

4k

4.8. **Method E: Split Body System** (Exs. **4l-4n** and Section 9).  In this
method the body is regarded as being comprised of two separate parts; the upper
body (hands and arms) and the lower body (legs and feet).  Thus, positions and
steps for the hands are written as if only standing on the hands; positions and
steps for the feet are written as if only standing on the feet.  There are two
'place' locations, one for the hands and one for the feet.

There are two ways of writing with the Split Body System, either by
notating the foot and hand positions or by positions of the feet and directions for
the arms (as in Method C above).  However, *torso direction and level must*
*always be shown.*  Ex. **4l** shows a 'crab' position with the hands further apart
than usual, illustrated in **4m**.  In a 'crab' position on feet and hands, the torso
faces up but is not arched.  In **4n** the same position is shown with arm directions
indicating placement of the hand supports.  Note that the Split Body Key is used
in these examples to indicate usage of this method.  This key is comprised of the
Standard Key to which has been added a second horizontal line suggesting the
split between upper and lower halves.[11]  (For 'crab' positions see also 10.4-
10.5.)

4.9.    This brief survey of the analytical methods employed provides
background for evaluating the advantages of each.  As will be seen, some
situations indicate that one or the other method is more appropriate.

## Method E: Split Body System

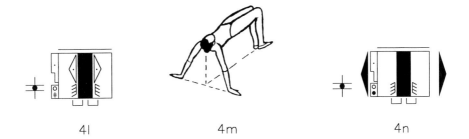

41                4m                4n

# 5  Method A: Central 'Place'

5.1.  Positions on hands and knees or hands and feet can be written with conventional direction symbols.  They are analyzed as open positions in which the hands are usually forward and the feet (or knees) backward of 'place'.  This analysis is not unlike that of '4th position' in upright standing.  This method of writing mixed support situations grew out of the basic rules of directional description established early on in the Laban system.[12]

5.2.   Method A was established by Albrecht Knust.  He wrote: "The points of support of the hands and feet in standing and walking on all fours are indicated in relation to 'place'.  Place is that point which is halfway between the point of support of the hand farthest in front and the point of support of the foot farthest behind" (Knust 1979: 483).

5.3.  Ex. **5a** shows standing on hands and feet.  With the direction 'place' being roughly centered in the waist, the hands are forward of 'place', the feet backward of 'place'.  Level indications used here show that the legs are bent and the arms normally extended.  The feet are together.  It is assumed that the hands are in their own tracks, shoulder-width apart, rather than strictly forward of the feet.  Ex. **5b** is similar, the position being on hands and knees.[13]

5.4.  Ex. **5c** is very similar to **5b** but the arms are bent so that the torso is directed forward low, the chest being closer to the floor than the pelvis.  In **5d**, illustrated in **5e**, the arms are shown to be contracted four degrees.

5.5.  **Distance.**  The following examples can be read in terms of relative or exact distance measurement.  Relative or 'general' interpretation of distance entails that the step-lengths are read according to what feels like a 'natural/ comfortable', 'small', 'very small', 'large' or 'very large' step.  Exact distance in which step-lengths are defined more precisely is identified by the exact sign: * .

5.6.  **Relative Distance.**  Ex. **5f** reads as a variation of **5a**, the right hand being farther forward and the left foot farther backward, as illustrated in **5g** (see also **4e**).[14]  In **5h** the hands and feet are a very large distance apart, the arms and legs normally extended, as illustrated in **5i**.  (For relative distance measurement see *Kneeling, Sitting, Lying* Section 35.6-9.)  Instead of writing the distance measurement signs across the center line of the staff, as shown in **5h**, they may be written separately for each column, as in **5j**.[15]

## Method A: Central 'Place'

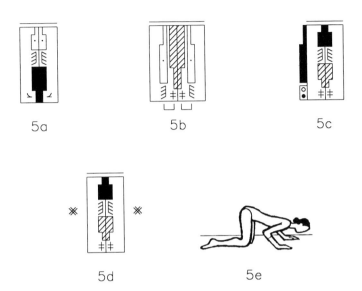

5a     5b     5c

5d     5e

## Relative Distance

ball of     ball of
left        right
foot        foot

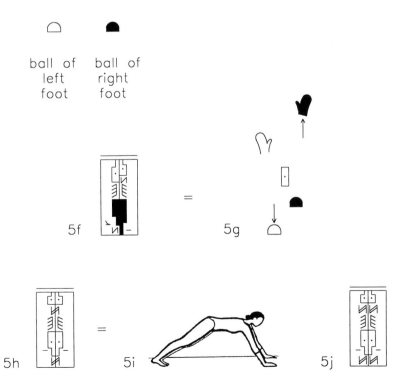

5f     =     5g

5h     =     5i     5j

5.7. **Exact Distance.** Knust states: "The length of steps in the forward direction is judged from the point of support which is farthest behind and the length of steps in the backward direction is judged from the point which is farthest in front. Simple direction signs (without a space measurement sign below them) indicate a distance of one step length. In standing on all fours this means the length of the trunk. A wide sign below a direction sign means $1^1/_2$ step-lengths, and the double wide sign means 2 step-lengths. A narrow sign below the direction sign indicates a $^1/_2$ step-length." (Knust 1979: 483).[16]

5.8. In **5k** the left hand is separated from the right foot by $1^1/_2$ step-lengths, the left foot stands 1 step-length behind the left hand, and the right hand is 1 step-length in front of the right foot. The distance between the right hand and left foot is a $^1/_2$ step-length. As shown by dotted horizontal lines and arrows in the illustration of **5l**, these distances are measured strictly along the forward-backward dimension, regardless of track. As usual, it is assumed that the hands are in the tracks of the shoulders and the feet more or less in neighboring tracks. (For tracks see Section 18, 19 and Appendix A.) The point of measurement for determining direction and level when supporting on the whole hand is the middle of the base of the hand (i.e. the heel of the hand, near the wrist); for the foot it is the middle of the part of the foot supporting.[17] (For exact distance measurement see the <u>Advanced Labanotation</u> issue *Kneeling, Sitting, Lying* Section 36.)

5.9. The writing of positions for mixed support situations as presented in this section can be made more specific by adding torso and arm directions and degrees of flexion/extension.

5.10. The movement in **5m**, a Knust example, is one of walking forward on hands and feet.[18] He writes: "A four-beat gait on all fours in the sense of the equestrian 'walk'. The step of one hand is followed by the step of the foot of the other side." For **5n** he states: "A two-beat gait on all fours in the sense of the equestrian 'pace'. The hand and foot of the same side are placed at the same time." Although the progression is all forward, steps on the feet are expressed as being backward. Note also the indications of distance; the hands are judged from the furthermost backward support, the feet from the furthermost forward support.

5.11. In **5o** the performer starts on feet and hands, the torso being forward horizontal. Three steps are taken on the feet. They do not walk backward as the notation immediately suggests, instead each foot steps on the same spot as in the starting position, **5p**. For the steps to travel backward the distance has to increase, as shown in **5q** where the left leg will be fully extended on the third step.[19]

# Method A: Central 'Place' (continued)

## Exact Distance

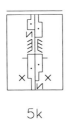

5k

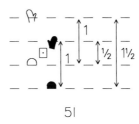

5l

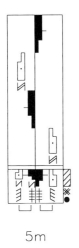

5m

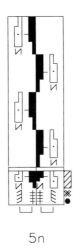

5n

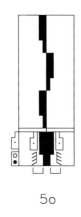

5o

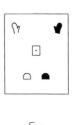

5p

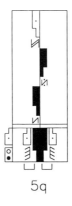

5q

**5.12. Disadvantages of Method A.** One of the problems with the Method A way of notating 'all fours' situations is that direction and distance are determined in two different ways. Direction is judged from place (i.e. the center between the four supporting parts) whilst distance is judged from the farthest supporting body part(s). When stepping continuously the center point ('place') is constantly moving, thus it is often not an easy reference point to locate. In addition, the use of backward direction symbols for the steps on the feet which are in fact progressing forward, does not give an immediate visual impression that all supports are, in fact, moving forward. Another disadvantage is that all the steps may be of the same length, while the distance indications do not give an immediate message concerning this fact.[20]

5.13. In **5r**, after sliding the right heel diagonally forward from a high kneel on the left knee (as if moving into a split), the right hand takes weight and the body turns $^1/_2$ while supported on the right hand and right foot. This ends in the position of **5i** (repeated here). Note the angling indication for the left leg in the gesture column showing the angle and hence degree of weight shift to the right foot. As the turn begins, the right hand takes weight and is, therefore, placed in the support column.

A 'resultant' bow is used to link the end of the turn to the new position. This shows that placement of the right foot and right hand are the result of the turn, they *are not lifted off the floor*. This is comparable to the use of a bow in **5s** to state the position arrived at for the left leg at the conclusion of the turn.[21]

At the end the direction symbols describe the resulting position, as in position writing, so the supporting parts relate to each other.

5.14. As mentioned before, in most 'all fours' positions the body parts are in a forward-backward relationship. However, other directions are possible. Ex. **5t** shows a very large 2nd position with straight knees and in which both hands are supporting between the feet. The hands are the usual shoulder-width apart. That they are slightly forward of 'place' is indicated by flat pins. (For use of tack pins see Appendix B.5-9.)

5.15. How a position is arrived at may be indicated in the starting position. Ex. **5u** is an *old way of writing* lying on the back as a starting position; the indications do not represent the actual position but rather the movement sequence used to arrive there. In this case first sit, then support backward on the shoulders.[22] Such statement of a movement sequence into a starting position can be a valuable aid when complex positions must be reached; one must read it from the bottom, as in reading movement. (For further Reading Examples see Sections 23-27.)

## Method A: Central 'Place' (continued)

## Disadvantages of Method A

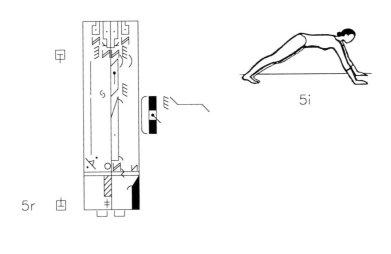

5i

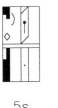

5r

5s

5t

5u

# 6 Method B: Isolated Body Part Signs in Support Columns

6.1. **Straight Path.** The following text explains in more detail the simple method presented in 4.5. Ex. **6a** shows walking forward on 'all fours' using the familiar gait pattern, in which a step on one hand is followed by a step on the other foot. The timing pattern here is intentionally uneven. This is a 'skeleton' description, the reader will take an ordinary, comfortable starting position. The direction of progression is not analyzed for each step, instead it is shown in a path sign. Only information that is needed is given.

6.2. In **6b** the hand and knee on one side of the body step forward at the same time, the vertical curved bow indicating the simultaneous movement. This bow is not needed for starting positions. While it is preferable to write the hands after the knees in the starting position, for the walking sequence, because the hand and knee step simultaneously, it makes no difference which symbol is placed first. With the broad staff in **6c** the simultaneity is visually obvious.

6.3. Ex. **6d** shows walking to the side. Here the hands step first, one after the other, followed by the feet. A familiar way of performing this is to 'close' with the left hand, placing it a shoulder-width near to the right; the left foot closing in to the right in a similar fashion. When distance is not important, this simple description will suffice.

6.4. In this method, the movement of **5o** (repeated here) would be written as **6e**. To reinforce the awareness of no traveling occurring, the path sign showing a place symbol (the standard description for no traveling) can be placed alongside. In **6f** the same is given in a broad staff. The equivalent of **5q** (repeated here) would be **6g** in which the path backward is designated specifically for the feet.

# Method B: Isolated Body Part Signs in Support Columns

## Straight Path

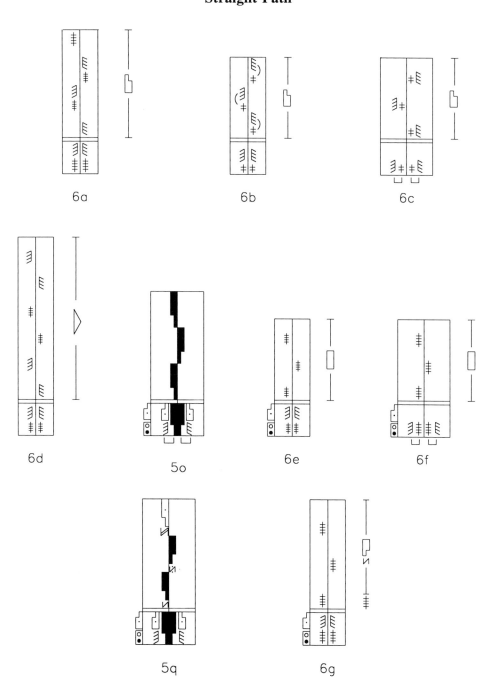

6a        6b        6c

6d        5o        6e        6f

5q        6g

6.5. **Validity.** In **6a-6e** and **6g** no statement is made regarding validity of support indications. In 'all fours' situations a new support does not automatically cancel the others (see 21.4). It is understood that the first step on the right hand does not cancel all the other supports. In many other related movements it is essential to show validity. The movement of **6h** is a way of traveling diagonally forward in which first the right hand steps in that direction, immediately followed by the feet and the left hand leaving the floor. The feet land one after the other, the left hand then 'catches up' before the right hand steps again toward the right forward diagonal and the action is repeated.

Ex. **6h** is a general statement but clearly records the type of gait used, since the action strokes in the leg gesture columns make clear that both feet leave the floor simultaneously after the step on the hand. If specific leg gestures occurred, the appropriate symbols would replace the action strokes. In **6i** release signs in the support columns show when the feet *and* when the hands leave the floor. Here the left hand is shown to lift much later. (For validity of support indications see Section 21.)

Note that the feet will have to land close to the right hand in **6h**, if the body is to travel in the stated direction.

6.6. **Circular Path.** If walking 'on all fours' occurs on a circular pathway, direction of stepping can be specified within the path symbol in the same manner as in walking on a straight path. In **6j** twenty-four 'steps' are taken on the hands and knees to produce the floor pattern of a semi-circle. The right side of the body is directed toward the imaginary center of the circle throughout.

6.7. In contrast, if stepping is sideward to the right while circling clockwise as in **6k**, the foot-end of the body remains directed towards the center of the circle. In such sideward 'stepping' the left knee and hand can be expected to close next to the right, no crossing over is likely in such a simple description. Note the small vertical bow meaning 'at the same time', linking the knee and hand sign.

6.8. Ex. **6l** shows standing on hands and knees facing the audience and then performing a quarter of a turn on the spot. In the process each point of support is picked up once. The exact performance, i.e. spatial adjustment to remain 'on the spot', is not stated.

## Method B: Isolated Body Part Signs in Support Columns (continued)

### Validity

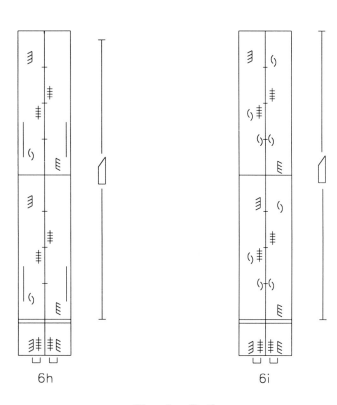

6h            6i

### Circular Path

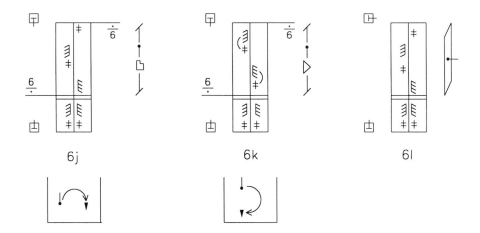

6j            6k            6l

6.9. **Ad Libitum.** If the order in which each part steps and the timing are not important a wavy ad lib. line can be used, as in **6m** in which the performer moves backward on a quarter of a circle to arrive at the left upstage corner and, having arrived, keeps turning around on the spot to face stage left.

6.10. **Circular Path Around a Focal Point.** In **6n**, from a squat the body leans to the left taking weight on the left hand. While the hand remains weight-bearing the feet 'walk around it'. Although only a general statement is made of this sequence (omitting analysis of direction for individual steps), it is desirable to state explicitly that the left hand remains supporting. For this reason a 'spot hold' is added in the hand support column. (For use of spot hold see Section 21.19.)

6.11. Walking around the left hand can also be indicated by stating it as the focal point (the center of the circle) for the circular path, **6o**. This indication is placed near the path sign. Alternatively, the sign for the body part or the focal point indicating the body part, may be placed *within* the path sign, indicating the axis for turning, **6p** and **6q** respectively.

6.12. Note that in **6n** there is no question about where the hand support is. The point of support is dictated by the directions for the torso and left arm. Because the support is written with an isolated hand sign no statement is needed in the support column with regard to direction or distance from the central 'place' which lies between the feet and the left hand.

## Method B: Isolated Body Part Signs in Support Columns (continued)

### Ad Libitum

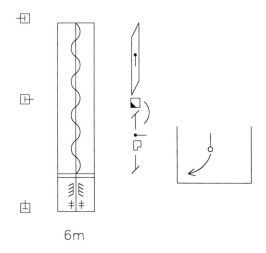

6m

### Circular Path Around a Focal Point

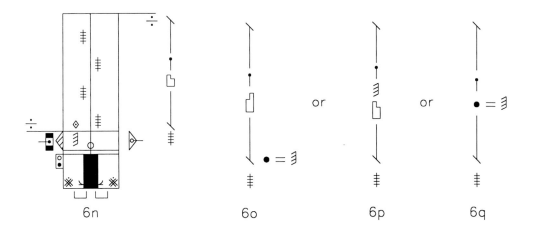

6n                    6o                    6p                    6q

# 7  Method C: Direction of Limbs to Clarify Supports

7.1.  In certain cases the location of a hand or foot support can be implied by writing the arm or leg gesture leading into the support.  Ex. **7a** illustrates how direction of stepping on the hands can be described by giving directions for arm gestures.  This avoids having to relate step direction and distance to a central 'place'.  From a high kneel, the torso inclines forward and the right arm extends downward so that the right hand can take part of the body weight.  The right hand is below the right shoulder.  The left arm moves slightly more forward so that the step on the left hand is more in front.  This causes the torso to travel forward slightly.  The right hand then steps in line with the left hand, under its own shoulder.  Then one after the other both hands step 'back' to end where they started.  The result of this sequence is akin to the step pattern of **7b**.  Note that in four-point or three-point supports, placement of weight on one part, here a hand, does not mean weight is taken off the other hand or the knees.  (For validity of support indications see Section 21.)

7.2.  Ex. **7c** illustrates use of gestures for arms and legs in writing a pattern walking forward with two 'steps' and then backward.  The right thigh moves forward before taking weight on the knee, at the same time the left arm moves forward to take weight on that hand.  The weight will be distributed equally between all four supports, causing the torso to shift forward slightly and all limbs to be angled more or less equally.  The support does not remain on four points, however, as the left thigh and right arm immediately move forward to prepare for the step on count 2.  As they lift to prepare for knee and hand to take weight on count 2, weight is shifted forward, so that direction of the left arm and right thigh become place low.  These resultant place low directions are automatic and usually need not be written.  Note that the resultant directions do not cause release of weight.  Of course, these directions will be cancelled when the right hand and left knee are placed backward of the supporting hand and knee.
On count 3 the right hand and left knee 'walk' backward (after the appropriate limb gestures).  Backward 'steps' are then taken on the right knee and left hand.  The resultant position is one in which the limbs are all angled, the right knee and left hand behind the left knee and right hand respectively.

7.3.  Stepping in 'place' is shown on count 3 of **7d**.  After the two forward steps, as in **7c**, the right hand ends up forward of the left and the left knee forward of the right.  The left arm and right thigh then move to place low before taking weight, thus count 3 produces a side-by-side relationship for both knees and for both hands.

## Method C: Direction of Limbs to Clarify Supports

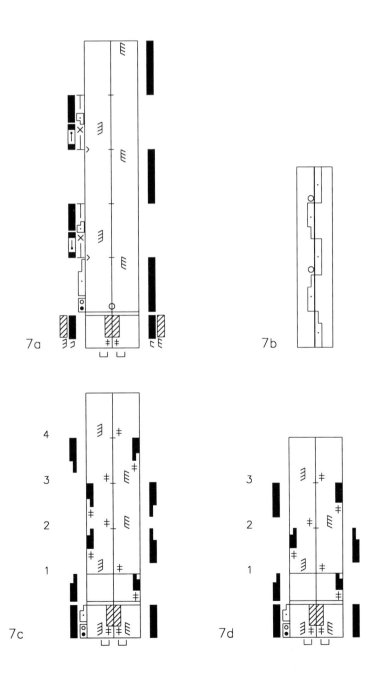

7.4.  Ex. **7e** starts in a sitting position, the hands placed close to the body. Weight is then taken on hands and feet as the unit shoulders-to-knees moves forward horizontal producing a 'crab' position.  (For terminology of 'crab' position see 10.4.-10.5.)

7.5.  Ex. **7f** is a more detailed recording of a transition from sitting into a 'crab' position.  This time, the torso inclines backward and, one after the other, the hands are placed well behind the hips and shoulders.  From there, the pelvis is lifted (travels up) off the floor, so the body ends in one line from knees to head, the head being in line with the torso.  While in **7e** nothing is stated regarding where the hands are pointing, in **7f** they specifically point backward (the arms having rotated outwards).  The end position is reached in such a way that as a result the arms end 'place low'.

7.6.  In **7g**, from standing on hands and knees, partial support is taken far behind the body on the right foot to enable the left foot to step underneath the body as a preparation for the jump far forward onto the feet.  Writing the step on the left foot as a flexed place low gesture followed by indication of support on the foot, avoids having to relate step direction to 'place' which, at this point, is theoretically between the hands as they are the only full supports.  The 'step' on the left foot could also be related to where the left hip is, using Direction-from-Body-Part (see Section 8).

7.7.  Release signs are given in **7g** in the support columns for the hands and left foot; for the right foot it is in the gesture column (see also 21.16-17). The gesture for the right leg will have taken the weight off the right knee.  A hold sign is needed at the end because weight is now only on the feet.

7.8.  The Time Sign placed in the addition bracket on the left of **7g** states that the movement is to be performed with much speed, i.e. very quickly.[23] Such statement allows the movement to be written with longer symbols, enabling easier reading.

# Method C: Direction of Limbs to Clarify Supports (continued)

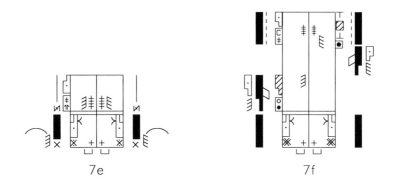

7e          7f

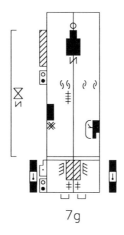

7g

# 8   Method D: Direction-from-Body-Part Indications (DBP)[24]

8.1.   Direction-from-Body-Part (DBP) indications state direction in relation to the location of a particular body part, the *reference part*.  DBP indications are mainly used for supports and for gestures touching the floor.[25]  They are most useful in describing steps in mixed support situations because it is often easier to relate direction to another body part, rather than to 'place'.  The reference part is usually another supporting body part, but it may be the same body part (i.e. where that body part was before) or a body part that is not on the floor. Conventional direction signs are referred to as *standard directions* to distinguish them from DBP indications.

8.2.   DBP symbols are direction symbols containing a body part symbol (the reference part).  They usually carry no indication of level (see 8.13-8.14). DBP indications are placed on the notation staff in the same way as standard directions.

8.3.   In **8a**, illustrated in **8b**, from a position 'on all fours', first the right knee steps to the right side of the right hand, then the right hand steps in front of the left hand.  In the first movement the right hand is the reference part.  In the second movement the left hand is the reference part.

8.4.   Performing the movement described by the DBP indications in **8a** entails changes in torso and arm directions.  These changes can be explicitly written if desired, but generally they are understood.

8.5.   **DBP - 'Place' Directions.**  If the moving part steps next to the reference part, leaving no appreciable gap, a DBP 'place' direction is used.  DBP 'place' directions in themselves mean that the body part steps *on* or *under* the reference part; such instances are rare and should be clarified using an 'above' or 'below' pin next to the place symbol.  For the more frequent instances in which the stepping part ends right *next to* (in front, behind, etc.) the reference part, such placement must be indicated by adding a black pin for the position (relationship). When the hand is stepping in place in relation to the shoulder, i.e. with reference to a part off the floor, the pin need not be added (see 8.36).  (For black pins see Section 18.)

8.6.  In **8c** the right hand steps in front of the left in a closed position. This is illustrated next to the notation.  In **8d** it steps next to the left hand as in a first position for the feet.  Ex. **8e** illustrates use of an 'above' pin to indicate stepping on the other hand.  For the right hand to support in 'place' below the left hand, as in **8f**, the left hand must release.

8.7.  **Distance.**  The DBP indications in **8a** make no statement about the distance between the stepping part and the reference part.  Comfortable body movement will dictate distances in general.  The illustration, **8b**, adjacent to **8a**, shows a possible performance.  There must be an appreciable gap between the knee and right hand after the first step and between the right and left hands after the second step, because otherwise 'place' would be used for the DBP direction and not sideward and forward.  (For distance see Section 17.)

### Method D: Direction-from-Body-Part Indications (DBP)

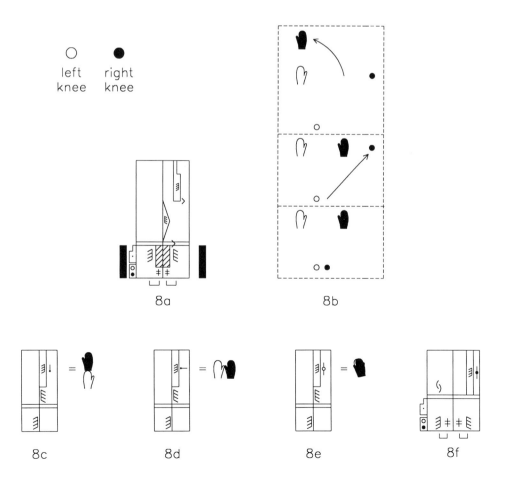

8a    8b

8c          8d          8e          8f

8.8. **DBP Examples.** Ex. **8g** shows a quick transition from standing to taking weight also on the hands (see also **8as** and **8at**). The hands then step sideward describing a $^1/_4$ circle around the feet. Note use of a spot hold for the balls of the feet; this allows the swivelling adjustment required.

DBP makes it easy to specify the direction of hand stepping. All DBP indications in this example have the right hand as reference part. The right hand steps to the side in relation to its previous location and the left hand 'closes' next to the right. (For use of a body part sign within a path sign see **6p**.)

8.9. **Touching Gestures.** DBP indications can also be used for parts that contact the floor without taking weight or take only partial weight. Ex. **8h** shows rising on the left knee from a low kneel, while the ball of the right foot is placed on the floor to the left of the left knee. The black pin indicates that the right leg crosses in front of the left leg.

8.10. **Point of Measurement.** Direction in DBP is judged as when using standard directions, i.e. in relation to the middle of the supporting part of the foot, the middle of the supporting part of the hand, or for other supporting parts, the middle of the area of support. (For a complete explanation see the Advanced Labanotation issue *Kneeling, Sitting, Lying* Section 36.)

8.11. If the reference part is a *limb* or a *body section*, DBP is judged in relation to the *middle* of that limb or section. In **8i** the ball of the right foot is placed next to the *middle* of the left lower leg. Note that no degree of leg bend is given for the right leg, the degree of flexion is dictated by the level of the kneel and the placement of the ball of the foot.

8.12. When DBP is to be judged in relation to the mid-point between two body parts, this can be stated by designating both parts simultaneously as the reference part. In **8j**, from a squat, the hands are placed down to take some of the weight, and then the right foot steps between the hands, illustrated in **8k**. Note that in this case a DBP 'place' symbol can be used without the addition of a pin sign (as used in **8c-f**).

# Method D: DBP (continued)

## DBP Examples

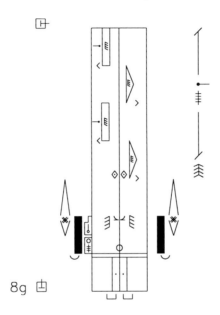

8g

## Touching Gestures                    Point of Measurement

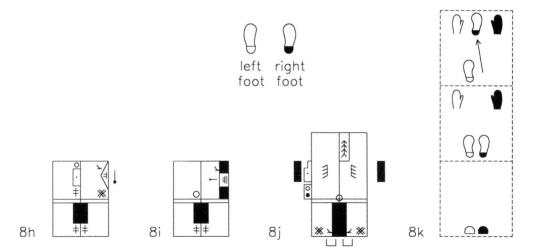

left   right
foot   foot

8h          8i          8j          8k

8.13  **Level.**  DBP indications often do not need to carry information about level.  Level of support may not be of prime importance.  It may be shown by other indications, or understood from context.  No level has been added to **8j**; the body configuration dictates what is needed.  In **8l** the step is forward of the right hand, no level is stated.

8.14.  Level for a step can be shown as in **8m**, **8n**, **8o** for low, middle and high level respectively.  When middle level needs to be specified, the dot in the symbol is placed *below* the reference part indication, which is placed slightly higher to attract the attention to the dot.  In these examples level indication has the same meaning as in standard directions written for supports.  Therefore **8m** means 'forward from the right hand, low level arm support' (i.e. with bent limb).

Leaving a separate space in low and high level symbols for the DBP indication is best handled as in **8m** and **8o**; middle level can be handled in a similar way, as illustrated in the alternative **8n** drawing.

8.15.  **DBP in Path Signs.**  It is sometimes convenient to use DBP indications in combination with path signs.  In **8p**, from a position 'on all fours' in which the legs are far apart, the hands 'walk' backward between the feet and then forward again to regain the starting position.  The DBP direction 'between the feet' for the hands is written as being the destination of the path backward.

Note that the necessary changes in torso placement are not analyzed here but the end position is indicated by a direction symbol preceded by the small vertical bow to state a resultant position.  In this example it indicates a return to the starting position of torso and arms (see <u>Advanced Labanotation</u> *Kneeling, Sitting, Lying* Section 39).

## Method D: DBP (continued)

### Level

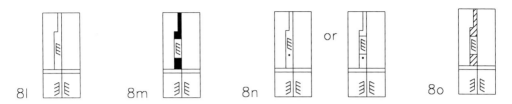

8l   8m   8n   or   8o

### DBP in Path Signs

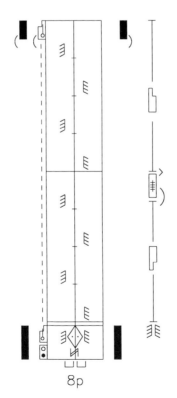

8p

8.16.  **Order of Reference.**  When DBP and standard directions appear simultaneously, this creates mutual cross-references between indications, bringing up the question in which order the references should be read.  In the majority of instances DBP indications refer back to a previous indication, however some refer to another indication occuring at the same time.   From these facts the following rules have been established for the general order of reference for DBP indications.

8.17.  **Rule 1:** *DBP indications which refer back to the location of a previous support are read first.*
          **Rule 2:** *When no DBP indication refers back to the location of a previous support, the standard direction symbols are read first.*

8.18.  **Writing a Position.**[26]  When writing a starting position, obviously no previous support exists, hence, if a DBP indication is used, the standard direction(s) must be read first.  This is true also of positions written as such in the course of a movement sequence.

8.19.  Ex. **8q** is a simple starting position on hands and knees with the knees apart and the hands exactly in front of the knees.  The standard directions for the knees are read first; this convention includes the idea of writing and reading the knee directions as if there were no weight on the hands.  Once the knee position is clear, the hand positions can be derived from it.

8.20.  If only one standard direction occurs simultaneously with one or more DBP indications, *the standard direction must be 'place' and it is read first.*  Ex. **8r** is a foot-kneel position in which the knee support is in middle level and the right foot is a step-length to the side of the middle of the left lower leg.  In spite of the fact that the body weight is not centered over the left knee, the kneeling direction is called 'place'.  The notation reads as an instruction of how to get into the position.

8.21.  In **8s** the standard direction for the left knee is read first as if no other supports occurred at the same time.  The left hand is then placed in front of that knee; the right hand sideward of the left hand; and the right foot between the hands.  The illustration, of **8t** is the interpretation of **8s**.  Exact distance must be specified if precision is required.[27]

# Method D: DBP (continued)

## Writing a Position

8q

8r

8s

8t

8.22. **Writing a Movement Sequence.** When writing a sequence of movements, DBP indications *can* refer back to previous positions. In accordance with Rule 1, such DBP indications will be read first.

8.23. **Previous Location.** DBP indications may relate to one of the following previous locations:

i)      *a static support,*

ii)     *the previous location of the same body part,* or

iii)    *the previous location of another 'lifted' part by using an (elongated) caret to reference this.*

Other indications can then relate to such a DBP support.

8.24. **Present Location.** DBP indications may also relate to:

iv)     *the present (new) location of another part.*

When such an indication occurs, another indication must be read first. This may be a standard direction symbol or a DBP indication which refers to a previous support. The following examples illustrate the various ways in which DBP indications can relate to another support.

8.25. **Reference to a Static Support, *(i).*** The following examples (except **8-8**) illustrate situations on all fours. The knees provide static supports as the reference parts for the DBP direction in **8u**. The right hand ends right in front of the left knee and the left hand forward of the right knee, illustrated in **8v**.

8.26. In **8w**, from a position on hands and knees, written as a 'fourth position' description, weight is taken off the knees and the feet 'jump' into a closed position in such a way that the right foot lands behind the right hand, in line with this static support, and the left foot closes next to the right. This is illustrated in **8x**. Releasing the hands from the floor the performer then rises to standing.

8.27. **Previous Location of Same Body Part, *(ii).*** In **8y**, from a position on hands and knees, the hands release from the floor and are replaced to the right side. The reference part for the left hand is itself and the same is true for the right hand. Thus the right and left hands both end to the right of their previous locations, as illustrated in **8z**. Note that in this example the starting position is written as a place description for the knees with the torso clarifying the starting position for the arms. (For use of Split Body Description see Section 9.)

# Method D: DBP (continued)

## Reference to a Static Support

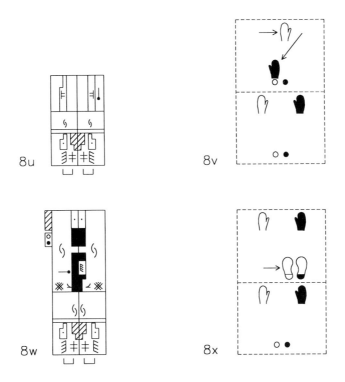

8u        8v

8w        8x

## Previous Location of Same Body Part

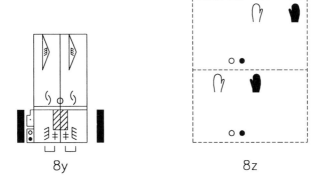

8y        8z

8.28. **Previous Location of a 'Lifted' Part,** *(iii)*. In **8aa**, illustrated in **8ab**, a jump to standing occurs from a foot-kneel support.[28]  A point is made of jumping simultaneously from knee and foot (in fact weight is placed momentarily on the left foot in rising; this is not written).  In reading the landing position, which determines the performance of the jump, the DBP indication is read first, as it refers to the previous support location of a lifted body part.  The landing is therefore in 1st position with bent knees, the left foot landing where the left knee was before the jump, the right foot in 'place' next to the DBP location.  Note use of the 'same spot' caret.

8.29.  Another way of indicating arrival in a position similar to **8u** is through use of an elongated zed caret relating to a spot, as in **8ac**.[29]  The logic is as follows: after the hands lift, the left hand arrives next to the previous location of the right hand, illustrated in **8ad**.  If no elongated zed caret were used, as in **8ae**, the position arrived at would be different, as shown in **8af**.  This is because the right hand would read the reference to the static body part (the left knee) first and the left hand would then locate its position in relation to the right hand.

8.30. **The Present (New) Location of Another Part,** *(iv)*.  In **8ag** the right hand must be read first (its new position established through referring to a static support) before the left hand is read.  The DBP for the left hand refers to the new position of the right hand; **8ah** illustrates the end placement.

## Method D: DBP (continued)

### Previous Location of a 'Lifted' Part

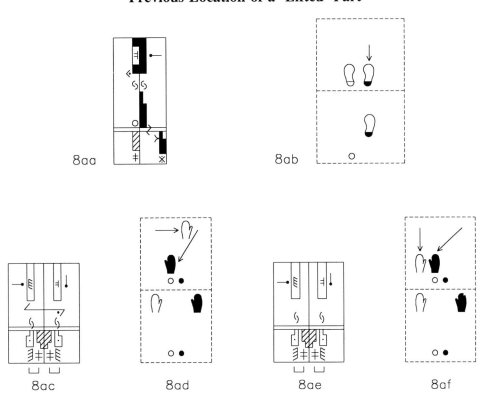

8aa 8ab

8ac 8ad 8ae 8af

### The Present (New) Location of Another Part

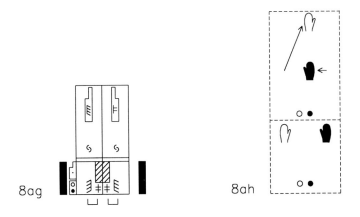

8ag 8ah

8.31.  In **8ai**, shown in **8aj**, the left foot jumps backward from where it was and the right foot arrives sideward of it.  Here the right foot refers to the new location of the left foot.  Therefore, the left foot indication has to be read first.  If the DBP indication were to refer to the previous location of the left foot an elongated caret would be drawn.

8.32.  In **8ak**, which starts on hands and feet, the feet spring up, the left foot landing sideward of where it was while the right foot lands in 5th position behind the left.  This action could also be described as the feet ending in 5th, having traveled sideward, **8al**.  This movement is illustrated in **8am**.

8.33.  Ex. **8an** starts in a wide 2nd position on the feet, the torso forward and the hands under the shoulders.  As the weight shifts over to the right foot the right hand steps forward of the right foot (the standard direction symbol being read first); at the same time left hand and foot release.  They then step forward, the left foot forward of where it was before, the left hand forward of where the left foot is stepping.  This progression is illustrated in **8ao**.

# Method D: DBP (continued)

# The Present (New) Location of Another Part (continued)

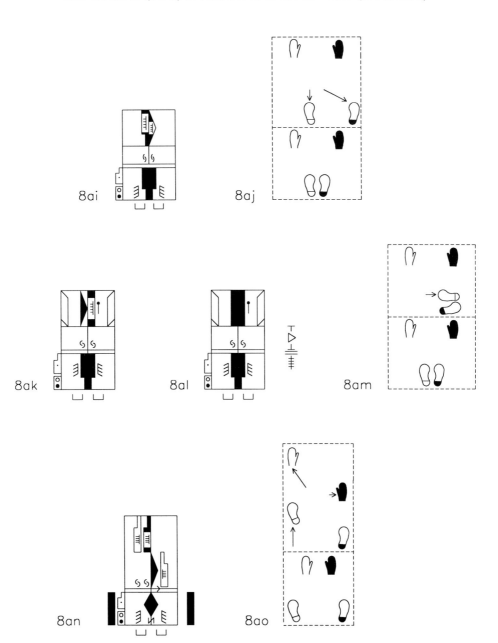

8.34. **Divided Front.** In a divided Front situation the body is twisted and different parts of the body have different Fronts.[30] For each clearly defined part DBP refers to the new Front of that part.

In **8ap**, the starting position shows standing on hands and knees facing the audience. The hands release and the torso wheels to the left while the kneeling sinks to middle level (note that the knees should not swivel).[31] This causes Front for the arms and their parts to change to stage left; the end position is illustrated in **8aq**. The Front sign here in brackets refers to the Front for the upper body. The DBP indications for the hands must be written and read according to *i)* (see 8.25-26). If it is more convenient to relate all DBP (and other) directions to the same 'untwisted' Front, the Stance Key may, of course, be used.

8.35. Note that, as with many other examples in this section, **8ap** is included for purposes of explanation only. If detail is important, the example will contain more indications. If detail is not important, a simple statement such as **8ar** may suffice.

8.36. **Reference to Part off the Floor.** Occasionally it is desirable to designate a body part that is not, or has not been, on the floor as a DBP reference. In **8as** a fall forward is caught on the hands just in time, with the hands taking support beneath the shoulders, arms in low level, before pushing the body up by stretching the arms. Note that, unless the relationship between hands and shoulders is particularly important, the simpler notation in **8at** will suffice.

## Method D: DBP (continued)

### Divided Front

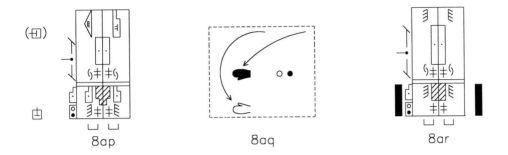

8ap                          8aq                          8ar

### Reference to Part off the Floor

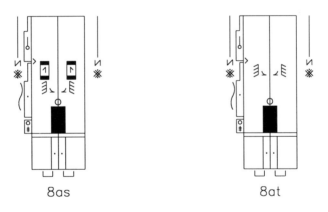

8as                                    8at

# 9  Method E: Split Body (SB)

9.1.  As mentioned before, one of the problems with Method A applied to notating 'all fours' situations is that direction and distance are determined in two different ways.  Direction is judged from 'place' (i.e. between all four supporting parts) while distance is judged from the farthest supporting body part(s).

9.2.  A relatively simple way to overcome this (and one which beginners easily relate to) was proposed by Maria Szentpál.  It regards the body as being comprised of two separate parts; one for the hands and arms and the other for the feet and legs.  Therefore, positions and steps for the feet are written as if one were only standing on the feet, and positions and steps for the hands are written as if only standing on the hands.  This method, known as Split Body (SB), is the way the performer often 'sees' and experiences the movement when complex configurations are not encountered.

9.3.  In SB the direction referred to as 'place' for the hands or elbows is under the shoulders, as in methods other than Method A.  For the knees and feet 'place' means that feet or knees are together under the pelvis.  Thus the knees/feet and hands each have a separate 'place' directions.

9.4.  Because it connects the lower and upper parts of the body, Szentpál used the placement of the trunk to show easily the direction and distance relationships between the positions of the hand and foot supports.  By indicating torso direction, level, and degree of flexion or extension, the distance between and the direction of the hands and feet can be shown (indirectly).  Szentpál states that for SB *"one always has to show the direction and level of the trunk."*  Whole torso placement is also often needed for the other methods.

9.5.  Initially, Szentpál introduced the use of blank direction symbols in the support column to attract attention to a different analysis.[32]  This was superseded by use of a special key for SB (see 9.6).

9.6.  **Split Body Key.**  The difference between Method E and other methods is made clear by using a Split Body Key.[33]  This key, **9a**, is based on the Standard Key, combined with double horizontal 'separating' lines to indicate the body being divided into two separate parts.  If the Body System of Reference is used, the key is modified to **9b**.

9.7. **Foot and Hand Positions.** In **9c**, illustrated with floorplan, **9d**, and figure drawing, **9e**, the performer is on hands and knees, the hands supporting in place under the shoulders, the knees apart in 2nd position. A middle level kneel and arms bent three degrees is shown in **9f** (**9g**, **9h**). Ex. **9i** (**9j**, **9k**) indicates support on hands and feet.

## Method E: Split Body

### Split Body Key

9a          9b

### Foot and Hand Positions

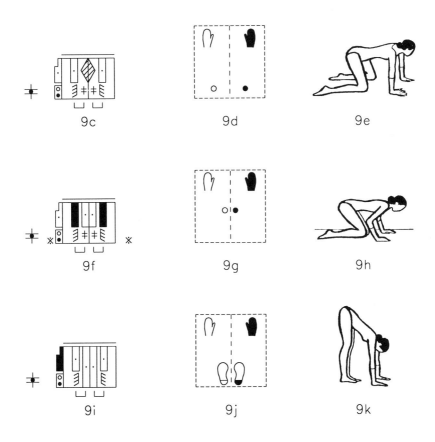

9c          9d          9e

9f          9g          9h

9i          9j          9k

9.8. A 4th position placement for both feet and both hands is given in **9l**
(**9m**, **9n**). Degree of bend is also given for each leg. For **9o** (**9p**, **9q**) the legs
are in a squat, the feet in 5th position. The hands are also in '5th position', the
right hand in front, both being on the center track. (For track pins see
Appendices A, B.) Note that no Split Body Key is given here; it is obvious from
the notation what the position should be.

9.9. **Walking Patterns.** Ex. **9r** starts on hands and knees, the torso
forward horizontal. The forward steps on hands and knees are all a comfortable
distance forward, therefore no distance signs need to be given.

9.10. In **9s** the 'all fours' position is on hands and feet. The pattern of
progressing forward is rhythmically uneven. After the step on the right hand
both feet release, the left one landing forward and the right joining it soon after.
A step forward on the left hand then takes place before this whole pattern is
repeated.

9.11. In **9t**, the level of the arm supports is shown specifically by addition
of flexion and extension signs in the arm gesture columns. The knees start place
middle, the arms in place and bent. As the right knee and right hand step
sideward, both arms straighten to normal (neither bent nor stretched). The left
hand and knee then close into place. The left knee then steps forward in middle
level, while the left hand also moves forward, the arm again bent. As the right
knee closes to 1st, the right arm steps in place and contracts, thus establishing the
position for the arms, as at the start.

9.12. In **9u** the movement pattern is similar to **9t**. In **9u** the right knee
and hand both step sideward high, the high support on the hand being on the
fingers (see 1.13). This is followed by a step in 'place' on both left knee and
hand, followed by the left knee and left hand stepping forward as in the previous
example. The right knee steps in place, as the right arm takes weight to the right
side, the arm being bent.

## Method E: Split Body (continued)

## Foot and Hand Positions (continued)

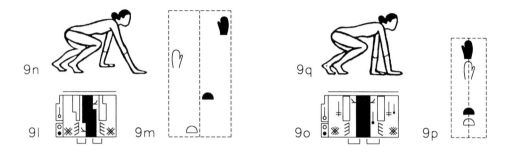

## Walking Patterns

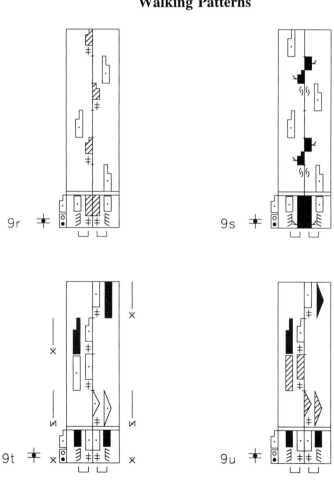

9.13. **SB with Gesture Indications for the Arms.** In practice, the SB method is sometimes combined with Method C, the hand/elbow supports being clarified by direction symbols in the arm gesture columns. The Split Body Key has to be added to indicate use of the SB method. The legs in **9v**, exemplified by the drawing in **9w**, are very bent, nearly in a squat, while the torso is horizontally forward leaning on the arms which point straight down. A position on hands and knees is shown in **9x** (**9y**); the hands are placed slightly toward the knees.

9.14. In the position on hands and feet in **9z** (**9aa**) the section from knees to chest is pointing backward. This means that the front of the torso faces upward. The hands are placed straight under the shoulders.

9.15. Ex. **9ab**, illustrated by the floorplan of **9ac** and the figure drawing of **9ad**, shows a position on all fours with the knees supporting in line with each other in 4th position, the right knee in front. The arms are side low and three degrees bent. In the position on hands and knees of **9ae** (**9af**, **9ag**) the torso is horizontal. The knees are in 2nd position, the right hand is placed on top of the left in the center track.

9.16. **Preferred Usage.** With this range of choices in writing (Method A, B, C, D, or E), the question comes up as to which is the preferred usage. It has been found that many notators combine Split Body with use of direction of limbs to clarify supports (Method C) with DBP indications (Method D). The context, the movement intention and other factors may dictate the choice. Of prime importance is that the information is clear and sufficient detail has been given.

## Method E: Split Body (continued)

## SB with Gesture Indications for the Arms

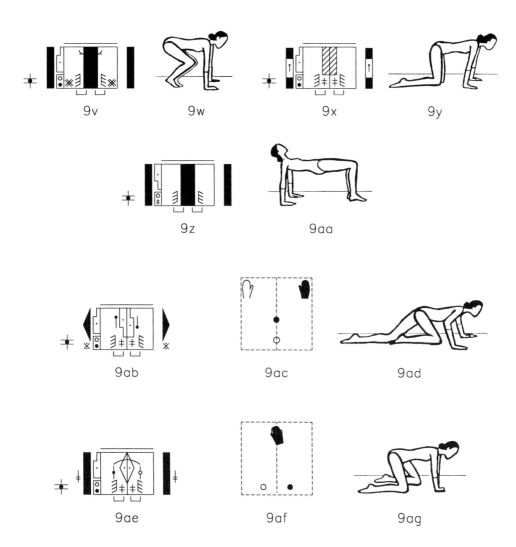

9v

9w

9x

9y

9z

9aa

9ab

9ac

9ad

9ae

9af

9ag

# 10 Torso Directions - Inverted, Augmented, Sections

10.1. In mixed support situations, indicating the direction of the torso is an important aid to the reader. In this way ambiguity is avoided and the need for other more specific details is often eliminated.

10.2. **Torso Directional Indication - Options.** In mixed support indications there are many more possibilities for spatial displacement of the torso than in standing. Therefore, inverted and/or augmented body section signs are often used. We start with inverted torso examples.

10.3. **Inverted Body Sections.** A particular body section is shown by two body part signs placed in a small vertical rectangle. The upper sign indicates the 'free end' and the lower sign the 'fixed end', the part in relation to which direction is judged. The free end moves as indicated in relation to the fixed end, i.e. takes direction and level from the fixed end.

As a rule, the end of the body section closest to the feet is designated as the fixed end and the other end, closer to the head, as the free end. However, in some circumstances it is the end of the body section closest to the feet that moves and thus the body sign is inverted to show that the lower part of the body is the free end. Ex. **10a** shows the generally used torso sign. Ex. **10b** is the inverted torso sign which indicates the lower part of the torso to be the 'free end' moving to a new direction. For greater distinction between **10a** and **10b** the inverted sign is often written as **10c**.

10.4. **Clarification of Terminology: 'Crab' Versus 'Bridge' Position.** Positions with the hands supporting backward of the feet (and with the back rather than the front of the torso facing the floor) may form a 'crab' position, as illustrated in **10d**, or a 'bridge' position, **10e**.

In a crab position, **10d**, the torso is not arched over the back nor is the head dropped back as in the bridge position. Otherwise the two positions have much in common. The notator needs to be aware of this potential confusion and must write sufficient detail to avoid it.

10.5. In **10f** the body is lifted from sitting, resulting in a 'crab' position. Because it is the lower part of the torso that moves rather than the shoulder section, it is appropriate to designate the pelvis as the free end for this movement, rather than the chest. Therefore, the inverted torso direction symbol is written.

In **10g** the more detailed inverted torso sign is used to draw attention to the inverted symbol.

10.6. Lowering the legs from a handstand into a bridge is shown in **10h**, illustrated in **10i**. The torso, chest to pelvis, is shown to be up. It then moves to forward high, forward being the direction in which the hands are pointing, the Front direction for the body-as-a-whole. As the inverted torso lowers to forward middle it contracts over the back surface before the feet reach the floor and take weight.

### Inverted Body Sections

10a    10b    10c

### Clarification of Terminology: 'Crab' Versus 'Bridge' Position

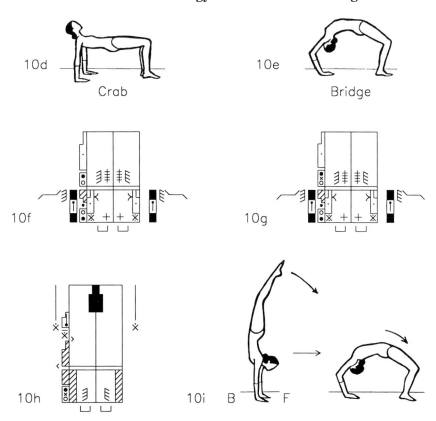

10d    Crab

10e    Bridge

10f

10g

10h

10i    B    F

10.7. Moving into a bridge from standing by bending the torso very far backward is shown in **10j**. The arms start up and are carried along as the torso arches and then bends backward. The knees bend and usually also the arms before the hands take weight. The arms are turned in so that the hands end pointing forward. Performers with flexible spines, who can fold backward to a much greater degree, will bring the hands closer to the feet. In this example, an inverted torso symbol is *not* used, because it is the free end (the chest) that moves rather than the pelvis end.

10.8. A bridge can also be achieved by rising from a supine position. In **10k** the legs start drawn in toward the hips, the soles of the feet on the floor. The arms are backward middle, very contracted so that the hands are near the shoulders. The hands are pointing forward, contacting the floor. The hands push downward and the arms stretch as the pelvis rises straight up; weight is taken on the feet and hands and the legs 'stretch' (literally approach the state of being stretched). Performers with flexible backs such as acrobats or contortionists, can achieve a bridge with straight arms and legs. Note the resultant end position for the torso. Because both ends of the spine move up, there is again no need to use the inverted torso sign in this example.

10.9. **Augmented Body Sections.** Augmented body sections are sections that include part(s) of the arms and legs and/or the head. They can be used to indicate clearly the alignment of body parts moving as a unit.

10.10. In the notation of **10l** statement of torso direction is essential because the relationship between supports is not indicated. In this example the augmented torso unit knees-to-chest is parallel to the floor. Other details such as the degree of knee and elbow bend, exact hand placement, etc., are left open. Ex. **10m** is another way of writing this basic position.

10.11. The notation of **10n**, which states that the (augmented and inverted) section chest-to-knees moves to forward middle, uses the most appropriate statement for this movement; it captures the essential information about the end position in a single directional indication, as well as indicating which is the free end of the moving body part.

10.12. An augmented body section symbol is also featured in **10o**. From a side sit with the body leaning on the right hand and the legs extended to the left, weight is taken on the right foot and the right hand, the right hip lifting off the floor as the body aligns from left foot to the chest (the free end).

Starting with the left hand resting on the left leg, the left arm lifts sideward in relation to the body axis. The position of the right arm, which results from the body movement, is also more or less to the side of the body axis and depends on individual body proportions. This will also affect the exact level of the torso (the unit of chest to foot).

10.13. In the middle level kneel of **10p** the torso, from right ankle to head, inclines diagonally backward in the opposite direction to the right leg gesture while a vertical line is established by the arms. The torso direction together with the left arm direction determines the spot on the floor where the left hand takes weight.

## 'Crab' Versus 'Bridge' Position (continued)

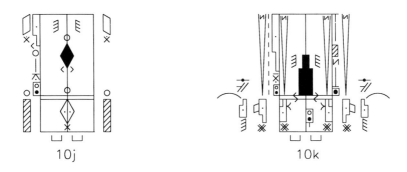

10j          10k

## Augmented Body Sections

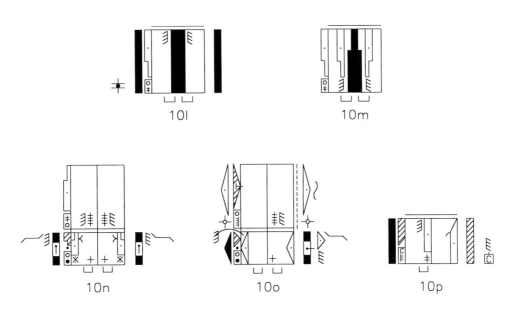

10l          10m

10n          10o          10p

# III REVOLUTIONS OF THE BODY

# 11 Turning Around the Vertical or Spinal Axis

11.1. When the body is erect, the vertical line of gravity and the longitudinal axis of the body coincide; there is no question of the performance of the signs of **11a** placed in the support column(s). When the body/torso moves away from the vertical, which is to be understood for **11a**?

11.2. **Rule 1:** *When the body is turning on a vertical support, as in 11b, the rotation signs of 11a mean turning, pivoting around the vertical line of gravity.* This is also the familiar interpretation of **11c**, in which the torso is inclined. Even when supporting on a bent leg, as in **11d**, the turning is around the vertical line through the support, i.e. the same vertical axis as in **11b** and **11c**. When the body is lowered to supporting on the knee, pivoting on the knee, even in a middle level kneel, **11e**, still retains the vertical axis.

11.3. **Rule 2:** *When the torso is horizontal, and no single support is retaining the vertical line, as occurs in a low kneel, 11f, or in lying, 11g, a rotation sign in the support column is always understood to be around the longitudinal (spinal) axis of the body.*[34]

11.4. **Statement of Axis.** Statement of axis is practical when examples are met where it is not immediately apparent as to whether the turn is around the body axis or the standard vertical axis. Ex. **11h** states rotation around the spinal axis and **11i** rotation around the vertical line of gravity axis. This same vertical axis is also understood in **11j**, the indication for horizontal wheeling. (For the difference between pivoting and rolling see also examples in <u>Advanced Labanotation</u> *Kneeling, Sitting, Lying* Sections 25, 27, and endnote 52).

11.5. In the low kneel of **11f**, because the torso is horizontal and so close to the floor and with weight completely on the lower leg (i.e. no vertical line of support), there will be an instinctive expectancy to roll, as when lying on the torso, rather than to swivel. This is also true of **11k**. However, to eliminate doubt in cases such as this, it is better to state the axis of turning. In **11l** rolling is indicated; in **11m** swiveling will take place. In this configuration, swiveling may require some outside help as well as a slippery floor.

## Turning Around the Vertical or Spinal Axis

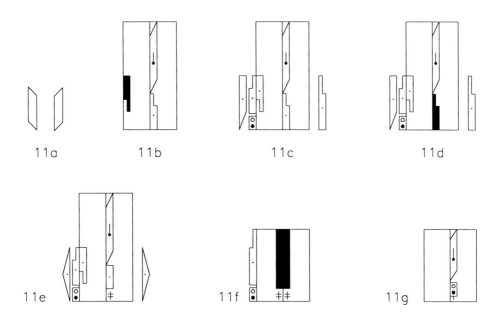

## Statement of Axis

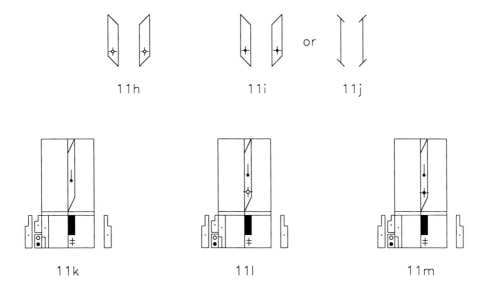

11.6. **Turning on All Fours.** When on all fours vertical supports exist but pivoting is difficult unless one or two supports are lifted. In **11n** and **11o** no statement of axis is necessary; the body situation, the one-sided release of supports and the space hold for the torso will make clear how the turn signs should be interpreted.

11.7. In **11n** the left foot and hand are lifted and turning takes place on the right foot and hand. After the half turn the left foot and hand are replaced. Another half turn then takes place on the left side supports. Note that level for the forward position of the torso is not specified. After the first half-turn the performer is in the 'crab' position of **10d**. After the second half-turn the body regains its starting position. The result of this sequence is traveling to the side, described here as being to the Constant right side direction (the room direction).
        The body configuration and weight placement of **11n** dictate an action which, because of the space hold for the torso, is akin to log rolling to the left (see 11.12).

11.8. In most all fours situations it is assumed that for hand supports turning is achieved through arm rotation rather than by swiveling on the supporting hand (previously discussed in Section 2). The performer prepares by placing the hand appropriately so that little, if any, swiveling need occur. However, because of the degree of turn in **11o**, there will need to be swiveling on each hand as well as on the feet. This necessary swiveling is a departure from the rule that normally swiveling on the hands is avoided.

11.9. Ex. **11o** shows placement of the turn symbols outside the staff for the movement of **11n**. For visual reasons, it is practical to make the turn sign more than one column wide so that they do not appear to refer to the arm or head (see Advanced Labanotation *Kneeling, Sitting, Lying* 27.7). Also indicated in **11o** is the torso position arrived at as a result of the space hold after each half-turn. These details facilitate reading. Ex. **11o** is more fluid than **11n**, because there is no gap, no pause between the turn signs in **11o**, whereas in **11n** the turning action is interrupted as the hand and foot are put down to take weight. (For small round destination bows indicating resultant positions see *Kneeling, Sitting, Lying* Section 39.)

11.10. **One-eighth Turn around the Vertical Line of Gravity.** Ex. **11p** shows $\frac{1}{8}$ turn to the left around the line of gravity while standing on both hands and both feet. Note that the turn sign covers all four support columns, the body as a whole turns, a new Front is established. The direction of the front surface of the torso remains unchanged. In **11q** the same occurs but with a space hold for the torso resulting in a diagonal torso direction. Placement of hands and feet is shown in **11r**.

## Turning on All Fours

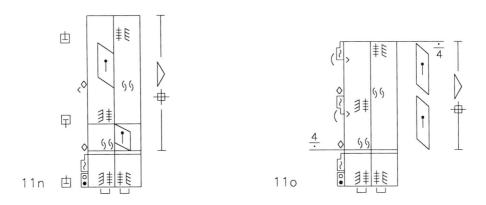

11n          11o

## One-eighth Turn around the Vertical Line of Gravity

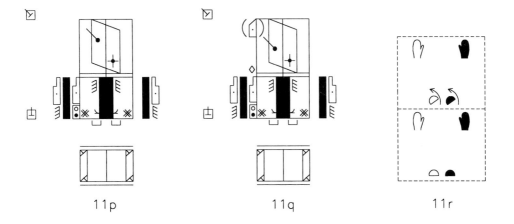

11p          11q          11r

11.11.  Because one-eighth turn around the vertical axis is a comparatively minor adjustment, the effect on hand supports may be swivel or non-swivel. When appropriate, non-swiveling can be shown for both hands and feet, as in **11s**.  In **11t** sliding is shown for the supports on both sides.  Here the unspecific curved bow ('hook') is used to avoid stating a particular part of the foot and hand.  If one needs to specify sliding for only one or other part, the indication needs to be written outside the staff, as in **11u**, illustrated in **11v**, where the left hand releases and the right hand is shown to have a sliding support.

11.12.  **One-eighth Turn around the Spinal Axis.**  While on all fours only a limited amount of torso rotation can be achieved without lifting any of the supporting parts.  Such turning, a rolling action of the torso which results in one shoulder being higher than the other, is best written in the torso column, as in **11w**.  It does not produce a change of Front.  This body turn could be the start of the movement of **11o** in that the effect of this rotation on the torso is similar to what happens in log rolling.  In log rolling a turn to the left always causes the left shoulder to move 'backward' and the right shoulder to move 'forward'; a rotation to the right produces the reverse result.

11.13.  **One-quarter Turn.**  The turning action in **11x** produces a rolling movement for the torso.  This is clearly indicated by the space hold for the torso. From 'all fours', if the degree of turn is $\frac{1}{4}$ or more, the arm and leg on one side of the body (here the left side) must be lifted off the floor.  During the $\frac{1}{4}$ turn of **11x** these limbs take a definite position, extending parallel to the floor.  Because the two supports on the right side remain, the turn must become a rolling action for the torso.  Diagram **11y** shows the ending position for the right foot and hand.  For this kind of movement it is almost impossible for the right foot not to swivel.  For this reason the expected foot print is shown in brackets.

Note that a release sign is written in the support column for the left hand as a visual help even though the left arm gesture indicates that the left hand is no longer supporting.  For the left foot no release sign is written; a leg gesture which cancels a foot support is common practice, also, the turning occurs only on the right supports.

11.14.  In **11z**, use of the Body Key in the turn sign eliminates the need for a space hold for the torso.  It may still be used, of course, to assist reading. Exact analysis of the path of the movement for the left limbs is necessary only if the movement is slow.  The example shows use of black diamonds to indicate the destination of an undeviating path for left arm and leg.  (For diamonds in directions for limbs see the <u>Advanced Labanotation</u> issue *Kneeling, Sitting, Lying* Section 32.)

## One-eighth Turn around the Vertical Line of Gravity (continued)

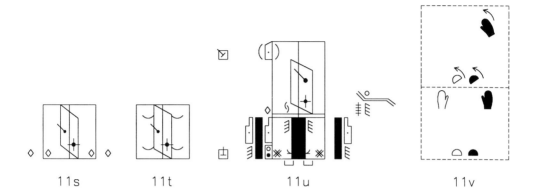

| 11s | 11t | 11u | 11v |

## One-eighth Turn around the Spinal Axis

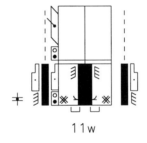

11w

## One-quarter Turn

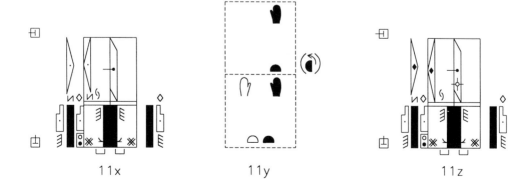

| 11x | 11y | 11z |

11.15.  In **11aa** the hands and feet are far apart and the weight placed so that the torso is almost forward horizontal.  The right hand is closer in; it is written with DBP, as being right diagonally backward of the left hand. Swiveling $^1/_4$ to the right occurs on the left hand and foot, the torso remaining spatially where it is (space hold).  The fact that the left hand swivels is shown in the gesture column through statement of the rotation for the hand combined with the double support bow indicating a sliding support.  The right foot becomes a touching gesture in front of the left leg (shown by the ball of the foot hook); thus weight is clearly taken off that part.

11.16.  Another version of the same movement is written in **11ab**, using the additional support columns.  Here the swiveling action for the left supports during the turn is specifically stated on the turn sign itself through use of the non-specific contact bows.  Attached to the wide turn sign, the bows refer to both supports.  Note that the right hand and the right foot are both shown to have released weight while still in contact with the floor.[35]  (For release of weight sign see 21.18.)

11.17.  **One-half Turn.**  As shown earlier in **11n** and **11o**, after a half-turn to the left the left arm and leg can be replaced on the floor so that a 'crab' position is reached, as in **11ac**.  While turning is usually written in the support column, as in **11ad**, in **11ac** it is indicated outside the staff in order to show the duration line for the right foot which indicates that rolling onto the whole foot takes the whole of the turn to be completed.  Hand position (the direction where the fingertips face) at the end of the turn is not important here, therefore this detail has been omitted.  (For duration lines in support columns see <u>Advanced Labanotation</u> *Kneeling, Sitting, Lying* endnote 36.)

11.18.  Indication for degree of leg bend in the starting position of **11ac** is modified by the subsequent movements; for clarity, lessening of the degree of bend is shown by decrease signs in the leg gesture columns.[36]

11.19.  **Change of Torso Direction.**  In **11ae** the rolling movement of **11n** includes a change of level for the torso, shown by an inverted body section. During the first half-turn the pelvis sinks, lowering almost to the floor.  The next half-turn leads to a return to its starting position.

## One-quarter Turn (continued)

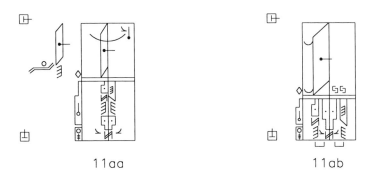

11aa            11ab

## One-half Turn

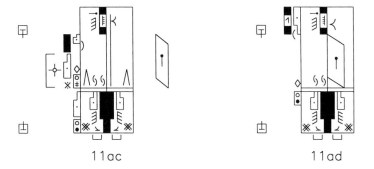

11ac            11ad

## Change of Torso Direction

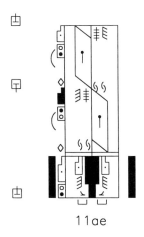

11ae

11.20.  As soon as the hands are released from the floor in a mixed support situation and weight is only on the feet/knees, the analysis of turning is as in standing (Rule 1 in 11.2).  In **11af** the hands and the left knee are released.  The turn is a pivot turn on the right knee, the right thigh being the axis around which the turn occurs. (See <u>Advanced Labanotation</u> *Kneeling, Sitting, Lying* Section 26.)

11.21.  Ex. **11ag** shows a movement similar to a 'blind turn', the lower legs retaining their direction so that no actual swiveling on the kneecaps occurs.  The pivot turn around the vertical axis with the torso horizontal is like a wheeling action, the shoulders remain level.  If a turn around the longitudinal body axis occured the right shoulder would end higher than the left.

11.22.  Ex. **11ah** is again the same movement, now described as torso wheeling.[37]  In **11af** and **11ag**, Front for the body-as-a-whole changes, but in **11ah** it is a turning action of the torso, not of the body-as-a-whole.  If it is convenient to rename Front as the right downstage corner (this depends largely on what follows) a secret turn sign can be added as in **11ai**.  The secret turn statement (the decision to rename Front), can also be placed as in **11aj**, outside to the left, thus linking directly to the new Front sign.  (For 'secret turn' see *Kneeling, Sitting, Lying* 31.9.)

11.23.  Ex. **11ak** shows a different timing for the $^{1/4}$ turn action of **11af**.  The turn is shown to occur in the upbeat and weight taken again on the hands on count 1.  (For exact timing see *Kneeling, Sitting, Lying* Section 34.)

11.24.  In **11al** a partial bunny jump (springing only with the feet) is shown with a $^1/_4$ change of Front.  As the legs lift, the hands swivel on the ground.  This springing motion of the legs partially releases weight from the hands, making it easier for the hands to swivel.  The swiveling is specified by the bows for non-specific sliding.  The same movement is written in **11am** but here the turn sign is placed outside the staff, sliding being shown with the double supporting bows.

# Change of Torso Direction (continued)

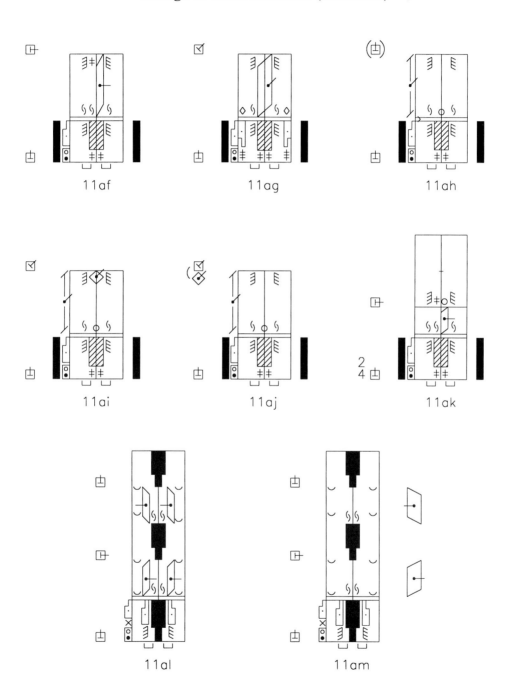

11af      11ag      11ah

11ai      11aj      11ak

11al      11am

# 12 Somersaulting

12.1. **Somersault - Analysis.** Somersault symbols are used when the body revolves around its left-right (lateral) axis. If the performer is standing upright, facing the audience, the axis for somersaulting forward or backward runs from stage left to stage right (intersecting the body). The axis remains horizontal whether the somersault is a roll on the floor or in the air. Somersaults are indicated by the appropriate forward or backward somersault sign as shown in **12a**. If the performer is lying on the left or right side of the body, the body axis for the somersault is now vertical, running from ceiling to floor (see **12i**).

12.2. The understood axis is defined in relation to the body, not in relation to space. If the body position changes, the relation of the axis to space may alter, but its relation to the body always remains the same. The equation of **12b** states that the Body Key is the understood system of reference for somersault symbols, and there is, therefore, no need to write this key in the somersault symbols.[38] (For Body Key see Hutchinson Guest 1970, p. 417 or <u>Advanced Labanotation</u> *Kneeling, Sitting, Lying* Section 33.9-33.11.)

12.3. **Somersault Rolls.** The most familiar form of somersaulting is a somersault roll in which the body does not leave the floor. Support is taken on different body parts during the roll. Somersault rolls, also known as forward and backward rolls in gymnastics, are written by placing the somersault sign in the support columns. Ex. **12c** is an abbreviated way of writing a forward somersault from standing upright, ending in a crouch on both feet. Exact performance is not stated. It is understood that the body 'curls up' as a preparation, the knees bending, the torso bending over the front, the head tucking in and the hands taking weight close to the shoulders to accommodate the action.

12.4. The fraction $^1/_1$ within the somersault sign indicates that one whole somersault turn is completed. (It is usually clearer to read than the numeral '1' by itself, particularly when written by hand.) At completion of the somersault, the front of the torso faces the same room direction as in the starting position. (For use of fractions and indication of degree see 12.11.)

12.5. Ex. **12d** is an outline statement for a somersault roll forward, starting upright and ending sitting on both hips (sitting bones). Degree is not indicated; it is self-evident from the support indication at the end of the somersault. Forward rolls result in traveling forward, backward rolls produce traveling backward.

12.6.  In **12e** the roll of **12d** is spelled out in detail by stating the respective supporting body parts and the preparatory crouch and torso bend.  No statement is made for the arms.  During such a roll, weight is usually taken on the palms of the hands, the upper back part of the shoulders, the back surface of the chest, the back surface of the pelvic area, and finally the hips.  At the end the torso bend and head tilt are no longer in effect.  Such statement of parts supporting sometimes requires placement of the somersault sign outside the staff, as in **12f**.

### Somersault - Analysis

12a    Forward    Backward    12b

### Somersault Rolls

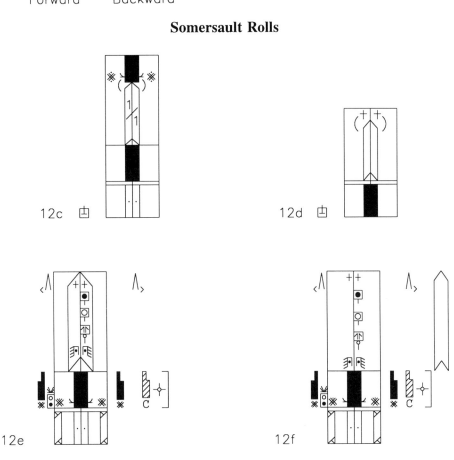

12c        12d

12e        12f

12.7.  Ex. **12g** shows a partial somersault roll backward onto the shoulders, starting from sitting.  The end position is a high shoulder stand, the 'candle' position.  The legs swing backward and then up to the ceiling, the end position is controlled by the hands grasping the sides of the waist.  The degree of somersault is $\frac{1}{2}$ .  (For shoulder stand see 3.5-3.6.)  Ex. **12h** shows a backward roll which starts and ends on the feet.[39]

12.8.  **Front.**  In most cases in which somersault symbols are used, Front is not affected by the somersault turn.  In the rolls of **12a-f** Front is the same previously established room direction throughout the movement.  The physical front of the body changes, but not orientation of the body-as-a-whole.

12.9.  In **12i** a $\frac{1}{4}$ 'somersault' occurs while the performer is lying on the right side of the torso.  At the start she is facing the audience.  As illustrated in **12j** (a bird's-eye view), the head end is displaced toward downstage and the foot end toward upstage; there is a $\frac{1}{4}$ change of Front.  Front changes because of the surface on which the body is supporting and the fact that the axis of this somersault turn is a vertical axis, as in an ordinary pivot turn.  Because in this context there is a change of Front, a black pin is used rather than the fraction $\frac{1}{4}$; the latter is more appropriate for a standard somersault, as it does not in itself involve a change of Front.

12.10.  The movement of **12i** is more frequently written as a turn around the Constant Vertical Axis, **12k**, or as wheeling of the body, **12l**.  (For analysis of wheeling see <u>Advanced Labanotation</u> *Kneeling, Sitting, Lying* Section 28.)

12.11.  **Indication of Degree of Somersault.**  When Front does not change, the amount of turn is indicated with numerals (whole numbers or fractions) (as in **12c** and **12g**).  If Front changes (as when lying on the side), the degree of turn is indicated with black pins, **12i**.  *Black pins in turn signs always indicate the amount of change of Front.*

## Somersault Rolls (continued)

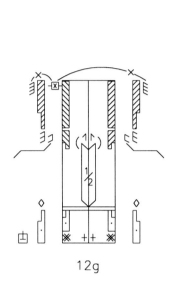

12g

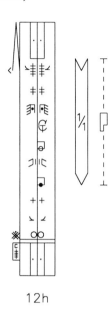

12h

## Front

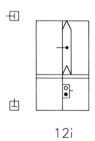

12i

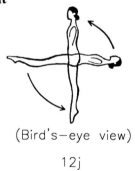

(Bird's—eye view)

12j

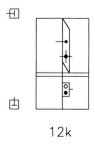

12k

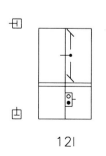

12l

12.12. **Somersaulting in the Air.** If the somersault occurs in the air, the somersault sign can be placed outside the staff or across the support columns with 'air lines' added for leg (or arm) gestures. Both placements give direct statements and are easy to read.

12.13. In **12m** a preparatory jump leads into a forward aerial somersault. Nothing is stated regarding body configuration in the air; the easier manner of performance is for the body to be curled up. The somersault sign is placed outside the staff and since there is a gap in the support columns, it is understood that aerial movement takes place.

12.14. As stated in 12.12, when the somersault sign is written in the support columns, to distinguish between a somersault roll on the floor or a revolution in the air, leg gestures or air lines must be added. Ex. **12n** shows the addition of air lines in the leg gesture columns to indicate that the somersault is an aerial one.

12.15. Such use of 'air lines', which parallel the rule for cancellation of supports in standing, can sometimes be too indirect a statement to be practical, particularly for the arms. An alternate method, used to show somersaulting in the air and to avoid any ambiguity, is to place a release sign within the somersault sign, as in **12o**. This states 'aerial somersault' in a direct way (see also **12ae**). Similarly, a retention sign can be added as in **12p** (see also **12t**) to indicate somersault rolling during which the body does not leave the floor.

12.16. In **12q**, the fact that each somersault is in the air is indicated at the start of each somersault sign through use of the release sign. In **12r** the release signs indicate air-borne somersaulting but the degree has been omitted as being self-evident because of the following support.

12.17. The pattern of **12q** and **12r** is written with airlines in **12s**. Both parts of the somersault in this example are in the air, i.e. there are no supporting body parts while turning, the action strokes for the arms cancel the hand supports.

12.18. In **12t** arm and leg gestures are written but the somersault is not in the air. The retention sign added within the somersault sign specifies that the body does not leave the floor.

## Somersaulting in the Air

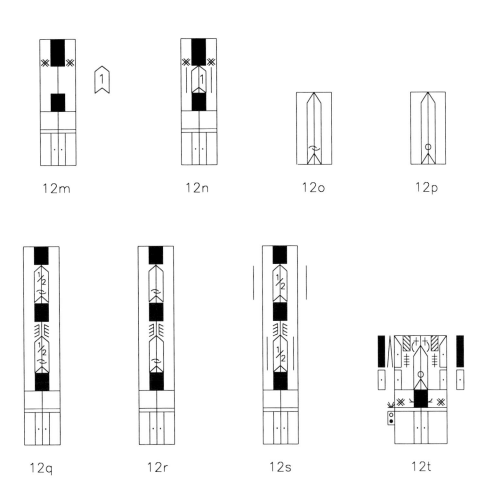

| 12m | 12n | 12o | 12p |
|---|---|---|---|

| 12q | 12r | 12s | 12t |
|---|---|---|---|

12.19.  **Indication of Trampoline.**  As stated in **12u**, a boxed TR can be used to represent the trampoline.  Such indication for a prop would need to be glossarized at the start of the score.

Here support on the trampoline is indicated only at the start.  It is not necessary to repeat the indication of support on the trampoline since the subsequent landing is on the same spot.[40]  Note that in this example the revolution is placed outside the staff on the right.  If the body travels, restating the relationship with the trampoline by using a new support bow is clearer as in **12v**.  This example shows jumping forward and landing on another part of the trampoline surface; supporting is understood still to be on the trampoline.  This is because a column has been given to the object, here a trampoline.  In contrast, when the performer is to jump off the trampoline onto the floor, this is shown by extending the support bow beyond the object column as in **12w**, or by writing the letter T in a box, the sign for *terra*, i.e. the floor, as in **12x**.[41]  As an alternative, contact (i.e. being supported by the trampoline) can be shown to be finished by a release sign placed alone at the appropriate place in the trampoline column or if need be the trampoline indication can be repeated with the release sign, **12y**.

If needed, various areas of the trampoline on which supports occur can be designated (see the Advanced Labanotation issue on handling props).

12.20.  **Traveling.**  As with log rolling, somersault rolls on the floor produce traveling.  In contrast, somersault actions in the air are rotations around the left-right body axis and do not in themselves produce traveling (see **12u**).  In **12z** the path sign explicitly states that forward traveling occurs during the roll.  Such clarification is not normally needed.  With the path sign of **12aa**, the performer deviates to the left (veering toward left backward diagonal) during the roll.  How this is achieved has not been spelled out.

## Indication of Trampoline

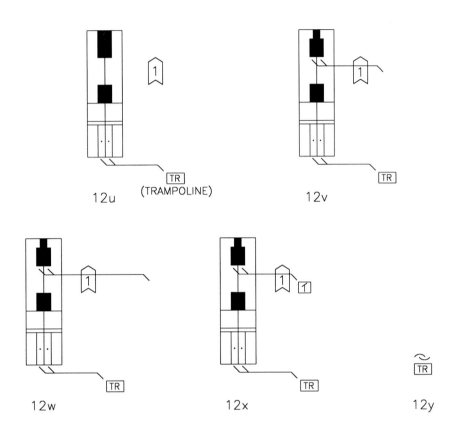

12u          (TRAMPOLINE)                    12v

12w                          12x                          12y

## Traveling

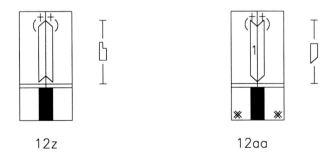

12z                                      12aa

12.21.  In **12ab** running forward and springing into a handstand provides the impetus for a somersault in the air.  The feet land slightly apart (for use of tacks see Appendix B).  During a double somersault, as in **12ac** illustrated in **12ad**, the arms and legs are usually drawn in toward the body.[42]

12.22.  Ex. **12ae** shows in some detail the double forward somersault of the illustration of **12ad**.[43]  The fact that the somersault is in the air does not in itself imply traveling; this is expressed by the forward directions for landing on the feet.  The notation allows for central placement of the somersault sign.  The release sign has been added to speed reading.

# Traveling (continued)

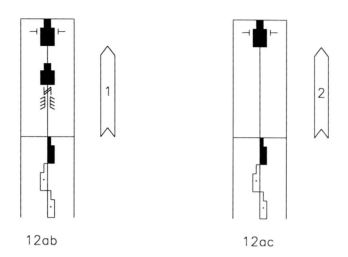

12ab                    12ac

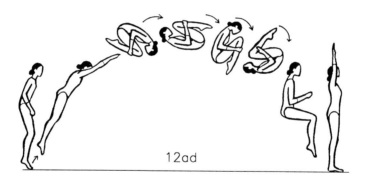

12ad

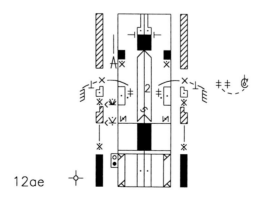

12ae

12.23. **Somersault Written with Direction Symbols.** In many cases somersault actions can be written as a sequence of steps and gestures, i.e. using direction symbols but no somersault signs. Ex. **12af**, a controlled handstand into a back-bend followed by standing up, is analyzed as a series of steps and gestures. Although the body does in fact perform a whole somersault forward in the process, the rotational aspect is not as prominent in **12af** as in the previous examples. The movement is appropriately described without somersault symbols.[44]

From standing upright, the hands take weight forward of the feet; the performer goes into a handstand, the left leg lifting backward before the right; the legs continue to move through place high to forward taking the pelvic area and waist with them. The body passes through a 'bridge' position as the feet take the body weight forward of the hands. Coming upright is aided by pushing (shifting) the pelvic area forward. In practice, at this point some pushing off from the hands occurs. The section ankles-to-hands comes up sequentially ending place high, as a result the arms will end up.

## Somersault Written with Direction Symbols

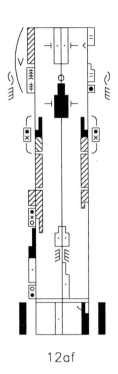

12af

# 13 Cartwheeling

13.1. Cartwheeling can be to the right or to the left. The appropriate cartwheel sign is written in the support column(s) or to the right, outside the staff. Ex. **13a** shows the signs for cartwheeling to the left and to the right.

13.2. **Cartwheel - Analysis.** In a cartwheel the body is rotating in the lateral plane around its forward-backward (sagittal) axis. As with the understood axis for somersaulting, the cartwheel axis is defined in relation to the body (see also 12.2): if the body position changes, the relation of the cartwheel axis to space may alter but its relation to the body always stays the same. In other words, the understood system of reference for cartwheeling (as for somersaulting) is that of the Body Key, **13b**.

13.3. If the performer is standing upright facing the audience and then performs a cartwheel to the right the axis of rotation runs from the audience to upstage. In the process, the front surface of the body remains facing the audience. However, the dancer's 'Front' does not remain constant but changes in the process.[45]

13.4. **Front.** Front is the relationship of the performer's personal front (his or her 'forward' direction) to the Constant Directions in the room or on stage. (For 'Front' as a technical term in Labanotation see also Advanced Labanotation *Kneeling, Sitting, Lying* 33.14.) When remaining in the upright position, changes of Front are easy to follow. In moving into or through upside-down situations, determination of Front requires more careful consideration.

In standing, any pivoting causes Front to change. Somersaulting causes the body to rotate but does not affect Front. Unlike somersaulting or pivoting, analysis of Front in cartwheeling is not straightforward. It is an interesting phenomenon, in terms of change of Front, that a full cartwheel can only be broken up into two $^1/_2$ cartwheels, and that the two $^1/_2$ changes of front occur close to each other.[46] This can best be understood by looking at a full cartwheel in four stages.

13.5 The movement progression of a standard cartwheel illustrated in the series of figures in **13c**, shows the performer facing the audience at the start (seen here from the back). After a quarter cartwheel revolution the position of the trunk is comparable to lying on the right side of the body facing the audience, (ii); Front has not changed. Another quarter cartwheel results in support on the

hands, (iii). In the handstand reached after half a cartwheel, Front is not where
the front surface of the body is facing (to the audience) but toward the opposite
direction (upstage). Awareness of this Front is heightened when the back is
arched and the head lifted, (iv). If from this position the feet were to be lowered
as in (v), it is quite clear that a half-change of Front has occurred; the body has
suddenly turned 180° and Front is toward upstage. Note that figures (iv) and (v)
are here for explanatory purposes only. After another quarter revolution the
original Front is restored, (vi), a position equivalent to lying on the left side. The
last quarter, used to return to the upright stance, (vii), does not affect Front any
more than the first quarter.

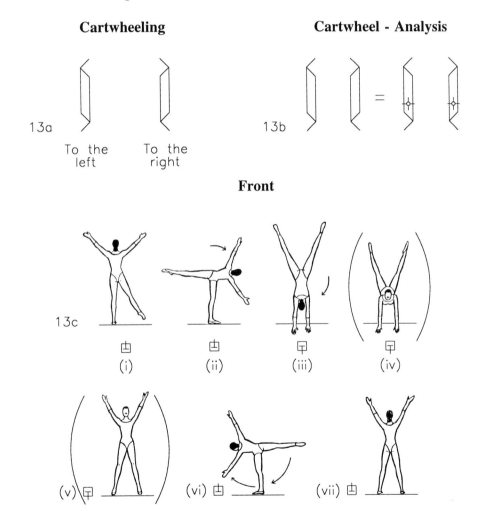

**Cartwheeling**          **Cartwheel - Analysis**

13a          13b

To the          To the
left          right

**Front**

13c          (i)          (ii)          (iii)          (iv)

(v)          (vi)          (vii)

13.6.  The following analysis of a cartwheel, **13d**, is designed to focus on the exact moments of change of Front.  Fig. (i) shows the starting position, the figure facing the audience.  The moment of change occurs when the old support, the right foot, is relinquished and weight is taken completely on the new support (the right hand), i.e. between (ii) and (iii).  Front is now toward upstage, as is quite clear when the second hand is placed on the floor, (iv).  The next change of Front occurs the moment when the left hand lifts and the left foot takes weight, (v).  From there until the conclusion of the cartwheel, (vi), Front is again to the audience.

13.7.  **'Blind Turns' (Non-Swivel Turns) on the Hands.**  In stepping on the hands in a cartwheel, in order to avoid swivelling, the arms prepare by rotating into the direction of the revolution.  Thus in **13d**, the right hand at the moment of (ii) will be placed to point upstage, as will the left hand in (iv).  This rotation of the arms provides a $\frac{1}{2}$ 'blind turn' which helps to explain the sudden half turn change of Front.  Ex. **13e** shows the feet at the start and how the hands will be placed.

13.8.  **Basic Notation.**  Ex. **13f** is a basic statement of a cartwheel to the right.  One full cartwheel is completed.  In contrast to somersault rolls, for which the arms and legs are usually brought in close to the body, in a standard cartwheel the four extremities are usually extended outward like spokes on a wheel so that support can be taken on one part after the other.  The arms are more or less held in the same relation to the body as in the starting position.  (See **13m** for specific directions for arms, legs, and torso.)

13.9.  The sequence of supporting parts may be written in the support column.  Ex. **13g** shows a standard cartwheel to the right in which respectively the right foot, the right hand, the left hand, the left foot and finally the right foot are shown to take weight, the sign for cartwheeling being placed outside the staff.  Front at the end is toward the same direction as at the beginning, i.e. to the audience.

13.10.  During the cartwheel of **13g** the performer travels to stage right.  This step direction is indicated in the path sign of **13h** which states undeviating traveling to the right.  The same statement can be made in terms of the room direction, **13i**.  In **13j** the cartwheel sign is placed across the support columns and the supporting body parts are placed within it.  Such placement is not always practical for exact timing, therefore placement of the cartwheel outside has a clear advantage.  The Constant Key given in **13k** governs the step direction.

## Front (continued)

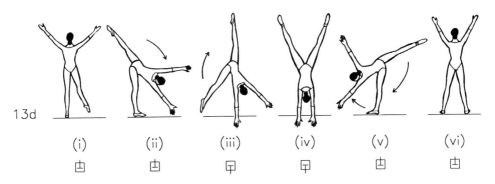

13d  (i)  (ii)  (iii)  (iv)  (v)  (vi)

## 'Blind Turns' (Non-Swivel Turns) on the Hands

13e

## Basic Notation

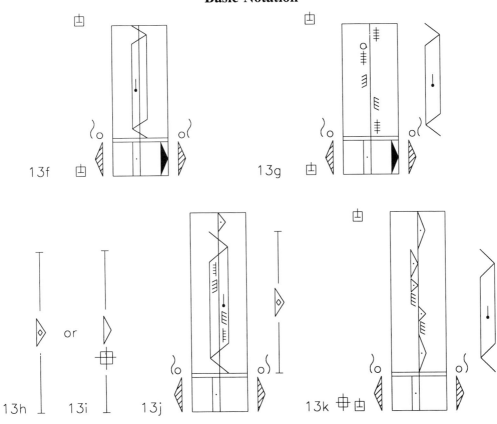

13f    13g

13h   13i   13j   13k

13.11. The required rotation of the legs and arms to produce the smooth 'blind turn' action for a cartwheel is spelled out in **13l**, which again uses Constant Cross directions. Normally, these rotations are understood and, as in **13j**, not actually written. In **13m** a cartwheel to the right is spelled out fully. Note use of the Constant Directions Key to facilitate interpretation of the direction symbols. (For Constant Key see Hutchinson Guest 1970, p. 241 or the <u>Advanced Labanotation</u> issue *Kneeling, Sitting, Lying* 33.12.)[47]

13.12. **Indication of Degree of Cartwheel.** In **13n** only half a cartwheel is performed. The performer then lowers the legs backward to return to his/her feet and ends up facing the opposite direction. Note that the arms are held more or less in their body-related side high position.

13.13. The rule that amount of rotation is shown with a *black pin* if Front changes and with a *fraction* if it does not (see 12.11) applies to cartwheeling as follows:

A black pin is used for a full cartwheel (see **13f** and **13g**) and for half a cartwheel (see **13n**). A fraction or numeral is used when only a partial cartwheel occurs and no change of Front. An example of this is shown in **13o** where a trampoline performer springs into a $^1/_4$ cartwheel to the left, landing on the left side of the body; then bounces $^1/_2$ cartwheel to the right, landing on the right side; and finally does $^1/_4$ left to land on his feet again. There has been no change of Front. Fractions may also be needed, when cartwheels are combined with other forms of rotation and a full cartwheel occurs but not a full change of Front (see **13p**, **13s** and **13v**). In any case, the Front sign should be restated for clarity and to facilitate the reading process.

## Basic Notation (continued)

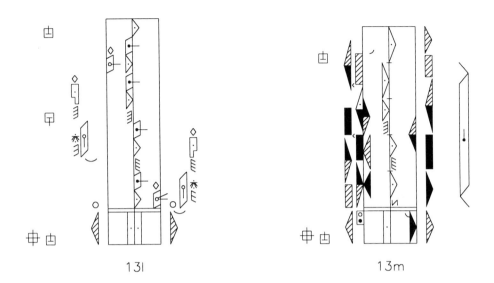

13l                    13m

## Indication of Degree of Cartwheel

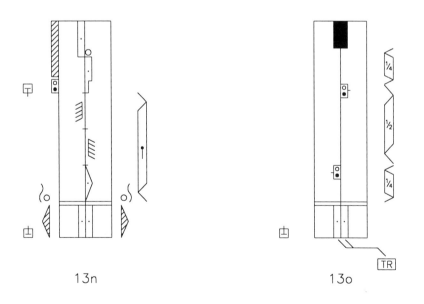

13n                    13o

13.14. **Cartwheeling with Different Step Directions.** So far we have dealt with pure cartwheeling during which the body stays within one plane. Cartwheeling may be combined with different step directions and ways of turning to create other forms, as shown in the following examples (**13p-13w**).

13.15. **'Diagonal Cartwheel'.** In **13p** a cartwheel occurs traveling on a diagonal line. It is a full cartwheel in the sense of passing through foot-hand-hand-foot supports, returning to the upright situation. The cartwheel sign placed outside gives an immediate message for the overall movement. This movement is basically the standard cartwheel of **13j**, but traveling in the right forward diagonal direction rather than to the side. This full cartwheel brings the performer back onto the feet, but, if no extra turning has been introduced, Front in the ending position is to stage left rather than to the audience, only a $^3/_4$ change of Front occurs. Progression in the same diagonal direction is shown through use of the Constant Key.

13.16. The same movement of **13p** is written in **13q** from the understood Standard Key. The traveling that takes place is written outside the staff as a Constant Key direction. Here leg and arm rotations and blind turns have been indicated. Note the $^1/_8$ blind turn on the right foot at the start.[48] The legs are shown to touch when they are up. Ex. **13r** shows the foot and hand placement on the floor for the diagonal cartwheel.

13.17. In **13s** the movement of **13q** is simplified and analyzed in terms of the rotations that take place. While the body revolves one full cartwheel in the sense of returning to the upright situation on the feet, it has accomplished only $^3/_4$ of a change of Front. This change of Front results from an unseen, unfelt $^1/_4$ turn to the left which is 'absorbed' in the cartwheel action. This $^1/_4$ turn is stated here in the adjacent turn sign for purposes of explanation. The traveling factor is added in the path sign (see also **13h**).[49]

13.18. A diagonal cartwheel could as well be analysed as a rotation around a diagonal axis; either a somersault for which the side-to-side axis has been turned $^1/_8$ to the right, as in the sign of **13t**, or as a cartwheel for which the sagittal axis has been turned $^1/_8$ to the left, as in **13u**. (For rotations around a diagonal axis, see Section 16.)

## 'Diagonal Cartwheel'

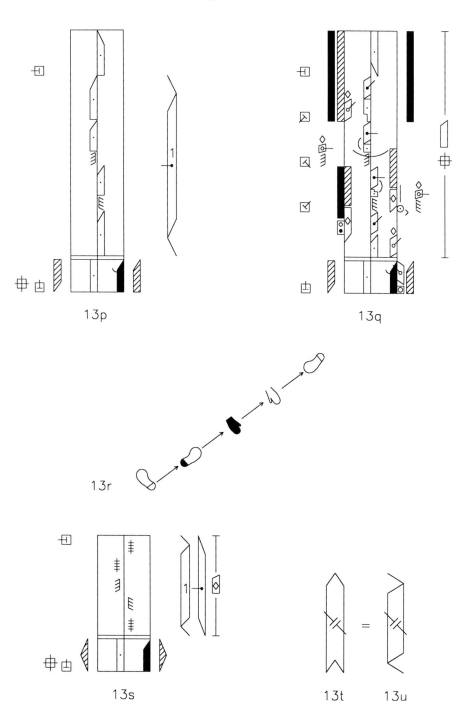

13p

13q

13r

13s

13t  13u

13.19. 'Forward Cartwheel'. A so-called 'forward cartwheel' places the hands and feet on a path directly forward of the starting position, **13v**. Ex. **13w** shows the placement of the hands. Some people, when beginning a 'forward cartwheel' with the right foot, twist the chest to the left, thus giving the initial impetus the feeling of starting a sideward cartwheel. The chest twist disappears once the weight is taken on the hands. For a full 'forward cartwheel', as spelled out here, only a change of front of $^1/_2$ results. This is because this rotation is a mixture of a somersault and a cartwheel occuring at the same time.

13.20. **Cartwheeling in Sitting and Lying.** Cartwheeling in the sense of rotating around the body's forward-backward axis is also possible in sitting and lying. It should, however, be stressed that cartwheel signs do not usually produce the clearest or most appropriate way of writing these movements. The following examples compare different analyses.

13.21. Ex. **13x**: from sitting, a $^1/_4$ cartwheel to the right produces lying on the right side of the body, the legs will remain in the previous forward direction. This movement is usually written as **13y**. The fact that in the starting position the legs are extended in front of the body, not in line with the torso as in standing upright, does not basically affect the determination of the cartwheel axis; here, because of the floor, the axis is located in the right hip. The leg placement enables one to think of the legs as providing the axis of the turn. The legs are understood to retain their spatial direction.

13.22. The same movement could be described as rolling to the right around the axis of the right leg, **13z** (for body part signs for axis of rotation see 16.11-16.13). Note the appropriate use of a fraction for degree of cartwheel rotation because there is no change of Front (see 13.13). Reiterating the Front sign clarifies this fact.

13.23. When lying on the back (supine), as in **13aa**, and body-based cartwheeling takes place (i.e. the form of rotation which would happen if standing up), illustrated with bird's eye view in **13ab**, the revolution will be around the vertical line through the center of the body. Such cartwheeling to the right causes Front to change in the opposite direction. As seen here, a $^1/_4$ cartwheel to the *right* (judged from the body) causes a $^1/_4$ change of Front to the *left*. This can be very confusing for the reader.[50] When lying prone, the same degree of body-based cartwheeling produces the *same degree* of change of Front. It is more practical to describe this action as wheeling around the vertical axis.

13.24. In **13ac** the sign for wheeling is placed in the support column. The whole body wheels $^1/_4$ to the left around its center, i.e. the top of the pelvis; the extremities, here the hands and feet, describe a $\frac{1}{4}$ circle. In **13ad** the wheeling action is indicated as a rotation around the constant up-down axis; this produces the same result.

### 'Forward Cartwheel'

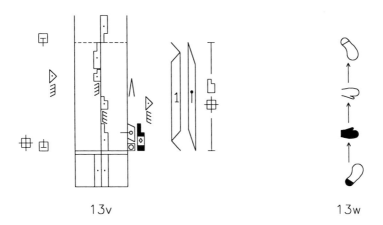

13v                                    13w

### Cartwheeling in Sitting and Lying

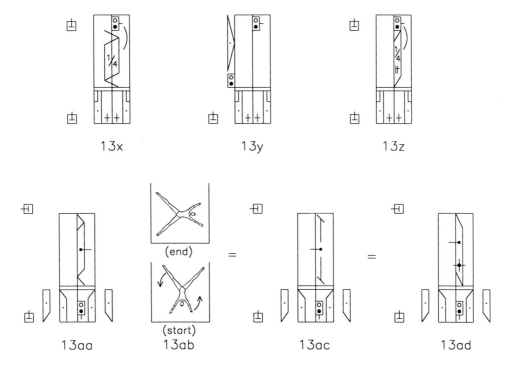

13x            13y            13z

13aa        13ab        13ac        13ad

13.25. **Cartwheeling in the Air.** Ex. **13ae** is the outline notation of half a cartwheel in the air. The action consists of jumping from standing and landing in a handstand on the same spot on the trampoline, facing the back. Writing options for cartwheels in the air are analogous to those for somersaulting in the air (see **12m-12s**). The jump may thus be notated alternatively by placing a release sign within the cartwheel sign or by placing the cartwheel sign outside the staff (in these cases action strokes as in **13ae** are not needed).

13.26. Ex. **13af** shows jumping 'on all fours'. The front of the body is facing down. In this context, cartwheeling $^1/_2$ to the right (viewed from the point of view of the body) is the same as turning to the right around the Constant Vertical Axis. This latter example, **13ag**, is the better description and most likely the first choice. Note the release sign within the turn sign.

13.27. The fact that a jump occurs (supports leave the trampoline) at the same time as the cartwheel turn, is indicated in **13af** by action strokes for the arms and legs. In **13ag** the release in the standard rotation sign indicates a spring. In **13ah** the same movement is expressed by placing the sign for rotation outside the staff and the release signs in the support column.

# Cartwheeling in the Air

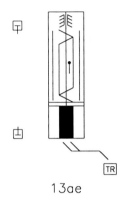

13ae

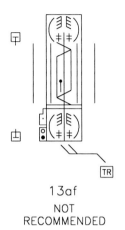

13af

NOT
RECOMMENDED

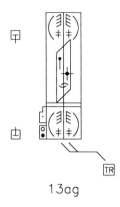

13ag

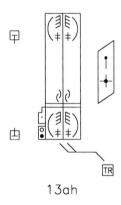

13ah

# 14 Somersault and Cartwheel Paths

14.1. The somersault and cartwheel revolutions discussed in Sections 12 and 13 denote rotation of the body around an axis that intersects the body. They are notated with *rotation signs*.

Somersault and cartwheel *path signs* denote very similar revolutions of the body. The difference is that the axis of rotation now lies outside the body. While they belong to more advanced acrobatics, presentation here may help to clarify the previously discussed rotations and revolutions.

14.2. Somersault and cartwheel path signs parallel the use of the signs for horizontal circular paths. As has been shown, floor contact determines whether and how traveling takes place during turns. In working with a trapeze, through which large spatial displacements are possible, somersault and cartwheel paths are more applicable. The facts concerning such paths are presented here in simple examples.[51]

14.3. Ex. **14a** shows the forward and backward somersault path signs. The axis of rotation for a forward somersault path is parallel to the left-right axis passing through the body, but it lies outside the body in front of the performer. For a backward somersault path it lies behind him/her.

14.4. Ex. **14b** shows cartwheel paths to the left and the right. The axis of rotation is parallel to the forward/backward axis through the body. If the path is to the left, the axis lies to the left of the performer; if it is to the right the axis lies to his/her right.

14.5. Perfect somersault and cartwheel pathways occur only through the aid of outer mechanical help, e.g. a swing. If the swing has metal 'ropes', there is the possibility of making complete circles. In **14c** a backward somersault path is occurring. Because the person is facing the direction of progression, this path may be experienced as a forward somersault path, but in terms of direction of somersaulting, it is a backward circular path. In **14d** the person is facing sideways, hence for him/her it becomes a cartwheel path to the right.

## Somersault and Cartwheel Paths

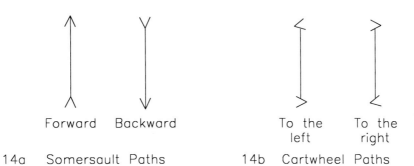

Forward　　Backward　　　　　To the　　To the
　　　　　　　　　　　　　　　　　left　　　right

14a　Somersault Paths　　　　14b　Cartwheel Paths

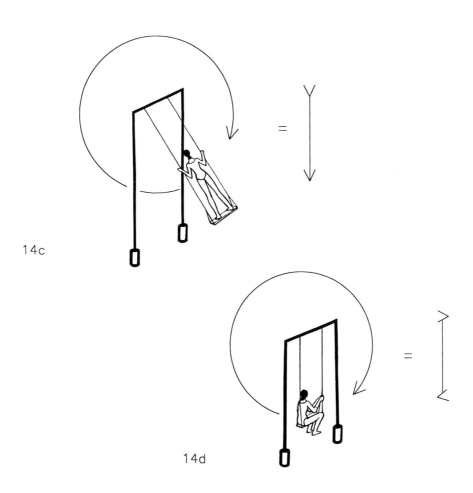

14c

14d

14.6.  Change of Front is analyzed in the same way as for somersault and cartwheel revolutions.  The figure drawing of **14e** shows spatial displacement of the body after $^1/_4$ and $^1/_2$ of a forward somersault path.  As in somersaults, Front does not change.  The degree of rotation is accordingly indicated with a fraction (see 12.11).  The front of the body remains directed toward the axis of the circular path throughout.

14.7.  Ex. **14f** shows placement of the body in space after $^1/_4$ and $^1/_2$ cartwheel path to the right.  The right side of the body is directed toward the axis of circling throughout.  As in cartwheels, it is understood that $^1/_2$ a cartwheel path causes Front to change by 180° (see 13.4-6).  Degree of cartwheel is therefore indicated by a black pin.

14.8.  These drawings are schematic to illustrate the analysis; in actual practice, when initiated by the performer alone the curve described in the air is less symmetrical, its actual shape depending on the initial direction and degree of force expended in the take off and the effect of gravity.  The degree to which aerial paths can be achieved depends on the height of the spring and the distance traveled; when a spring board or trampoline is used, the 'flight' can be increased. Describing it as a somersault path can give the reader a spatial image that will help in the execution of the movement.  These matters also depend on the aim of the notation and the degree of precision needed.

14.9.  Exs. **14g-h** show in outline notation a forward dive from a diving board (labeled D) into water (labeled A, from the Latin 'aqua').[52]  The body is shown to penetrate the water.  During the jump the arms move overhead so that the hands are the first to touch the water.  The displacement of the body is as in the illustration of **14e**.
  Note that to indicate the body entering the water, a line is drawn from the center of the staff to link the staff with the sign for the water.[53]  The double x sign shows entering ('penetrating') the water.

14.10.  In **14h** a full somersault around the body axis is combined with the half somersault path resulting in 1 $^1/_2$ revolutions so that the dive again enters the water hands first.

## Somersault and Cartwheel Paths (continued)

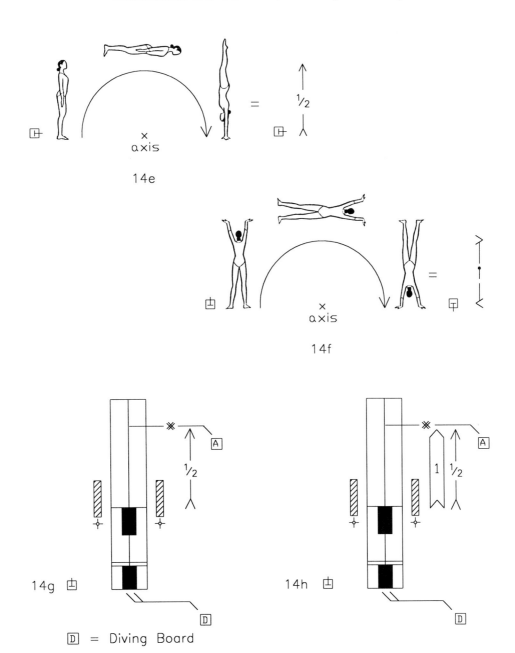

14e

14f

14g

14h

D = Diving Board

14.11.  It is not always necessary to analyze somersault and cartwheel paths as such.  The first movement of **14i** (a 'dive' forward roll) may resemble $^1/_2$ a somersault path in the air but can be written as shown; the performer ends stretched out on the back.

14.12.  Ex. **14j**, earlier discussed as **12ae**, is a double somersault executed while traveling forward.  If there is enough rise into the air while traveling this can be felt as being the same as a $^1/_2$ somersault path during which the body revolves an additional $1$ $^1/_2$ turns around its left-right axis, **14k**.  The latter way of writing has the advantage of pointing out that most of the turning action occurs in the middle of the sequence.  If the description of **14k** is used the direction of the legs at the landing is not forward but 'place'.  This is because **14j** shows traveling through directions in the support column and **14k** shows it by a path sign.

14.13.  Ex. **14l** describes a full somersault backward during which momentary support is taken on the hands (a back-flip).  Traveling backward is shown in the support column.  The initial backward folding of the torso gives impetus to the aerial backward somersault.  Instead of using the somersault sign, this could be described using two half backward somersault path signs, **14m**.  Ex. **14n** illustrates the notation.

# Somersault and Cartwheel Paths (continued)

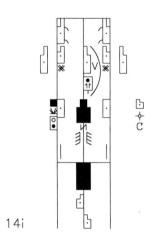

14i

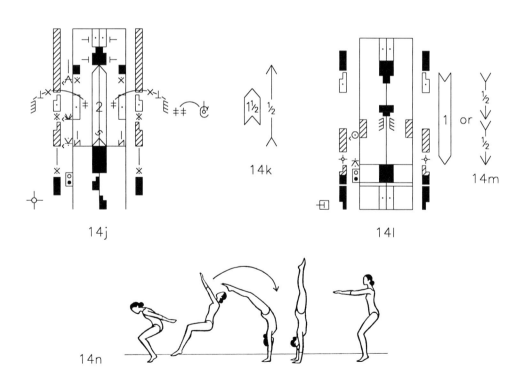

14j

14k

14l

14m

14n

14.14 **Distance.** Distance in such traveling is usually given in a general statement. When a long trampoline is used it can be schematically divided into sections which are labelled. When two people are on the trampoline simultaneously, it can be important to know where each one lands. For our purposes here, some simple examples are given for three ways of indicating distance.

14.15. In **14o** a long distance upward is stated in the path sign alongside the staff. The somersault circular path should be vertically longer than a standard, comfortable path. An extra long distance for landing backward, i.e. horizontal displacement, is shown in **14p**. The addition of a short straight path to the same basic movement, **14q**, also states distance in terms of horizontal displacement. Timing will affect distance in that more time in the air requires a greater height. Such height will be balanced against the amount of horizontal displacement indicated.

# Distance

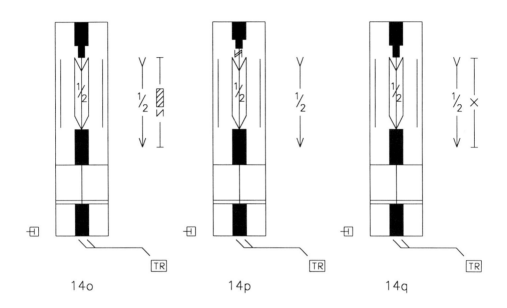

14o            14p            14q

# 15 Combined Revolutions of the Body

15.1.  The preceding sections discussed revolutions of the body around one of the principal axes, i.e. the up-down, the forward-backward or the left-right axis.  These axes may be defined in relation to the Standard Cross, the Body Cross or in relation to the room (the Constant Directions).  They may intersect the body or lie outside it, as in circular paths.  In all these cases the axes are easy to identify and the effect of a simple rotation around one of them can be calculated without difficulty.

While a few simple combined forms were given in the last sections, in this section more complex possibilities are explored.  The reader should bear in mind that Labanotation strives to give a simple and accessible description of human movement without omitting vital information.

15.2.  Revolutions of the body may be more complex than the forms hitherto described for two reasons:
-      different types of revolution may take place simultaneously, e.g. somersault and pivot turn, cartwheel and somersault;
-      a revolution may not be around an easily identifiable axis such as the left-right body axis or a Constant Vertical Axis, but around *two dimensional (diametral) or three dimensional (diagonal) axes* (see 16.2-5).

15.3.  A complex rotary action, in which the body revolves around more than one axis at the same time, may occur when it is supported on the floor (as in 'break dancing') or when it is in the air for a period of time, as in diving or tumbling, e.g. on a trampoline.

15.4.  In simple log rolling, as in **15a**, the head-end of the body remains directed toward the same room direction.  Another simultaneous rotation may cause this body orientation to change.  Thus **15b** and **15c** illustrate an example of floorwork combining two forms of rotation, 'log rolling' and 'wheeling'.  As the body rolls to the right the head-end and foot-end describe half a horizontal circle to the right around the pelvis (center of the body, the axis for the wheeling).  The performer will end again prone, on the belly, but facing upstage (i.e. feet toward the audience).  The 'wheeling' action is defined as occurring around the Constant Vertical Axis, **15b**.  The Body Key has been placed in the 'log rolling' sign as an aid to distinguish it from the wheeling action.  Use of the horizontal path sign in **15c** has the advantage that the sign itself states the vertical axis and there is less need for the Body Key reminder in the log rolling symbol. (For full explanation see the <u>Advanced Labanotation</u> issue *Kneeling, Sitting, Lying* Section 29.) In **15d** and **15e** the wheeling indication has been placed outside the staff. For some people this placement facilitates reading.

When log rolling, the body's orientation in relation to space (the Front direction) is constantly changing. It is therefore impractical to relate the axis of a wheeling action also to the Body Cross, i.e. to describe it as part of a cartwheel.

15.5. Actions which are basically rotations can be described, when the body is on the floor, through changes in placement of the body weight together with directional changes for parts of torso and limbs. These may cause a change of Front without the geometrical axes of turning being described. In **15f** the torso directions spell out a sequence which is basically a backward somersault.

In contrast, in aerial turns (such as occur in diving) the movements need to be described in terms of revolutions of the body and combinations of revolutions.

### Combined Revolutions of the Body

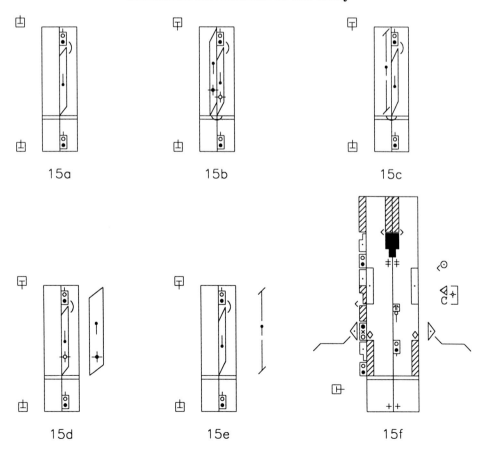

15a        15b        15c

15d        15e        15f

15.6. **Analysis.** Before going into further detail on the combination of two forms of rotating in relation to the body-as-a-whole, a more familiar but related exploration of head movements may help in understanding what takes place. The main difference is that the head is limited by its attachment to the body, whereas the body-as-a-whole is a 'free agent' as it travels through space.

15.7. The point to be investigated is the use of a body reference in contrast to an outside reference. The forward head tilt of **15g** is followed by a rotation around the head axis, the left ear ending in front of the chest. The rotation does not affect the spatial direction of the head tilt. In **15h** the rotation occurs first, followed by the tilt. The direction for this tilt is taken from the front of the free end of the head. Thus the end position is with the nose close to the right shoulder. The sequence of these two movements has produced a different result. The key of **15i** to determine Front from the twisted part can be given for clarification, but it is not usually needed as this is the standard rule in Labanotation for statement of direction for a twisted part.[54]

15.8. In **15j** the forward tilt is followed by a $^1/_4$ wheeling to the right, the end result is the same as **15h**. The nose will be near the right shoulder. This is because the axis for a head rotation in its upright state, as at the start of **15h**, is the same axis as for the wheeling in **15j**, i.e. a constant vertical axis. In **15k** the head turns first then tilts into the Stance forward direction, i.e. toward the previously established front. The resulting position is the same as for **15g**.[55]

15.9. When such tilting and turning occur at the same time, as in **15l**, the result is a skew (three dimensional) curve, a movement possible for a limb or the torso but not, under most circumstances, for the body-as-a-whole. The end result is as in **15h**. In **15m** use of a space hold for the forward direction produces rotation on a spatially retained movement; the end result being the same as **15g**. The same movement could also be written with the Stance Key, as in **15n**, the movement being a simultaneous performance of **15k**.

15.10. Ex. **15o** illustrates the difficulty of relating two combined rotations both to a body axis. It shows simultaneous somersaulting and pivoting actions. The resulting skew curve works for limbs which are attached to a stable base, but does not function for the whole body in ordinary unaided circumstances. Such combinations, however, can occur in underwater swimming, where the performer has control of change of direction through pressure against the water. Note that the end result of this combined rotation cannot be calculated by simply taking one rotation first and then adding the other: this is demonstrated in **15p** and **15q**. In **15p** the body is first subjected to a quarter of a somersault, then to a quarter of a pivot turn (a 'roll') to the right. In **15q** the pivot turn comes first, followed by the somersault. For each case the ending position is different.[56]

## Analysis

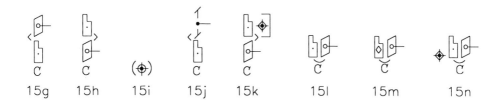

| 15g | 15h | 15i | 15j | 15k | 15l | 15m | 15n |

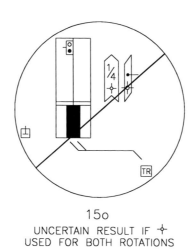

15o

UNCERTAIN RESULT IF ✛
USED FOR BOTH ROTATIONS

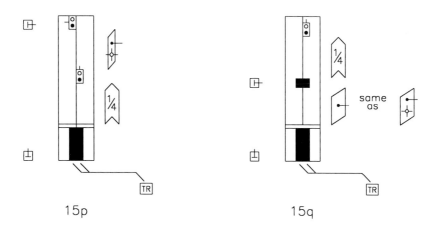

15p                    15q

15.11. In the above examples of **15m** and **15n** the forward head tilt can be equated with a $^1/_4$ forward somersault path for the extremity, the top of the head, **15r**. The end position will be with the left ear facing down in front of the chest. In a similar way, the body, while traveling on such a path, can additionally revolve around its own axis.

15.12. Because of the law of inertia, somersault and cartwheel aerial paths have a spatially controlled trajectory.[57] For instance, once the body has taken off from a diving board, the path in the air is set by the direction and force of energy on the take-off; the path follows the natural pull of gravity and cannot be changed, no matter how much the body twists and turns within that path.

15.13. In **15s** one of the rotations has been defined as a turn around the Constant Vertical Axis. The end position is the same as in **15q**, not as in **15p**. It is important to observe that if in **15p** and **15q** the Constant Vertical Axis is used for the turn sign, the end result (i.e. ending lying on the front) will be the same whether the turn comes before the somersault or after.[58]

15.14. In performing an ordinary cartwheel, a turning action produced by foot and hand pressure can make the path curve, as in **15t**. The step direction is, of course, affected by the circular path.

15.15. **Spatial Retention for Revolution or Path.** Analogous with its application within direction symbols, a space hold may be placed within somersault and cartwheel turn signs to indicate that the axis of rotation established at the start does not change its spatial orientation even if the body is in the process of turning. If in **15u** the original cartwheel path is maintained (shown by a space hold), the $^1/_4$ rotation to the right (here written with a rotation sign) will cause it to end as a forward walk-over, producing a straight path.

15.16. In **15v** the direction of the forward somersault is maintained, it does not change because of the $^1/_4$ rotation to the right. In **15w** this same direction of rotation is described in terms of the Constant Cross, an automatic spatial retention for the somersault.

15.17. Because **15v** starts facing Front, the somersault sign of **15w** will produce the same form of rotation, but, if one starts facing stage right, as in **15x**, the forward rotation toward the audience would produce the action of cartwheeling to the left in the body. The result will be to end on the left side of the torso with no change of front. In **15y** the additional $^1/_4$ rotation produces a change of front and ending lying on the back.

## Analysis (continued)

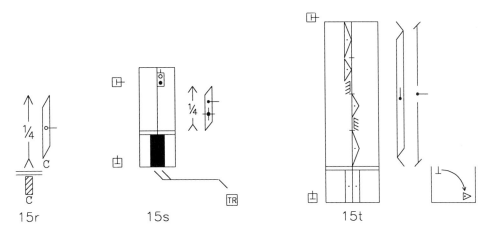

15r          15s          15t

## Spatial Retention for Revolution or Path

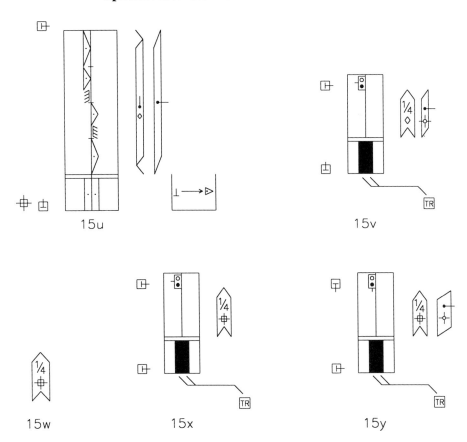

15u          15v

15w          15x          15y

15.18. **Turn With Somersault.** Ex. **15z** shows a very basic example of a somersault path combined with a turn, known in gymnastics as a 'twist'.[59] The movement here consists of jumping from a handstand on a trampoline to standing upright. With the somersault path alone, the performer would still face downstage at the end. Because of the added half-turn around the head-foot axis of the body, in the ending position s/he faces upstage. Note that here no space hold or Constant Key has been given for the somersault path, as such spatial retention can be understood.

15.19. The description of **15z** links with what takes place when one turns while walking on a circular path. The path continues in the same direction despite other turning actions taking place. This is illustrated in the simple example of **15aa**. The half-turns around the body do not affect the circular pathway; on the contrary, the pathway influences the turns by augmenting them slightly when turning in the same direction as the circling and diminishing them slightly when turning in the opposite direction.

15.20. Ex. **15ab** describes a similar exercise to **15z** in which a half somersault rotation bringing the body upright is combined with a half-turn. The somersault is forward and includes traveling, which may feel like forward traveling because of the upside-down starting position. However, backward direction symbols are written, because the direction is judged on landing after the half turn; you end facing the trampoline.

15.21. In **15ac** a backward somersault with a full 'twist' is notated in some detail. It should be noted that the figure illustration of **15ad** is spread out to make the action clearer. This well-known gymnastic pattern is often performed so that the performer lands on the same spot. The overall action is of a full somersault backward during which a full turn around the head-foot axis takes place. The turn and the somersault around the body start simultaneously, creating in principle the problem of **15o**. Therefore, in **15ac** the somersault is related to the starting direction by the addition of the white diamond within the somersault sign.

15.22. If traveling backward occurs, as suggested by the illustration of **15ad**, then the backward somersault action would be described partly as a path and partly as a rotation as shown in **15z**. Direction symbols for the landing would then be used.

## Turn with Somersault

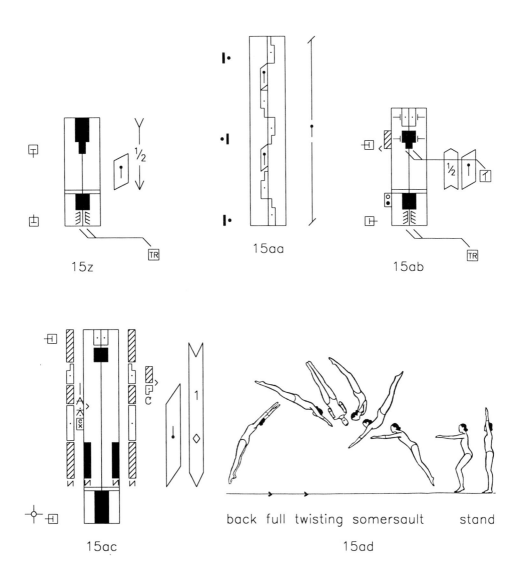

15z

15aa

15ab

15ac

back  full  twisting  somersault      stand

15ad

15.23. **Overlap of Actions.** Rotations may overlap rather than coincide. In **15ae** the somersault path and the turn around the head-foot axis have started before the somersault. The direction of the somersault can therefore only be expressed by use of a Constant Cross Axis, in this example the somersault relates to the side-to-side room axis.

15.24. **Turn and Cartwheel.** In **15af**, person A, standing with her back to the audience, jumps sideward into the arms of three partners, B, C and D (see floorplan). During the jump A performs a very quick $^1/_2$ turn around her head-foot axis, facing the audience at the end, and landing supported on her left side.

15.25. Although A will not describe exactly a $^1/_4$ of a cartwheel path in the air, the displacement could be written as in **15ag**, the spatially controlled $^1/_4$ cartwheel replacing the torso direction and the straight path sign in **15af**.

## Overlap of Actions

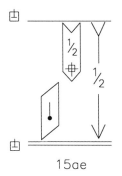

15ae

## Turn and Cartwheel

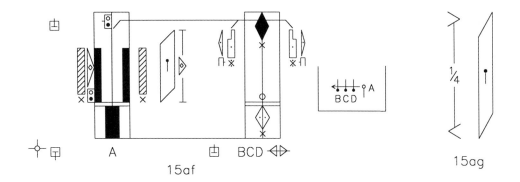

# 16 Other Axes of Rotation

16.1.  The dimensional axes in the body are easily identifiable; when upright facing front, they coincide with the fixed axes of the Constant Cross. Rotation can also take place around other axes.  The specific axis is stated by placing two opposite 'pin' signs within the rotation sign, **16a**.

16.2.  **Diagonal Axes.**  A diagonal (three dimensional) or diametral (two dimensional) axis can be described by placing within the rotation symbol the two pins that symbolise the two opposite directions between which the axis runs.  In **16a**, the cartwheel revolves around the left-forward-middle/right-backward-middle diagonal axis.[60]

16.3.  The axis of **16a** is applied to **16b**, as illustrated in **16c**.  This axis lies between the normal somersault and cartwheel axes.  The revolution around this axis can also be described using a somersault sign, **16d**.  There is no difference in result, the difference lies in whether it is seen or experienced as related to the one form or the other.  The drawing of **16e** shows a person about to revolve around a horizontal bar representing this same axis.[61]  In **16f** a box is used to illustrate the same thing.

16.4.  Turning around the same axis as in **16b** or **16d**, but in the opposite direction, can be indicated as in **16g**, using either a cartwheel to the left or a backward somersault symbol.  The axis pins are the same; the cartwheel or somersault signs are therefore in the opposite direction.  Note that the pins, used to state the axis, refer to the Standard Cross; when stating the Constant Key, pins will refer to the Constant Cross of Axes and a 'Constant Key axis' can be given.

16.5.  An axis may also be a *body part*; such an axis can be designated by placing the body part sign within the rotation sign, as in **16h**, which shows a backward somersault around the knees, as might occur on a trapeze.  (For body part axes see 16.11-13.)

## Diagonal Axes

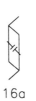

16a

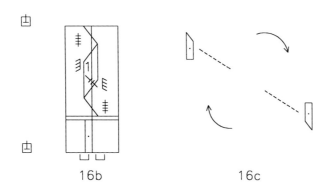

16b                    16c

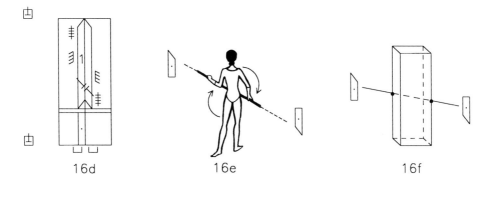

16d            16e            16f

16g                    16h

16.6. **Degree of Rotation.** By convention half and full degrees of cartwheeling are indicated by black pins, when they cause an equivalent change of Front. As mentioned before, fractions are used when the degree of cartwheeling does not produce an equivalent change of Front (see 13.13). In this respect cartwheeling is different from somersaulting (see 12.11). Because in **16b** the revolution is a mixture of cartwheel and somersault and a full change of Front does not take place in the process, the full revolution is better written with a numeral. It is important to give the Front sign at the end.

16.7. **Indications for Body Orientation.** For determining orientation of the body at any time the abbreviated signs of **16i** are valuable.[62] In addition to indicating Front (i.e. room direction) in the usual way, the signs for the surfaces of the torso (front, back, right, left, etc.) can be abbreviated to: (i) and (ii) for front and back sides; (iii) and (iv) for right and left sides of the body. The sign of (v) indicates the line of the spine, from which are derived (vi) for the 'head-end' and (vii) for the 'foot-end' of the body. Orientation can be determined at any point by stating the facing direction of just two of these surfaces. It is essential that *the surfaces chosen are at right angles to each other*. In (viii) the performer is facing the audience with the right side of the body facing down. In (ix) the foot end is up while the right side is facing stage right. One of the co-ordinates needs to be a Front sign, or directions need to be defined in terms of the Constant Cross.

16.8. Such statements can be used for clarification as well as pin-pointing moments in complex lifts in which one dancer changes position by the manipulation of two or more others. As these are orientation indications they are placed at the left of the staff.

16.9. **Range of Pins for Axes.** When pins are used for axes, 'flat' pins (tacks) symbolize horizontal axes, white pins high and black pins low directions. Thus **16j** and **16k** show rotation around the axis running from left side high to right side low. Such a revolution could occur when supported on a slanting pole. This axis lies between the left-right and the up-down body axes, illustrated in **16l**, and can therefore be indicated either with a somersault or a standard turn sign, as in **16k**. This same axis is illustrated with a box in **16m**.

16.10. The revolution of **16l** is analysed in **16n**, which shows the orientation of the torso after each $\frac{1}{4}$ rotation. In determining orientation two body surfaces can prove easier to determine than Front. In **16n** the orientations of the front and top end of the torso are shown. Note also which body surface or edge faces down at each juncture.

## Indications for Body Orientation

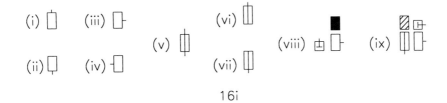

16i

## Range of Pins for Axes

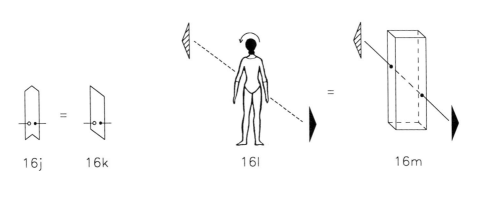

16j  16k  16l  16m

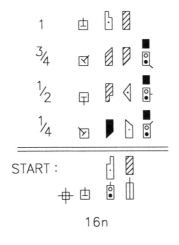

16n

16.11. **Body Part as Axis.** As mentioned briefly before, in certain cases it is practical to indicate that rotation takes place around a part of the body. This may be a part of the torso (other than the understood center), the head, ankles, etc. or the longitudinal axis of one of the limbs or a section of a limb. In **16o** the axis for the somersault, the knees, indicating that the performer is somersaulting around his/her knees, as on a trapeze, is stated outside the staff, the meaning is quite clear. The body part sign can also be placed within the rotation sign. However, body part signs placed in a rotation symbol in the support column, as in **16p**, usually indicate support, placement of weight, therefore designation of axis needs to be clear. In **16q** the focal point sign is placed next to the knee sign thus placing the related information together.

16.12. In **16r**, while lying supine, an unwritten outside agent is causing the body to rotate around a vertical axis located at the ankles. This form of rotating could also be written as wheeling, **16s**. Because the turning in these two examples is resultant, i.e. not initiated by the person themselves, dotted lines for passive movement are used. In **16t** the axis is the shoulder area. This rotation can result from an impetus initiated by the performer, or might be initiated by an outside person causing a resultant path, as in **16u**; here the wheeling has been written outside the staff. When a rotation of this kind is placed outside the staff the meaning of the body part is clear.

16.13. In **16v**, from sitting upright with the legs out diagonally, the body rotates around the axis of the right leg onto the right side of the body. A similar example was previously discussed in **13z**. Here the rotation is actually a cartwheel-like action for the torso. The placement of the right leg results in $^1/_8$ change of Front. It is important to note that the angle of the limb in relation to the body affects the degree of turn and hence change of Front. The new Front is stated and a $^1/_8$ secret turn added for clarification. The secret turn is placed within the staff when there is room; or it may be placed just before the new Front sign. (For secret turn see <u>Advanced Labanotation</u> *Kneeling, Sitting, Lying* 31.9.)

16.14. In **16w**, from lying, a 'left shoulder' backward somersault roll takes place around the left arm. This axis of rotation, which is similar to the diagonal axis previously illustrated in **16c**, causes $^1/_8$ change of Front to the right. Because an ordinary somersault does not produce a change of Front, this example illustrates the device of showing change of Front by using a 'secret turn sign'. The change of Front is resultant in that it depends on the stated axis of rotation, the left arm and its spatial placement. In this case the 'secret turn' is $^1/_8$ of a turn to the right. Here the secret turn is placed adjacent to the new Front sign to clarify why a change of Front has occurred. Angling is used for the concluding kneel to show it lower than a middle level kneel.

## Body Part as Axis

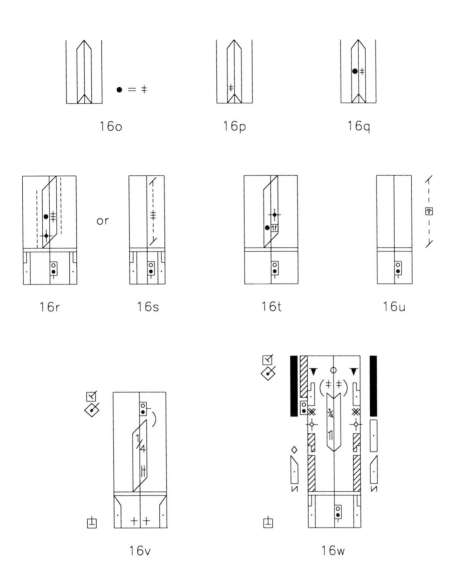

16o     16p     16q

16r     16s     16t     16u

16v     16w

# IV CLARIFICATIONS

# 17 Distance

17.1.  In paragraphs 5.5 - 5.11 information about measurement and statement of distance is given.  Details are explained in the <u>Advanced Labanotation</u> issue *Kneeling, Sitting, Lying* Sections 35 and 36.  All rules apply to multiple support situations in the same way as to simple kneeling, sitting and lying.  This section is limited to additional remarks.

17.2.  Statement of distance may be made for some supporting parts and not for others.  In the starting position of **17a**, the legs are very far apart; this is stated by means of distance indication.  The hands are exactly below the shoulders; this is stated through DBP indications.  The distance between hands and feet results from the torso placement, here shown to be flexed but without statement of level.[63]

17.3.  Exact statement of distance is illustrated in **17b**.  The feet are exactly half a standard step-length apart.  The hands are forward of the feet and therefore also exactly half a standard step-length apart (i.e. the same as judged for the feet).  The distance the hands are forward of the feet is half a step-length.  The four points of support are therefore each on the corner of an imaginary square on the floor, as illustrated in **17c**.

17.4.  Ex. **17d** shows a starting position with DBP.  First the 'place' direction for the knee is read, then the DBP direction (8.20).  The distance measurement symbol is therefore placed underneath the DBP indication, and not centered as in **17a**.  The DBP indication shows that the right foot is half a step-length to the right of the left lower leg.

17.5.  In **17e** the foot of the right leg gesture is to the right of the left knee; the measurement sign here for the right leg gesture refers to the degree of bending at the right knee joint, thus dictating the distance between the right foot and the left knee.  This measurement sign does *not* state the distance between the right foot and the right hip as it would if it were written in the support column.

# Distance

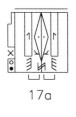

17a

17b

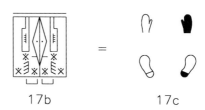

17c

17d

17e

# 18 Use of Black Pins for Tracks

18.1. This section is concerned with what in Labanotation is assumed to be the normal track for walking (stepping) sequences on the feet, knees, hands, or elbows, i.e. the *understood* performance. Also investigated is how specific tracks have in the past been indicated by black pins through describing the relationship of the legs. Section 19 presents Track Pins and how these may be used for gestures and supports. An exposition on Track Pins is given in Section 19 and Appendix A.

18.2. **Tracks - Feet.** In **18a** the feet are placed beside each other. The direction 'place' indicates that weight is supported under the center of gravity. When both feet are supporting, weight is shared between them and 'place' lies between the two feet. When walking forward, **18b**, the feet maintain the side-by-side relationship, each walking in its own track, **18c**. When standing on one foot weight is centered over that support, **18d**. Subsequent walking, **18e**, will still be with each foot placed in its normal track.

18.3. The question often arises as to the correct interpretation of the simple statement of **18a**. Because many people naturally stand with the feet slightly apart, should it represent this stance? Or should it mean feet together, touching, feet nearly touching, or feet specifically placed under the hips? The logic of the meaning of 'place' points to *feet together*, since *for supports 'place' is beneath the center of weight*. When supporting on one foot, there is no question that the support is under the center of weight. When supporting on both feet, each is as close to the central line of gravity as possible.[64]

Many forms of Western dance (e.g. ballet and ballroom dance) take **18a** to be the notation of the 'closed' foot position in which the feet are together, touching, i.e. a '1st position'. However, anthropologists require a simple indication for the legs, supporting slightly apart. The parallel alignment used in contemporary dance is with the feet aligned under each hip socket.

18.4. A specific performance of feet in place can be made explicit in the notation. Ex. **18f** states that the legs are touching; this is expressed more specifically in **18g** where the feet touch; **18h** specifies that the legs are turned out so that the feet point to the side (90° turn-out) with the heels touching. In **18i** the feet are shown to be slightly apart, a minor sideward displacement, which will result in the feet being approximately under each hip socket. If the flat pin is placed within the place symbol, as in **18j** the displacement will be a third toward the sideward direction, a larger displacement than **18i**. If the description should be in terms of relation of the support to the hip socket then DBP can be used, as in **18k**. Note the difference in autography between the flat sideward pins and the signs for right and left hips.

18.5. In **18l** a slightly straddled walk is shown; each step is displaced slightly sideward. The approximate resulting tracks are shown in **18m**. The even wider base of **18n** gives greater stability and hence such a walk is used by babies, old people and drunks. In this walk the feet do not pass near each other. In **18c** the tracks in which the feet walk are side by side; in **18n** the tracks are wider apart, an extra 'track' lying between them, illustrated in **18o**.[65]

## Tracks - Feet

18a    18b    18c    18d    18e

18f    18g    18h    18i    18j    18k

18l    18m    18n    18o

18.6. **Black Pins for Sagittal Tracks.** The need to be specific about tracks for both feet and arms resulted in the invention of special track signs (see Section 19). Before these became part of the system, tracks had been specified with black pins which indicated the *relationship of the feet, one to the other*, and, by extension, relationship to the center line of the body. This use of black pins, which is still applied today, is presented here.

18.7. Starting with the known, **18p**, the normal (established) side-by-side relationship of the feet when together, illustrated in **18q**, needs no pins. If pins were used for this relationship, they would be the sideward pointing black pins of **18r**, meaning each at the side of the other. If pins were added to normal walking forward, they would be written as in **18s**.

18.8. In what in ballet is called the 5th position relationship of the feet of **18t**, the right foot is in front. This is shown with a comfortable turn-out of the legs in **18u**. If the feet are parallel, the position would be as in **18v**. One foot stepping in front or behind the other instead of each in its normal track is shown in **18w**. This usage indicates tightrope walking. Ex. **18x** illustrates placement of the feet on the center line, this line cutting through the center of each foot. The same with parallel feet is shown in **18y**.

18.9. A 3rd position of the feet in ballet is shown in **18z**, the right foot in front as illustrated in **18aa**. Use of this pin in sagittal walking steps, **18ab**, produces the path of **18ac**, i.e. use of an inbetween path, the legs less crossed over, as if each step came from a third position; one $1/4$ of each foot is across the center line. With the feet parallel, walking forward with 3rd position pins exists, but provides a rather subtle difference between walking in parallel 5th and walking in parallel 1st position, hence seldom needed.

## Black Pins for Sagittal Tracks

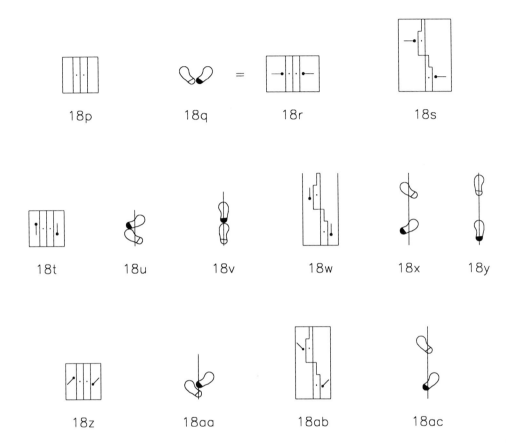

| 18p | 18q | 18r | 18s |

| 18t | 18u | 18v | 18w | 18x | 18y |

| 18z | 18aa | 18ab | 18ac |

18.10. **Black Pins for Lateral Tracks.** For clarity in the illustrations, the following examples are given with parallel feet. Starting in 1st position in **18ad** the right foot steps to the right, the left foot then steps across in front of the right leg. The width of the legs causes crossing steps naturally to be placed more forward or backward of true side. Hence the more forward track for the left foot in **18ae**. The step on the right foot which follows on count 3 will be in line with the left foot, on its center track. This pattern is illustrated in **18ae**.

18.11. If these steps are repeated continuously, it can be seen that the performer's path will veer slightly forward. In Western folk dances where stepping patterns such as **18ad** are common, usually performed in a circle, the dancers will instinctively adjust the step direction enough to remain on the sideward line. If the front/back crossings are alternated, illustrated in **18af**, this veering is automatically corrected, the crossing behind, illustrated in **18ag**, counteracting the forward displacement. When writing Hungarian folk dances, Maria Szentpál needed to be accurate, thus instead of the general statement of **18ad**, she would write **18ah**, spelling out the displacement that the right leg needed to make, illustrated in **18ai**. Note the letters CL to indicate the center line between the feet in this progression.

18.12. In walking sideward it is possible to stay on the true sideward center line by placing the foot carefully in line with the other foot after crossing in front or behind. In **18aj**, after the right foot steps to the side, the left foot crosses over in front of the right and is then placed exactly in line with the right foot. This pattern repeats but with the left foot crossing behind and ending in line with the right foot, illustrated in **18ak**. The pins are read in sequence, the crossing being performed first. Note that the center line runs through the middle of each foot. Such tight crossings are familiar in ballroom dancing as well as Spanish Flamenco.

18.13. A 3rd position relationship of the legs is written in **18al**, illustrated in **18am**. The idea of each foot stepping in a 3rd position in relation to the other leg must be kept in mind. For the left foot it is a crossed 3rd. The center line cuts through $1/4$ of each foot.

# Black Pins for Lateral Tracks

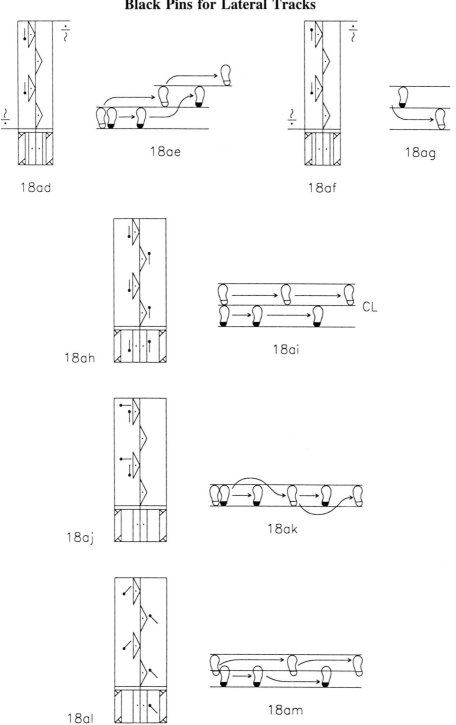

18ad

18ae

18af

18ag

18ah

18ai

18aj

18ak

18al

18am

18.14. **Sagittal Tracks for Knees.** In **18an** the knees are supporting in place: theoretically they should be together, legs touching, but in practice they are often slightly apart. This is because the knees are closer to the hips than the feet, and thus the width between the hip joints is more appreciable in kneeling than in standing on the feet; an absolutely closed position on the knees is less usual and less comfortable. Knees touching is shown in **18ao**. When walking on the knees, **18ap**, each knee is placed in its own track.

18.15. Details regarding placement of steps for knees can be specified as shown for the feet on page 129, Exs. **18i-18n**. If steps on the knees are long enough, as in **18aq**, they can be on the center line, one in front of the other. This relationship can also occur when thighs are inturned, **18ar**.

18.16. When the legs are outturned, the lower leg can be placed across to the other side, allowing the step on the knee to be again on the center line, **18as**. This example is an abbreviated statement, the leg action needed for such walking on the knees is spelled out in **18at**.

18.17. **Sagittal Tracks for Hands.** In **18au**, from a squat, the hands walk forward on the center line.

## Sagittal Tracks for Knees

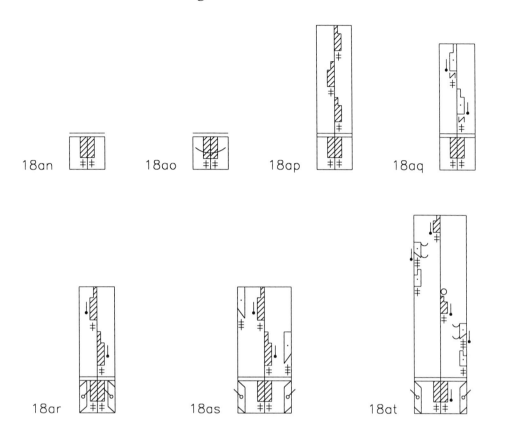

## Sagittal Tracks for Hands

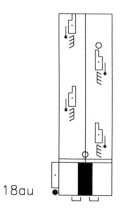

# 19 The Use of Track Pins⁶⁶

19.1. **Definition.** Track Pins are signs which indicate relationship to the center lines in the body. Track Pins placed next to a direction symbol indicate how that direction is to be interpreted.

19.2. **Normal Track.** The standard point of reference for direction - the hip for leg gestures, the shoulder for arm gestures - lies within the 'normal' track for that part of the body. This 'normal' track results from the build of the body, the legs being attached at the lower side of the pelvis and the arms being attached at either side of the chest.

19.3. **The Sagittal Tracks.** The sagittal tracks are wider for the arms than for the legs because of the width of the body between the arms. Each arm has its own point of reference, the shoulder, from where direction is usually judged. Between the normal tracks for the right and left arm lie three tracks across the body. These tracks can be considered roughly to be the width of the hand.

When the arms swing forward or backward, each follows its natural track at the side of the body. All sagittal directions for arms and legs naturally follow these tracks. This is the understood performance for any unqualified sagittal direction symbol. Reference can also be made to sagittal directions which emanate from the center line of the body, or from the intermediate body lines. Put another way, the direction of a sagittal gesture can be modified to lie within one or other of the sagittal 'tracks' of the body.

19.4. **The Sagittal Track Pin Signs.** The Sagittal Track Pins will first be explored for the arms. Ex. **19a** shows the basic sign for the sagittal (forward/back) center line, meaning 'in the center track'. This sign is based on the pin for 'center', **19b**. Note that for the sagittal sign the center line is unbroken. The next examples show the pins, derived from the center line pin, which indicate the different sagittal tracks. The pin of **19a** is modified to **19c** to show the forward sagittal center line and to **19d** for the backward center line. Ex. **19e** shows the intermediate tracks and **19f** the outer sagittal track pins.

19.5. Ex. **19g** shows the five sagittal tracks for the arms, seen from bird's eye view: i) - the center sagittal track; ii) - the intermediate sagittal tracks; iii) - the outer tracks. These last will rarely be used since they are the natural tracks. However, if the right arm should use the left arm track, as in **19h**, and the intent of the gesture has no connection with the idea of the left diagonal direction, **19i**, then this track pin would express the idea of forward in relation to the left arm track, as illustrated in **19j**.

### The Sagittal Track Pin Signs

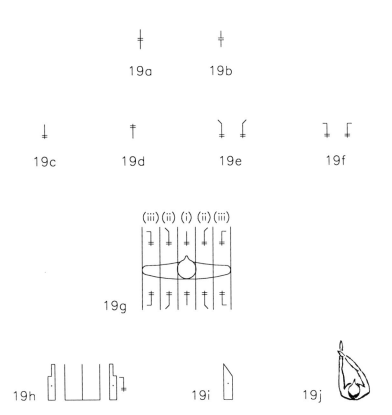

19.6. **The Sagittal Center Lines.** In certain instances the movement concept requires relating to the center line of a track rather than to the track itself. This is particularly true of the middle center line. Ex. **19k** shows the center lines within each track.

When a limb is centered in a track, it is in fact *on* the center line of that track. Placement of the extremity of a limb *next to the center line* is sometimes needed. For this the pins of **19l** and **19m** are used, the dot indicating 'next to' (rather than 'on') the center line. Ex. **19l** indicates the left of the center line, **19m** shows the right of the center line.

19.7. For the arms the part relating to the center line will depend on the rotational state of the limb. With the arms forward, **19n**, palms facing each other, illustrated in **19o**, the palm sides of the hands are close to the center line. With palms facing down, the thumb edge of the hand is at the center line, thus the hand as a whole is slightly further away from the center line, as illustrated in **19p**.[67]

19.8. When both hands are *on* the center line, as in **19q**, a greater sense of center line occurs when the thumbs are facing up, **19r**. Here the left hand is above the right. With palms facing down, as in **19s**, the width of the hand makes the performer aware of using the center track, rather than the center line.

19.9. These examples have explored arm gestures in relation to the sagittal center tracks and center lines. When used for supporting on the hands, the same relationships hold true. Further information on arm gestures relating to sagittal, diagonal and lateral tracks are given in Appendix A.

# The Sagittal Center Lines

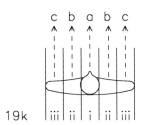

19k

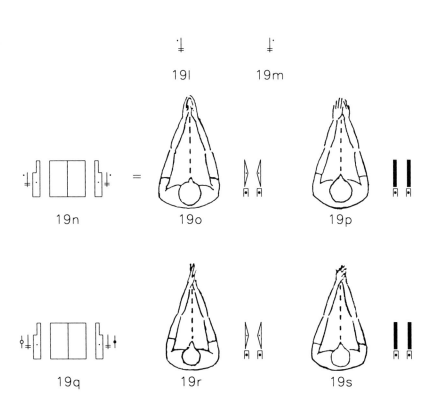

19l    19m

19n    =    19o    19p

19q    19r    19s

19.10. **Track Pins for Leg Gestures.** Tracks for leg gestures are needed more often for floorwork where placement of the legs may bear no relation to the familiar positions of the feet while standing. Because of the smaller separation between the hip joints (compared with the width between the shoulders for the arms), subdivision track pins are needed less often for the legs. To be taken into consideration is the differences in hip width and leg separation among different people, however, a standard, a 'norm' must be established. Ex. **19t** illustrates the tracks for the legs: i) is the center track, iii) are the normal outer tracks, while ii) are the tracks which lie between.

19.11. **Track Pins for Vertical Leg Gestures.** The same track pins are used when the legs are down. No exact performance is indicated for the general statement of **19u**. Feet together can be shown specifically as legs touching, **19v**, illustrated in **19w**. Legs not quite touching would be described as next to the center line, **19x**. Legs directly under the hip joint, in what is considered the anatomical alignment, can be shown with track pins, as in **19y**, illustrated in **19z**. This position can also be written with DBP, the legs being shown to be under each hip, **19aa**. The position with the legs slightly open, **19ab** could be written with the diagonal pins, as in **19ac**. Separation of the legs, may be written with displacement pins (tacks), as in **19ad**. However, with the statement of **19u** not being specifically defined, an exact meaning for **19ad** cannot be defined. (For a comparison in use of tack pins and track pins see Appendix B).

19.12. **Track Pins for Sagittal Leg Gestures.** In **19ae** the legs are forward while sitting; nothing specific is stated, most people will sit with the legs more or less together. Ex. **19af** specifies that each leg should be in front of its own hip, i.e. apart the width of the hip joints. In **19ag** the extremities of both legs are on the center line with the right leg above. In **19ah** the extremities of both legs are in the sagittal track of the left hip, the right leg being above. In this example leg contact is specifically stated. Track pins for lateral and diagonal leg gestures will be dealt with in Appendix A.

## Track Pins for Leg Gestures

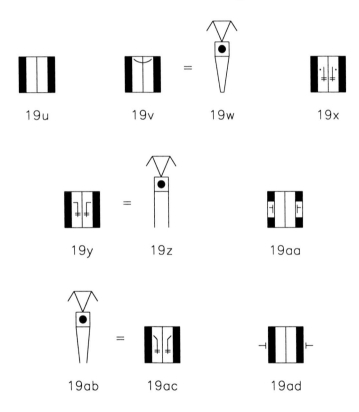

## Track Pins for Vertical Leg Gestures

## Track Pins for Sagittal Leg Gestures

19.13. **Track Pins for Supporting on the Hands.** Track pins are often needed to indicate the exact placement of the hand in taking a new support. The same pins are used with the same meanings, i.e. relation of the supporting direction to the body center lines and tracks.

19.14. In **19ai** the hands walk forward on their normal tracks (shoulder width apart). This placement is specifically stated in **19aj**. 'Tight rope' walking is shown in **19ak**, while **19al** shows use of the intermediate track between **19aj** and **19ak**.

19.15. **Track Pins for Supporting on the Feet.** Track pins applied to walking on the feet provide a somewhat different message from the black pins which show relationship between the feet. The two devices coincide when walking on the center line is indicated. Ex. **19am** and **19an** describe the same movement, the equivalent of tight-rope walking. In **19ao** each step is in front of its hip, i.e. the steps are a hip-width apart.

19.16. Between the tracks of **19an** and **19ao** lie the intermediate tracks illustrated as ii) in the diagram of **19t**. Thus, walking with the legs adjacent to each other, the normal walk of **19ap**, if written with track pins, would be as in **19aq.**

19.17. The width of these tracks in stepping depends on the degree of leg rotation. When the feet are parallel they occupy less width on the tracks; when markedly turned out the track appears to be wider. In fact, the center line of the track should run through the center of the foot whatever the degree of leg rotation.

## Track Pins for Supporting on the Hands

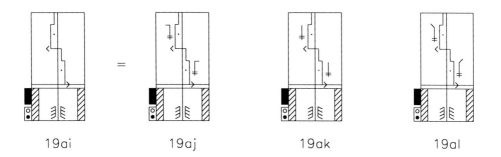

19ai          19aj          19ak          19al

## Track Pins for Supporting on the Feet

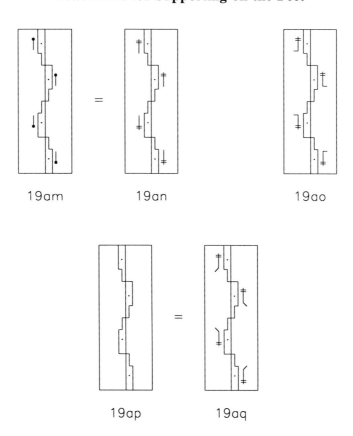

19am        19an          19ao

19ap          19aq

19.18. **Lateral Steps.** Track pins can also be applied to the side and diagonal directions. The sense of tracks in these directions is weaker, the hip width being less, and the application of the appropriate pins not visually so easy to understand. The need for lateral tracks has already been met in paragraphs 18.10-18.13. Logically the lateral track pins are the same as in **19t** but pointing to the side, as in **19ar**. Here (i) shows the center track, the dotted line being the center line; (ii) the intermediate tracks and (iii) the outer tracks. Applying these pins we have the notation of **19as**, which was described before with black pins, as in **19at**.[68]

19.19. Graphically such placement of the sideward pins is not practical, they consume too much lateral space; thus the decision was made to apply the sagittal track pins of **19ar** to the lateral direction as well as to the diagonal direction. This requires the reader to visualize the set of pins of **19ar** being rotated $\frac{1}{4}$ to the left to be applied to the right side directions. Thus the sequence of **19at** is correctly written as **19au**. In these examples, in which the fourth step crosses behind, the backward pointing track pins of **19au** look awkward. They are actually correct, but *the preferred way of writing this sequence is the familiar use of black pins*, as in **19av**.
Use of track pins for diagonal steps is discussed in Appendix A.

19.20. **Track Pins for All Fours.** The comfortable all fours position on hands and knees is shown in **19aw**, illustrated in **19ax**, each support in its normal track. For the hands the possible tracks of **19ay** exist. Though it is usually not necessary to use pins to notate the position of **19aw**, track pins can be added as in **19az**. Bringing the hands closer together would make use of the intermediate tracks of **19ba**, illustrated in **19bb**. Placed next to the center line is shown in **19bc** and illustrated in **19bd**. For placement on the center line one hand would need to be on top or in front of the other. In **19be** and its illustration **19bf**, the right hand is on top; in **19bg** and **19bh**, it is in front.

## Lateral Steps

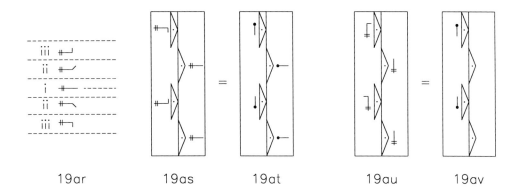

| 19ar | 19as | 19at | 19au | 19av |

## Track Pins for All Fours

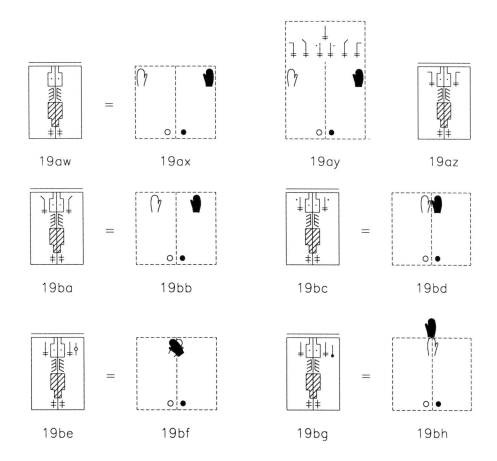

| 19aw | 19ax | 19ay | 19az |

| 19ba | 19bb | 19bc | 19bd |

| 19be | 19bf | 19bg | 19bh |

19.21.  In **19bi** all four supports are on the center line, the left hand some distance in front of the right and the right foot some distance behind the left, as illustrated in **19bj**.  In a similar example, **19bk**, the hands are together on the center line with the left hand in front; the feet are together with the right foot behind, shown in **19bl**.  The pins immediately next to the main symbols indicate track; the black pin for the left hand and the right foot indicate relationship to the paired body parts.

19.22.  Ex. **19bm** starts from a 'crab' position, on 'all fours' with the hands backward of the feet.  As the legs are very bent, the hands and feet are fairly close.  This example is written using method E (Section 9), i.e. the 'all fours' position is analysed using SB (Split Body).

Three steps are executed while the hands retain weight.  Track pins indicate that instead of stepping straight forward, the feet cross over slightly beyond the middle line of the body, i.e. into the track where the *other* foot would normally step.  The third step is on the middle line.  As a result of walking forward, the lower part of the torso (the pelvis) rises to the new direction stated for the inverted torso.  At the end the right foot is resting on the left knee.

19.23.  The starting position of **19bn** is similar to that of **19bm** but written using Method A (see Section 5).  The feet mark a rhythmic pattern by clicking together in the air (this rhythm needs appropriate footwear, such as boots).  After each 'jump' track pins indicate that the feet land in a solid position, i.e. farther apart than usual, in the tracks of the hips.  If black pins were used, as in **19bo**, it would mean the feet are together, side by side, not in the more separated tracks.

Note that the forward directions in **19bn** reflect the position of the feet forward of the hands, and not forward locomotion, so in fact they land on the same spot.  After the three jumps and the spring onto the right foot, the two stamps occur also without traveling forward.

19.24.  Ex. **19bp** is the same sequence as **19bn**, but written using SB (see Section 9).  The message is immediately clear that the feet always land on the same spot.

## Track Pins for All Fours (continued)

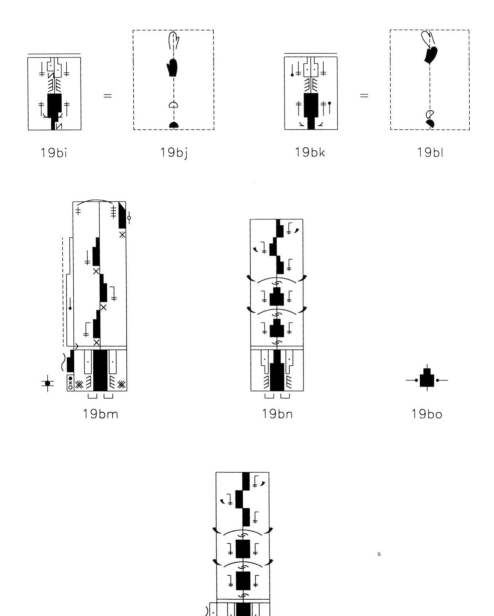

19bi        19bj        19bk        19bl

19bm        19bn        19bo

19bp

19.25.  Ex. **19bq** shows diagonal placement of hands and feet with the right arm off the floor gesturing diagonally high.  The advantage of analyzing this position as an open position between hands and feet is that the exact position and rotation of the torso need not be determined.  From this position the right hand 'steps' in a closed position next to the other hand, the diagonal pin indicating that the position is like a crossed 3rd position on the hands judged from before the turn.  In order to reach this position the chest twists as the right arm crosses the body.

The 'step' on the right hand is followed by a turn on all supporting parts except the right leg, which releases (lifts from the floor) and closes next to the other foot after the turn.  In addition, a space hold is added for the left hand to emphasize non-swiveling.  The end position is stated as a standard position on hands and feet with the feet together and the hands forward, close together (as shown by the track pins).  The ending for the feet could also have been written as **19br**, which shows the right foot closing next to the left.  The ending relationship for the hands could also be shown with side-by-side black pins as in **19bs**.

19.26.  **Diagonal Steps on All Fours.**  A similar diagonal 'all fours' position is featured in **19bt**.  Directional indication is achieved here by DBP symbols relating to the previous point of support of each moving part.

Track pins modify the directions so that all supporting parts are placed in the diagonal center track in the body.  The result is stepping on one line, as if walking on a narrow ledge.  Without the track pins, the result would be as if walking on four parallel bars placed closely together.[69]

19.27.  Ex. **19bu** shows the same diagonal steps, but this time from an open position in which the hands are forward of the feet, and not in a diagonal direction as in **19bt**.  This means that the hands step on one line, the diagonal line that runs across the center point between the hands; the feet step on another line that runs on the center point between the feet.  This differs from **19bt** in that walking is as though on two parallel bars, not on one line.

19.28.  **Lateral Steps on All Fours.**  Ex. **19bv** shows an alternative way of stepping 'on all fours' while turning on the spot (see **6l**).  In the starting position, the hands are further apart from the feet than in the standard position 'on all fours'; this will facilitate the ensuing movement.

First the left foot steps sideward of the right foot.  The black pin indicates that the left foot crosses in front of the other foot, the track pin states placement on the sideward center line.  Then the left hand steps sideward to establish a wider distance between the two hands.  The right foot steps to the side of the left foot (this will automatically be on its sideward center line, as in all open sideward steps) and the right hand steps in 'place', i.e. under its shoulder. This pattern is repeated three times.

All these step directions are governed by, and therefore modified by, the indication for turning (rotation without traveling); during twelve steps one whole turn should be achieved.

19.29. For immediate recognition of the type of rotation to be performed, it is helpful to add the Standard Key, **19bw**. For turning 'on the spot' the spot hold sign can be placed within the turn sign, as in **19bx**.

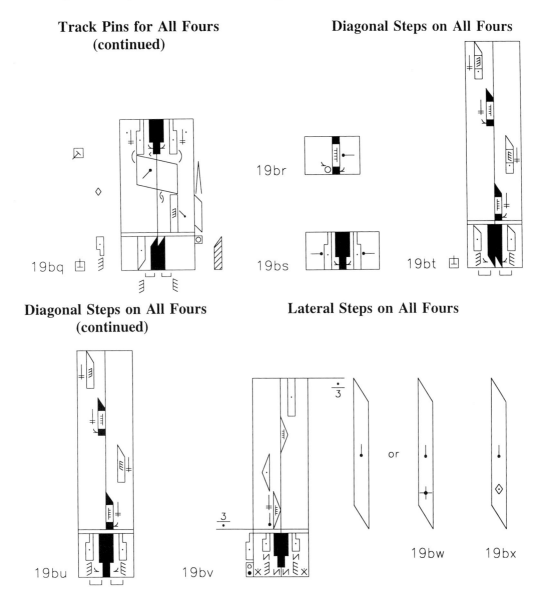

**Track Pins for All Fours (continued)**

**Diagonal Steps on All Fours**

19bq   19br   19bs   19bt

**Diagonal Steps on All Fours (continued)**

**Lateral Steps on All Fours**

19bu   19bv   19bw   19bx

# 20 Use of Columns

20.1. The use of columns in the notation staff deserves consideration in relation to mixed support situations because, for reasons of layout, it is often practical to have more than the two usual support columns.

In **20a-c**, the shaded columns indicate support columns; all others are gesture columns. Any number of gesture columns may be added on both sides.

20.2. Ex. **20a** shows standard use of columns in what has come to be called the 'narrow staff'. Columns 1 are the support columns; in columns 2 leg gestures are written; in 3 body gestures and in 4 arm gestures.

20.3. Ex. **20b** shows the *expanded* or *broad* staff, now more commonly used. This staff allows for Inner Subsidiary Columns (ISC), the extra columns between the support and leg gesture columns (1 and 2), which can be used for symbols that modify a leg gesture or a support indication and generally provide space for easier reading.[70] It is now also fairly common usage to leave an extra column between the body column (3) and the columns for movements of the whole arm (4) as shown in **20b**.

20.4. If the narrow staff is used and there are more than two supporting parts, two indications must be written in the same support column. In simple notation, this is often possible (see **4b**, **4e**, and **4g**). In many mixed support situations, however, it is desirable to have a separate support column for each supporting part (see **4c** and **4f**). The ISC can be designated as a support column by tying it to the center column with an angular horizontal staple. These staples are usually placed beneath each staff as in **20c**; the arrangement with four support columns then applies to the whole of the staff. The staples must be repeated at the beginning of each new staff, if the designated support columns are to continue.

20.5. If supporting body parts are to be the same for an extended period of time, pre-staff indications show that the columns have been assigned to particular body parts by placing the symbols for these parts in the appropriate columns *below* the horizontal line at the beginning of each staff, as in **20d**. Each body part then keeps to its own support column.

20.6. The particular body parts for the support columns can also be indicated by placing the signs for these parts *after* the baseline, as in **20e**.

Movement symbols which follow pertain to the stated body part until otherwise indicated. For clarity, carets can be added to each subsequent symbol. After a change of part has occurred, a subsequent return to the initial part must be restated.

20.7.  Doubling the support column may not take away the need for an ISC for leg gestures. For complex scores, the staff of **20f** is recommended.

## Use of Columns

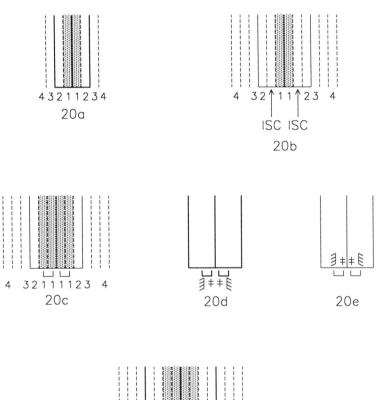

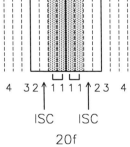

20f

20.8. During the progression of the notation the ISC may need to be named as a support column as in **20g**. The column will remain a support column until cancelled by the angular horizontal staple linking the ISC with the gesture column.[71] In **20h** a step forward on the left hand is followed by a left arm gesture at which time the ISC is shown no longer to be a support column. In many cases the context of the movement indicates clearly that the ISC was only needed briefly as a support column. However, to remove any doubts it is better to make the cancellation statement.

20.9. **Floorwork Staff.**[72] When supporting on the torso or its parts, it has been necessary to place the indications in either the left or right support column even though the right or left side of the torso is not featured. The Floorwork Staff was devised to simplify the writing of supports through avoiding this left-right division.

20.10. The center line in the standard staff is removed and a frame is placed around the support and ISC columns, **20i**. Everything inside the frame is understood to be a support; the problem of whether to place the torso on the right or left side of the staff is removed and the inclusion of the ISC columns allows more room when supporting on 'all fours'.

20.11. The bottom and top of the Floorwork Staff frame visually alerts the reader to the start and finish of this special staff.

20.12. **Indication of Timing.** Count marks ('ticks') may be placed on the frame of the Floorwork Staff, as in **20j**, or on the outside staff line, **20k**. The usual tick marks could be ambiguous and consequently, dots, as in **20j** and **20k**, are more appropriate. Slanted tick marks, **20l** and **20m**, could also be used.[73]

20.13. Exs. **20n** and **20o**[74] show how the Floorwork Staff would appear on a score when it starts and ends within a measure. **20n** shows 5 measures of 2/4. The Floorwork Staff is shown to 'enter' on count 2 of measure 2 and 'exit' on count 2 of measure 4. The dots placed on the left of the Floorwork Staff indicate the timing quite clearly.

20.14. Ex. **20o** shows 3 measures of 3/4. The Floorwork Staff 'enters' on count 3 of measure 1 and 'exits' on count 2 of measure 3. In this case the counts are indicated by dots being placed on the left side of the main staff.

## Use of Columns (continued)

## Floorwork Staff

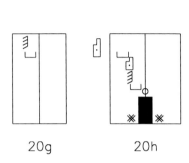

20g          20h

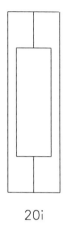

20i

## Indication of Timing

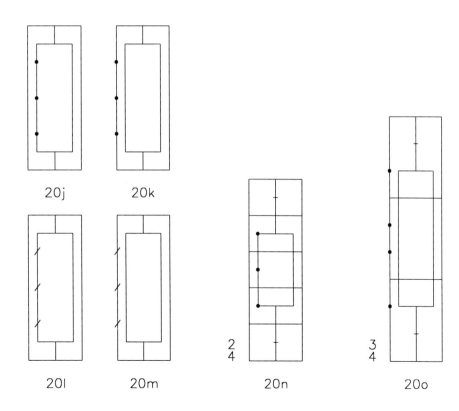

20j          20k

20l          20m

$\frac{2}{4}$     20n          $\frac{3}{4}$     20o

20.15.  **An Example of Floorwork Staff.**  In **20p**[75], from standing on
both feet, the left foot takes a long diagonally backward step.  The performer
lowers, turning $\frac{1}{8}$ on both feet to arrive in a very low crossed foot-kneel facing
downstage right.  At this point the Floorwork Staff begins.  The performer sits
diagonally backward on the left hip.  Rolling $\frac{1}{8}$ to the right the body lowers to
end supporting on the back of the torso.  The legs then swing up and backward
towards the floor producing a partial backward somersault so that the support is
only on the shoulders.  This provides impetus to roll forward, arriving briefly on
the hips with the legs open diagonally forward, very flexed, ready for the small
quick spring onto the feet into a low second position.  Note that the duration for
this phrase is shown by a Time Sign at the start not to be exact.

# An Example of Floorwork Staff

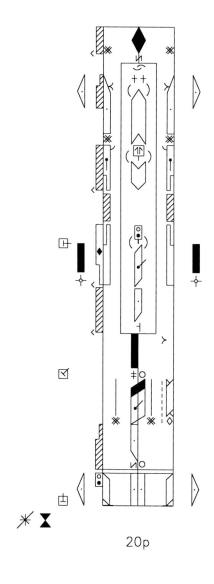

20p

# 21 Validity of Support Indications

21.1. The validity rules discussed in this section are illustrated in many examples throughout this issue. Validity for support indications can be summarised by dividing these indications into two main categories.

21.2. **Category 1. Supporting on the Feet, Knees or Foot-knee.** The standard rule is: *A gap between movement symbols in both support columns means cancellation of the support(s).* This fundamental rule of Labanotation is primarily applied to the feet, the consequences and details of which can be found in any textbook.[76] When the body is supported only on the feet, on the knees (paired kneeling), or in a mixed foot-kneel, retention of support is stated with a retention sign. This sign is also used for retaining weight on one support when another steps into a double support.[77]

21.3. In **21a** the right foot remains supporting, when the left foot steps forward, ending in a fourth position. The same happens in **21b** for the knee supports. In **21c**, after the right leg steps forward in *plié*, the left leg kneels in place next to the right foot. The performer then remains in this position for one count before stepping to the side onto the right foot in *plié*; the left knee support is cancelled as no hold sign is stated for the knee on this count. Ex. **21d** shows a similar sequence in which the left knee continues supporting when the right foot steps to the side.

21.4. **Category 2. Supporting on Other Body Parts or on 'All Fours'.** *A gap following support indications in the center columns for weight on hips, torso, elbows, hands, head, etc. does not indicate springing into the air. Nor does a gap indicate springing into the air when on 'all fours'.* According to this rule no lifting of such parts will occur unless:
  a)  a gesture (shown by a specific direction symbol or an action stroke) written for that part negates its weight-bearing state or,
  b)  a release sign for that part is written in the appropriate support column.

However, in a series of transferences of weight (i.e. 'stepping') on parts other than the feet only, it is automatically understood that each limb lifts to take the new step and continue the progression. At the end of this progression the limb(s) is understood to retain weight. Note that whether hold signs have been used or not, *no lifting occurs* without either a) or b) above. Thus if a hold sign is forgotten it will not change the movement.[78]

## Supporting on the Feet, Knees or Foot-knee

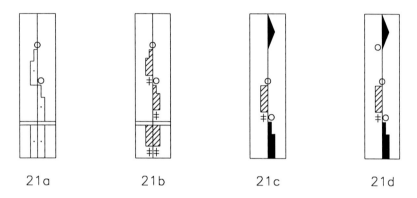

21a         21b         21c         21d

21.5. Examples are presented below in which a support is: (i) understood to be retained (automatic retention); (ii) explicitly retained; (iii) released by indication of a particular gesture; (iv) released by indication of an action stroke; (v) released by indication of a release sign; (vi) released while contact is retained by indication of a weight release sign; (vii) open statement, result not specified.

21.6. **Automatic Retention.** In an 'all fours' situation a new support indication does not automatically imply that all the weight is taken by the new supporting part. In **21e** the step forward on the right hand does not mean that the other three supporting parts are lifted.

21.7. In **21f**, because the hands are being put down (i.e. an 'all fours' position is achieved), no hold sign is added for the knees. There is no question as to whether springing from the knees occurs; they are understood to retain weight (see 21.4).

21.8. The carets in **21f** refer to the knees. If the intention is to transfer weight to the feet, which previously had no weight, then a 'zed' caret is used, linking the new support to the leg gesture column, **21g**. To help the reader, **21f** can also be written as **21h** by repeating the knee symbol.

21.9. In **21i** (**4.g**) walking forward (i.e. stepping) occurs on the hands and knees. At the end of the progression weight is on both hands and both knees. Ex. **21j** shows four steps forward in a handstand. After the fourth step no springing into the air follows. Whether the right hand releases or retains weight is left open.

21.10. **Explicit Statement of Retention.** In **21k**, at the end of the same walk as in **21j**, retention of weight on both hands has been specifically stated.[79] In **21l**, the right hand is shown to release at the end.
   Note that, in the starting position of **21l** an inverted wrist-to-pelvis sign is used, indicating this section to be upright.

21.11. **Release by Indication of Gesture.** In Category (iii) above, the retention of a support can be cancelled by indication of a gesture. Indeed, the gesture of a limb implies release of that limb from the floor. In **21m** this is true for the left leg and the right arm.

21.12. In **21n**, supporting on the shoulders and the feet results from raising the pelvis and the resulting direction for the section shoulder-to-knees.

## Automatic Retention

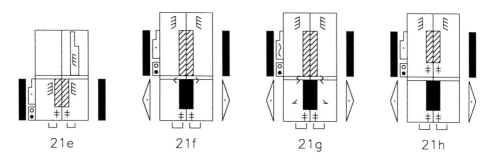

|  |  |  |  |
|---|---|---|---|
| 21e | 21f | 21g | 21h |

## Explicit Statement of Retention

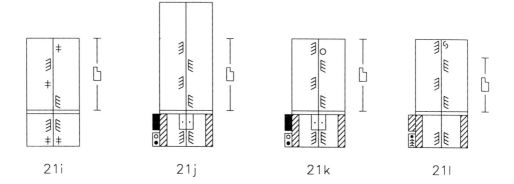

|  |  |  |  |
|---|---|---|---|
| 21i | 21j | 21k | 21l |

## Release by Indication of Gesture

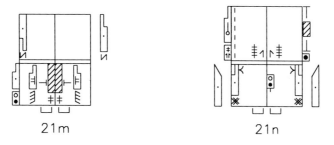

|  |  |
|---|---|
| 21m | 21n |

21.13. **Release by Indication of Action Strokes.** The cancellation of support by a limb gesture can also be shown using an action stroke, the indication for an unspecific gesture, in the appropriate limb column(s).[80] Written for the arms they imply release of support on the hands or elbows; for the legs they imply release of support on the feet or knees (see also **21m**).

21.14. In **21o**, while on all fours, the right arm makes a gesture releasing weight from the right hand. The hand then takes weight forward. This is followed by a left leg gesture leading into a low forward step at which point both arms and the right leg are shown to gesture, releasing weight from the hands and right foot. On count 4 all weight is on the left foot and the regular foot-support rules apply.

21.15. Ex. **21p** shows a 'bunny hop': from standing on hands-and-feet, the feet 'jump' forward into 'place' (beneath the center of the body), landing next to each other. Next, all four supporting parts leave the floor. Landing forward is on the hands with the feet supporting immediately after. Ex. **21q** provides a general recording of the manner of locomotion used in **21p**.

When applied to mixed support situations the device of using action strokes is not always practical. In examples such as **21o** or **6.h**, it is convenient, because hands and feet are written in the same support columns; use of release signs in the support columns would require four support columns.

21.16. **Release by Indication of Release Signs.** Cancellation of a support by a release sign in the support columns provides a direct statement; the information is where the reader needs to find it, since concern is centered on the supporting condition (see **21l**).

In **21r** a release sign is used to show both feet lift at the same time; this is crucial to the nature of the gait. Without the release signs each foot would lift one after the other in time to take the next step, following the rule concerning consecutive 'walking'. (This example was earlier presented with additional release signs for the hands in **6.i**.) A more detailed example is **21s** which shows a possible and more specific performance of **21r** using DBP.

## Release by Indication of Action Strokes

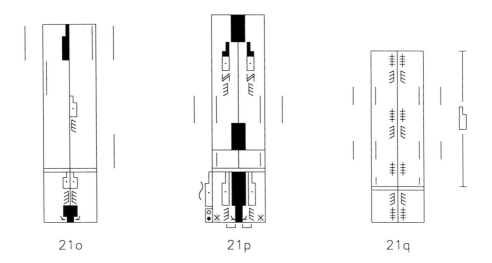

21o                                21p                                21q

## Release by Indication of Release Signs

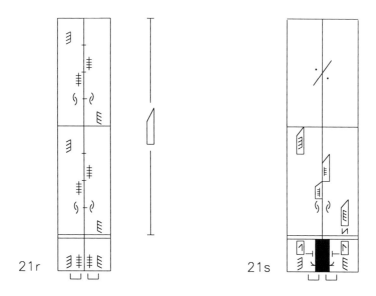

21r                                              21s

21.17. Ex. **21t** shows a movement similar to **21p** using release signs. In **21u** it is clear from context that the hips leave the floor, however, it is helpful to state this by adding release signs in the support column. After the starting position of **21u**, in which the hands take some weight, the hands are not lifted but become major supporting parts simply by taking more weight. At the end of the example they retain some weight, again without lifting. It is recommended that validity for angular bows is specified by retention or release signs placed either directly above the bow or in the column of the part for which the bow is written.[81]

21.18. **Weight Released, Contact Retained.** The release sign of **21v**, used in the previous examples, means total loss of contact with the floor. The sign for release of weight, **21w**, means that contact is retained but without weight, weight is lifted (released). The choice of which way the sign is drawn depends on legibility. The release weight sign is derived from the angular support bows of **21x** and intentionally relates in shape to the more commonly used release contact sign of **21v**. Ex. **21y** shows a simple example of release of weight while standing, i.e. weight is momentarily taken off the right foot and then replaced, but contact remains. In **21z** the performer starts in a sitting position, leaning backward with weight on the hands. Slowly weight is taken off the hands while the abdominal wall contracts. The hands remain in contact with the floor, only the weight is released.

21.19. **'Spot Hold' for Retention of Weight.** Use of a 'spot hold' for retention of weight is appropriate when adjustment needs to be made for that supporting part, e.g., a slight adjustment of weight on a supporting hand or foot to enable it to swivel and accommodate the movement, as in 'walking' on the feet around a supporting hand. Such a situation already occurred in **6n** where the feet walked around one supporting hand. In **21aa** the right foot stays on the same spot and swivels as needed while the hands describe a quarter circular path around it.

## Release by Indication of Release Signs (continued)

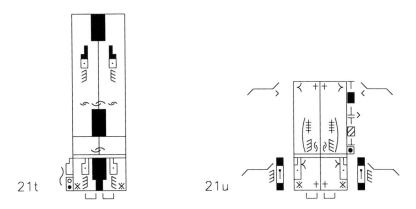

21t

21u

## Weight Released, Contact Retained

21v

21w

21x

21y

21z

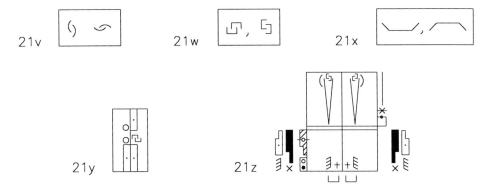

## 'Spot Hold' for Retention of Weight

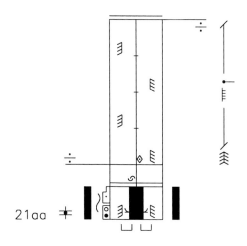

21aa

# 22 Miscellaneous

22.1. **Retention Signs and Pre-signs on Center Staff Line.** When hold signs for two supporting parts are written in the center support columns, one retention sign can be centered on the middle line of the staff to take care of both supports, **22a**. A separate retention sign may be used for each support, **22b**.

22.2. In a similar way, simultaneous release for both center support columns can be written with one sign, centered as in **22c** or individual release signs can be used as in **22d** (see **21r, 21s, 21t, 21u**). The release sign covering two support columns can be further stretched to accommodate three or four support columns at the same time, **22e**.[82] Releasing three or four support columns can also be written with individual release signs, **22f**.

22.3. Distance measurement signs applying to both center support columns are usually centered across the middle line of the staff, **22g**; shown in the mixed support situation of **22h**. However, it may be more appropriate to write a separate symbol for each column, **22i**. In a mixed support situation separate signs may be clearer, **22j**.

22.4. **Part of Foot Contacting in Mixed Support Situations.** For the standard levels of support (low, middle, high) the part of the foot taking weight is automatically understood. In other situations the part of the foot being used may need to be stated. In standing 'on all fours', when the hands are forward of the feet, support is often not on the whole foot but only on the ball of the foot. Generally speaking, this need not be specified. Ex. **22k** produces the understood performance of **22l**. However, use of specific foot hooks allows differentiation between supporting with the foot almost flat on the floor, on the ball of the foot, on the forced arch, etc. (For specific indication of other parts of the feet in mixed supports see **22p**.)

## Retention Signs and Pre-signs on Center Staff Line

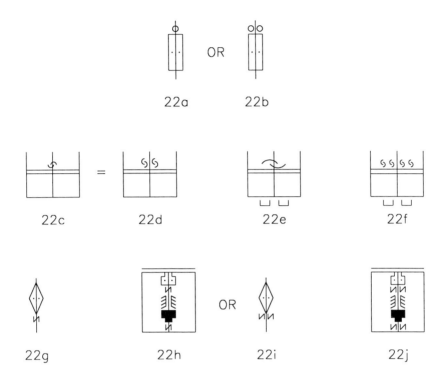

## Part of Foot Contacting in Mixed Support Situations

22.5. **Layout.** As discussed in Section 4 for mixed supports many
different writing options are available to the notator. For accurate descriptions
which require extra symbols the choice depends largely on what placement on the
staff is easiest to read. The more complex the statement, the more attention
should be given to clear layout. The series **22m-r** show statements of the same
type of movement with different degrees of detail and different layout solutions.

22.6. General statements such as **22m** are easy to read. There is no risk of
the reader missing symbols or putting the information together in a wrong way.
From standing on hands and feet, **22m** shows rolling around the spinal axis.
First the turning is on the left hand and foot, swivelling taking place, then it is on
the right hand and foot. The hand and foot will be replaced on the floor at a
comfortable, expected location.
    Note that at the start of the movement the right hand and right foot are
shown to release at the same time; the rolling around the body results from the
simultaneous turning on the left hand and foot together with the spatial retention
for the whole torso. In this configuration rotation around the vertical axis is not
possible, a rolling action must occur. In **22n** rotation around the body axis is
shown, therefore the space holds for the torso are not needed. Use of the Body
Key gives a direct 'body rolling' message.

22.7. Ex. **22o** shows the same rolling combined with a $^1/_4$ circular path
around the hands. This variation of **22m** now includes more detail. The feet step
behind and in front of each other on a curved path. The hands have their own
columns (denoted before the starting position: see also 20.5) and are shown to
take weight beneath the shoulders half-way through the turns around the spinal
axis. The free arm is gesturing in the air. Note that at the start and end no level
is given for the sideward tilt of the torso; it is left open.

22.8. Ex. **22p** features an analysis of **22o** in use of parts of the foot.
Because of this the turning sign must be placed outside the staff. The duration of
changing from one part of the foot to another is shown by the vertical duration
line.
    In the starting position support is on the little toe edge of the ball of the
left foot. The right foot steps backward onto the ball of the foot and during the
step transfers weight to the whole foot at which point the left foot support
changes to the whole foot. It is subsequently lifted in anticipation of the next
step and the right foot rolls onto the little toe side of the ball of the foot. The
same process occurs with the left foot except that weight passes to the high balls
of the feet instead of the whole foot.
    Note use of a space hold within the step direction, which states the initial
placement of the foot; during the turning the transference of weight continues in

that same direction. Also, note that foot hooks only specify use of parts of the foot in the forward-backward (sagittal) build of the foot; for statement of *sides* of the foot supporting, the specific foot area signs of **22q** are used. Note the need here for the diagonal edge of the foot, shown by combining the two indications of **22q**.

## Layout

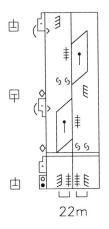

22m

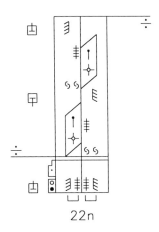

22n

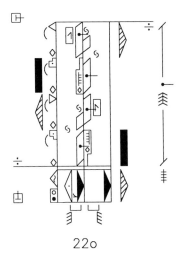

22o

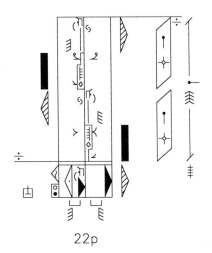

22p

22q

22.9. In turning around the spinal axis in 'all fours' positions, the question arises as to whether the turn signs should be placed inside the notation staff, as in **22m** and **22o**, or outside, **22p**. Outside placement leaves the support column and adjoining columns free for other symbols and often dispenses with having to calculate the degree of turning at each separate stage of the movement progression. On the other hand, inside placement is more easily seen and makes it possible to show how the turn interacts with other aspects of the movement.

22.10. In comparison, the way of writing of **22r** is cumbersome: a point is made here of having the turn indication cover all supporting parts but, unless the movement is slow, this overlapping hardly alters the result.

22.11 The way of writing of **22s** makes it possible to show by a vertical simultaneous bow that the step on the right foot and the turn partially overlap. The direction of the step is established before the turning begins. In **22t**, the amalgamated stepping and turning are shown to be completely simultaneous by the small vertical bow.[83] As in **22o** and **22p**, a space hold is shown within the step direction so that, during the action of turning, the transference of weight continues in the direction judged from the start.

22.12. A log rolling turn often results in a new position. When the turn sign is placed in the support column, a layout problem may arise because, in mixed support situations, signs needed to indicate the resulting position (such as pre-signs, hand signs, and/or DBP symbols) inevitably take up a certain amount of vertical space, i.e. time. When exact timing is being used care is needed in showing the moment of arrival.

In **22u**, from sitting, the pelvis is lifted taking the weight off the hips and onto the feet and right hand. A half-turn takes place on the right hand and right foot, the left foot releasing. The symbols for the end position take approximately one square; such positions are the result of the preceding movement. Note the short vertical bow connecting the turn sign indicates resultant placement; the whole movement is completed ending with the new position 'on count 1'.

22.13. In **22v** the new support to which the turn leads is written 'on count 1' as the turn finishes, i.e. at the beginning of the next measure. The torso is shown to be forward at the start, but levels for the torso, hands, and feet are not given, thus performance is left open.

# Layout (continued)

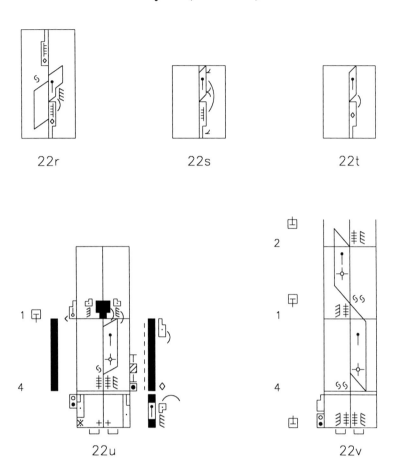

22r    22s    22t

22u    22v

22.14.  **Carets.**  In support columns, as in gesture columns, carets can be used to indicate that the movement is written for the *same body part* as stated previously in the same column.  In **22w**, also shown as **2h**, carets indicate that the steps are on the hands, otherwise they would be understood to refer to the feet.  Alternatively, the pre-signs can be restated as in **22x**.[84]

22.15.  In an 'all fours' situation for which four support columns are used and body parts are designated, as in **22y**, carets are not needed for movements of the same parts in these designated outer support columns.  Note use of spot holds here for the feet which allow a swiveling adjustment.

22.16.  **Same Spot Caret.**  The special caret designed to show the idea of a touch or a support happening on the same spot as a previous contact (usually on the floor), is derived from the *spot hold sign*, **22z**.  This sign divided in half produces the *'same spot' caret*, **22aa**.

22.17.  When a supporting limb is lifted off the floor and then replaced to where it was before, the 'same spot' caret makes clear that reference is not to a previously indicated part of the body.  The more general meaning of the caret 'the same' is pinpointed to mean specifically 'the same spot'.  In **22ab**, while 'on all fours', the right hand takes a step forward opened $1/_3$ to the diagonal; it then lifts, the arm gesturing sideward, before being placed again 'on the same spot' as before.

22.18  When a limb or part of the body remains in contact with the floor but changes from a support to a gesture or vice versa, in most cases the ordinary caret is clear, as in **22ac**, the meaning being 'the same'.  Here the right foot takes weight where the ball of the foot was touching.  After the left foot closes, the right becomes a gesture, the ball touching in 'place' where it was before.  However, use of the 'zed' caret, as in **22ad**, visually links gesture to support and vice versa and can therefore be particularly helpful in 'all fours' situations and floorwork (see also **21g**).

# Carets

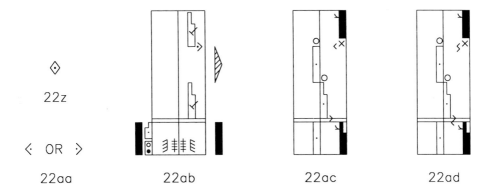

22w          22x

22y

## Same Spot Caret

22z

⟨ OR ⟩

22aa          22ab          22ac          22ad

22.19. **Momentary Auxiliary Support.** In floorwork the hands or elbows often help the performer to get into the next position by momentarily taking support on the floor. This is usually unstressed and can be dealt with simply by writing a hand symbol with an angular supporting bow indicating that the hand takes some weight, **22ae**. Here the moment of releasing the hand is shown. (For details on this way of writing see <u>Advanced Labanotation</u> *Kneeling, Sitting, Lying* Section 40.)

22.20. The hand support indications of **22ae** and **22af** do not in themselves have a specific time validity. A moment of weight-bearing is shown with no statement of retention or immediate release. Cancellation or retention should be indicated as needed; in **22af** the hand contact, which serves to help balance, is cancelled by the subsequent rising of the torso to normal standing.

Arm gestures can be indicated to show when the hands release, if such a degree of precision is needed in the notation.

# Momentary Auxiliary Support

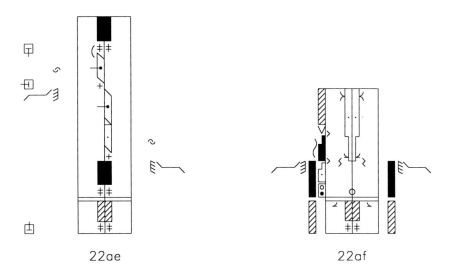

22ae                                    22af

# V READING EXAMPLES

# 23 Supporting on the Hands and Shoulders

23.1. **Supporting on the Hands.** In **23a**, a small excerpt from *Fever Swamp* by Bill T. Jones, P steps into a handstand, bringing the legs up one after the other.[85] G helps P stay up by holding P's ankles. Note that no hold signs are necessary for the hand supports.

## Supporting on the Hands

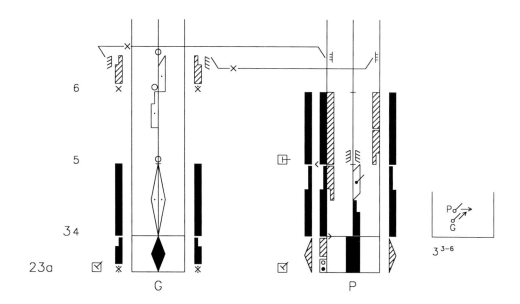

23.2. **Supporting on the Shoulders and Other Body Parts.** The next example shows an excerpt from *Icarus* by Lucas Hoving.[86] Breathing in, expanding the lungs (the inside of the chest) and breathing out, shown in **23b**, are both used in this excerpt. Also used are gathering ans scattering movements for the arms, **23c**.

23.3. Ex. **23d** presents the following sequence: From lying on the back with the legs contracted above the torso and the arms and palms of the hands flat on the floor, the inverted torso rolls sequentially (pelvis first) to a support on the back of the shoulder area as the legs extend up. The right leg then directs to the back to touch on the ball of the foot, then moves to the side, which initiates a roll to the right on the right shoulder ending in a position lying on the right side of the torso facing downstage. The legs end sideward left, the left arm is stretched backward and the chest arched. The legs and arms then contract, as the body rolls onto the right knee and left foot, the torso is bent forward and twisted to the left, the hands covering the ears at the end of the gathering arm movement. Breathing in, the performer rises onto his knee, arms quickly dropping and then quickly reaching upward with a scattering expression. He then sinks again, hands to ears. This rising and sinking is repeated before the upper part of the torso leans to the right and weight is taken on his right lower arm as a transition to rolling to the left onto the right hip and then onto the back, facing upstage. He ends on the back of the shoulder area, similar to the first movement, but with the left leg extended up, the right touching the floor in front without taking weight.

# Supporting on the Shoulders and Other Body Parts

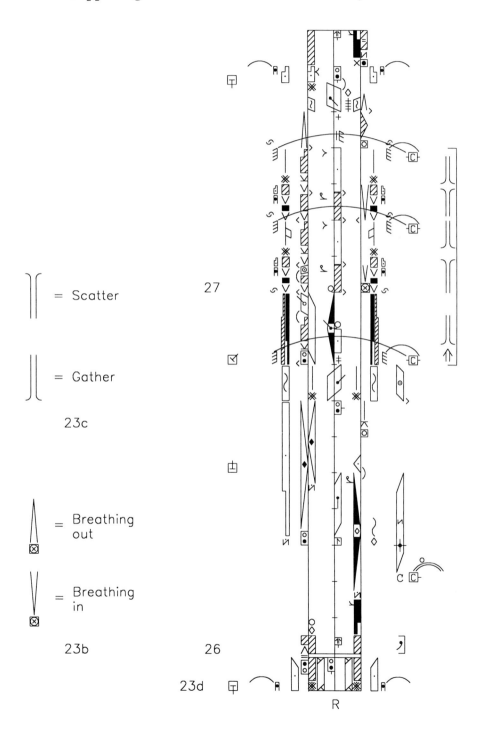

= Scatter

= Gather

23c

27

= Breathing
out

= Breathing
in

23b

26

23d

R

23.4.  Ex. **23e** is a Pilates exercise which, from lying on the back, goes into a shoulder stand, the legs both moving overhead, touching the floor behind.[87] Then, opening out and circling, as the body lowers again to lying, the legs end forward just off the floor.  After 4 repeats this pattern is reversed, the legs opening and sweeping to the back as the center of weight rises into the shoulder stand.  As the performer breaths out, the legs come together sliding over the floor.  The pelvis (actually the center of weight) then lowers and the body returns to lying on the back of the torso with the legs rising up sagittally.  While breathing out the legs lower to just off the floor in diagonal directions.

The torso movements are written here in terms of the center of weight lifting to place high and then lowering to middle level.  A shoulder stand high on the spine is indicated through weight ending on shoulders and neck.  These movements are good exercise for the abdominal muscles.  Note the inclusion of breathing, the timing of inhaling and exhaling.

## Supporting on the Shoulders and Other Body Parts (continued)

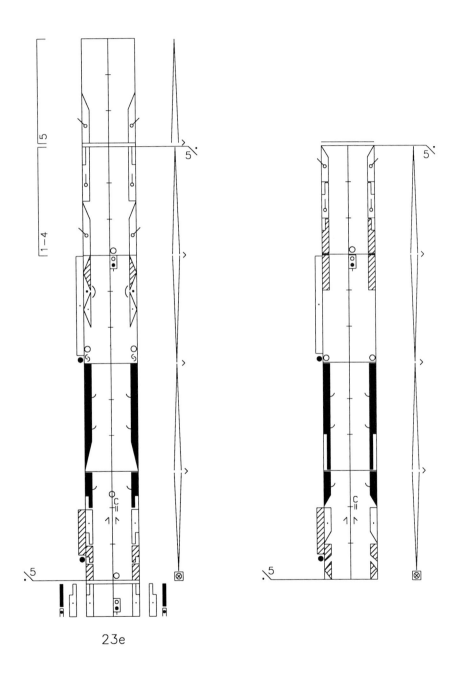

23e

# 24 On 'All Fours'

24.1. **Method A - Central 'Place'.** The following example shows a Limón Technique exercise.[88] In **24a** the performer starts standing on the feet. The torso hangs down, the hands touching the floor. Note that the notator of this piece chose to place the torso and augmented body signs outside the staff, on the right. The feet stay on the same spot while the hands walk forward, one after the other, until the body unit from ankles to shoulders is a little lower than forward high. Each step forward on the hands becomes longer, each distance being judged from the place direction established by the feet. The last step on the left hand will arrive on a line with the right because it is the same distance from place. To return to the starting position in the same manner, each step on the hands becomes a shorter distance from place. With this analysis the direction of each step is given as forward, although spatially the hands are traveling backward. Again the hands end in a line, both being the same distance from place.

## Method A - Central 'Place'

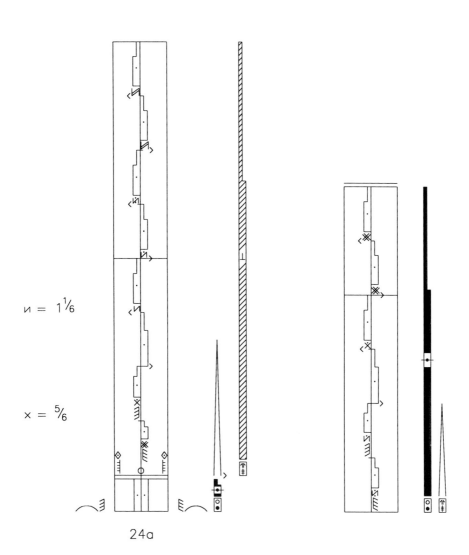

24a

24.2. **Method B - Isolated Body Part Signs in Support Columns.**  Ex.
**24b**, taken from *Bonsai* by Moses Pendleton, shows use of the Split Body Key
(see Section 9).[89]  From a position on hands and feet, the feet turn $^1/_4$ as the
hands release momentarily.  The notation then indicates how performer B walks
('gallops' in the score) a $^3/_8$ circle forward, the feet ending a step-length behind
the hands, the legs and arms bent.  B's head is between person Z's arms and his
hands close to and on the outside of Z's feet.  B's limbs stretch on count 1 of
measure 154; they contract 1 degree on count 2 followed by 2, 3, then 4 degrees
on counts 3 and 4.  The body then lowers even further to the ground, as it turns
$^1/_4$ on the feet, while the torso bends sideways and the hands maintain their
support.  The hands release on count 4 of measure 155 and the body ends in a
support on the left side of the torso, legs and arms contracted, the feet touching
the shoulder of the person to the right and the hands grasping the ankles of the
person to the left.

24.3.  In the excerpt from *Fever Swamp* by Bill T. Jones, **24c**, M slides the
feet backward as the legs stretch.[90]  The hands of L touch the shoulders of M.
Walking backward on a straight path on hands and knees, M passes under D's
legs before coming up to a standing position on the feet in *plié*.

## Method B - Isolated Body Part Signs in Support Columns

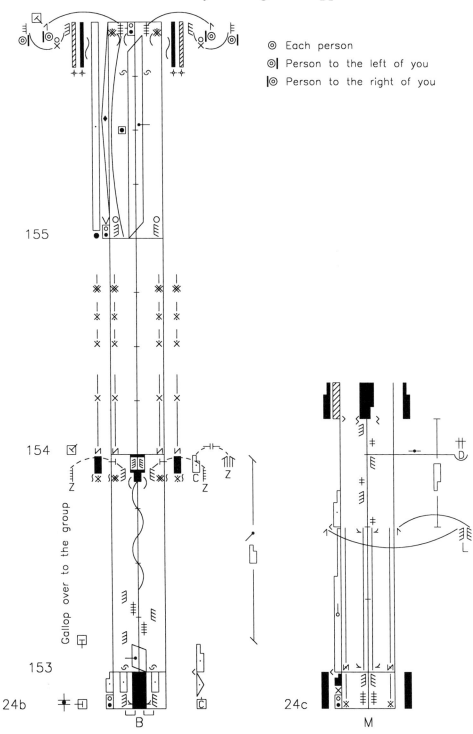

⊚ Each person

⊚| Person to the left of you

|⊚ Person to the right of you

24.4  In **24d** the mother (M) in Victoria Uris' *3 On a Match* "oozes along the floor", trying not to attract attention.[91]  She travels forward, using her right lower arm and left hand, dragging her pelvis.  Her path takes her straight forward under D, then circling $^1\!/_4$ to the left she slithers between D's legs.

### Method B - Isolated Body Part Signs in Support Columns (continued)

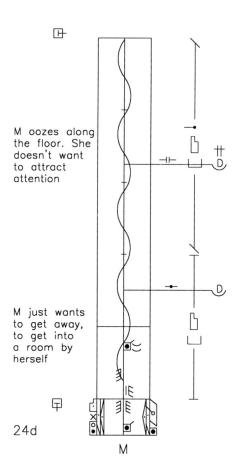

M oozes along
the floor. She
doesn't want
to attract
attention

M just wants
to get away,
to get into
a room by
herself

24d

M

24.5.  **Method C - Statement of Limb Direction.**  In **24e**, from *Fever
Swamp*, M tilts the torso forward low, the right leg going backward high as she
starts falling forward.[92]  L catches her right ankle in time to allow her to lower
onto her hands and lie down.  The arms gesture down just before weight is
supported on the hands.  Also the subsequent movements of the arms, a 5 degree
contraction and then extension, are given in the arm gesture column.   Stretching
her arms, she takes her weight back onto her knees, her body coming upright as
she swivels and simultaneously lowers on her left knee, leaving her right leg in
its old direction but off the floor.  She then takes weight on her right foot as the
torso twists to the right, arms now forward low.

**Method C - Statement of Limb Direction**

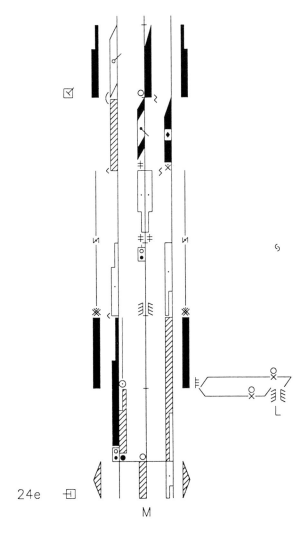

24.6. **Method D - Direction-from-Body-Part.** In **24f**, again from *Bonsai* by Moses Pendleton, a row of performers support on hands and feet with the head between the legs of the person in front and the feet on the inside of the hands of the person behind.[93] The right foot and left hand then step in front of themselves (indicated with DBP), then the left foot and right hand. The stepping goes on, the feet ending a step-length behind the hands, the head still between the legs of the person in front and the feet between the hands of the person behind. Note that although the hold signs for the hands in measure 151 reinforce the retention of support, they would not have been necessary (for validity of supports see Section 21).

24.7. Ex. **24g** is a floorwork exercise taught by Nina Wiener, in which weight is taken on various body parts.[94] The performer starts standing and swings the arms in a circle, while moving toward a position on hands and feet, the right foot a far distance backward of the hands. The position of the left foot is then given with a DBP indication: immediately next to the right. The feet slide backward, then the arms slide diagonally out, as the body lowers to lying down. A $\frac{1}{2}$ roll to the right ends lying on the back. The body then comes up, the right leg being positioned across the left leg and the right foot taking support exactly where it contacted the floor. With the added support on the left hand, the body turns $\frac{1}{2}$, ending in a position on both hands and feet, the torso inclined forward low. The left hand then steps forward of the left foot, while the right leg slides to left sideward middle behind the left leg. The right hand then steps a large distance sideward right of the left foot, as the weight is taken on the right hip. From this position the body rolls $\frac{1}{4}$ over the hips and ends facing stage left, lying down on the back with the arms sliding out to the side.

## Method D - Direction-from-Body-Part

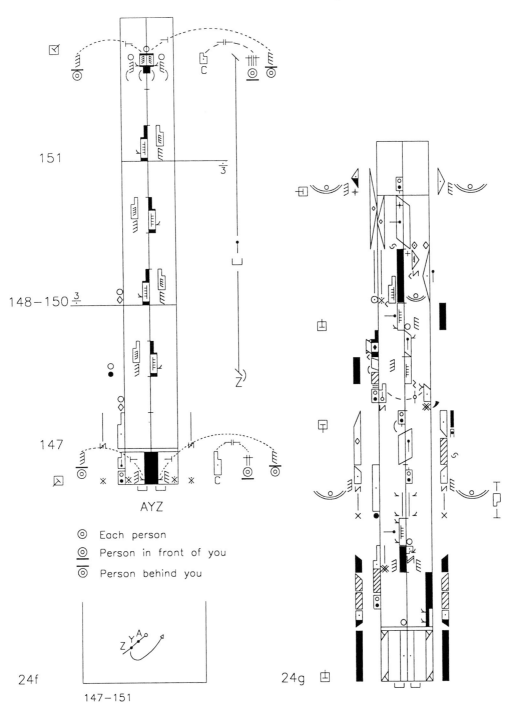

151

148–150 $\frac{3}{4}$

147

AYZ

◎  Each person

⦿  Person in front of you

⊚  Person behind you

24f

147–151

24g

24.8.  Ex. **24h** shows walking the feet up to the hands from lying down on the front.[95]  The arms stretch and thus raise the body.  Note the indication of the augmented body section from ankles to chest.  The right foot then steps a short distance in front of itself, then the left foot steps a step-length in front of itself, the right foot does the same.  The left foot then steps to the right of the left hand and the right steps immediately next to the left foot, so that both feet end between the hands.

24.9.  In **24i** the performer is on hands and feet, arms straight and the body inclined forward from ankles to chest.  The body turns $^1/_2$ to the right around its spinal axis, the right hand is then placed underneath the shoulder and the right foot immediately next to the left.  Because of the sideward pointing pin, it was necessary to add a wider staple to identify that the sign for under the shoulder relates to the hand.  The right foot then takes a low step backward of itself, followed by the left foot stepping next to it.  This results in a crab position (for crab position see 10.4).

24.10.  Ex. **24j** shows standing up from sitting on the hips with hand support.  Support on the hips is cancelled as the pelvis shifts forward high and the feet and hands take the weight of the body resulting in a crab position.  The pelvis shift leads into a low kneel; the torso rounds forward and the palms are placed beside the knees.  Weight is taken on the hands and also backward onto the balls of the feet in order to stand up.

24.11.  Ex. **24k** shows moving from standing to sitting on the right hip.  After lowering during a $^1/_4$ turn, the performer puts the right hand far to the right of the right foot before the hip sits sideward immediately next to the right hand.  Note that the gap after the turn sign in the foot support columns does not mean jumping; the support on the right hand immediately indicates an 'all fours' situation, this means that supports are automatically held, and specific cancellation would be needed.

## Method D - Direction-from-Body-Part (continued)

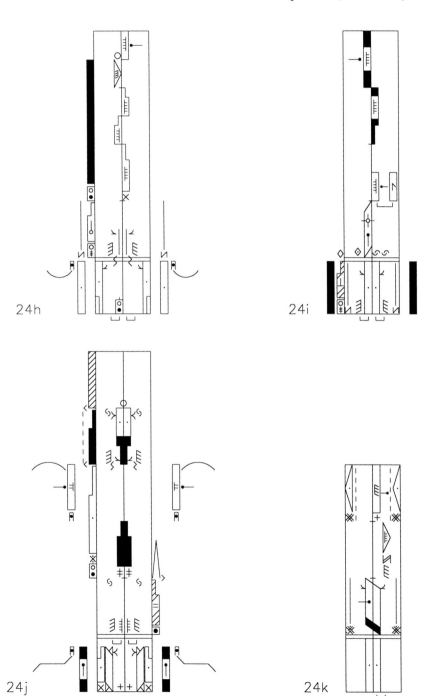

24h

24i

24j

24k

# 25 Turning

25.1. In ex. **25a**, another excerpt from *Bonsai* by Moses Pendleton, as there is no vertical support, rolling happens around the spinal axis (Rule 2 in Section 11).[96] Each roll starts from the feet and progresses through the body to

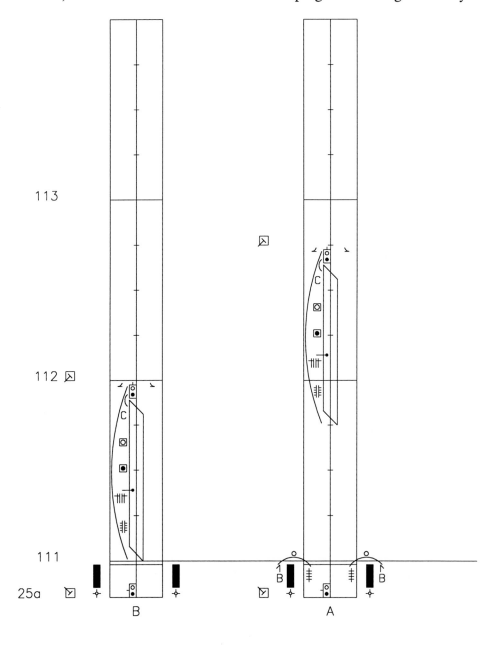

the head, i.e. the feet lead first, then the legs, pelvis, chest and head. Of interest is that the succession is passed on from B to A to Y to Z, as all form a single file; each person (except B) has his/her feet touching the shoulders of the person on the right. This contact is maintained during the roll.

## Turning

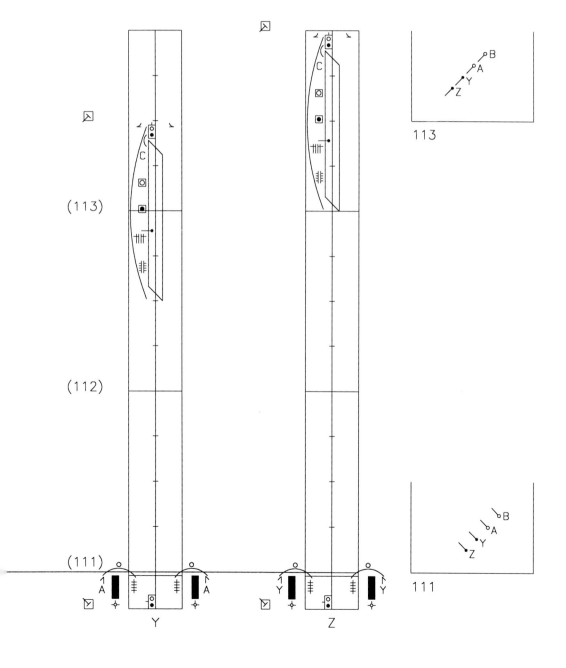

25.2  Ex. **25b** shows both partnering and floorwork for the father (F) and mother (M) in an excerpt from *3 On a Match* by Victoria Uris; the movements of the daughter which occur on another part of the stage during this sequence have been omitted.[97]  The father, facing upstage and lying on the left side of his torso, wheels through 'stepping' actions a $^1/_2$ circle around his left shoulder.  Note use of supporting bows for the feet.  The main weight is on the torso, but some weight needs to be taken by the feet during the stepping actions.  During this movement M moves with a $^1/_4$ turn into a position with her torso forward low, her right leg bent up in the air and the front of her chest on the floor.  From lying on his left side, facing downstage, F grasps M's waist and, taking her with him, he rolls to the right, the back of her torso lying for a moment on his front.  Both end on the right side of the torso, facing stage left.  Since there is no key in this turn sign and F is lying down, rolling (around the spinal axis of the body) is understood.  The last part of his $^3/_4$ roll takes F onto his right knee on which an additional $^1/_4$ turn occurs.  The mother has made a full rolling turn, ending on her right knee.  Both take weight on the right hand and knee as they move into a low kneel.  F releases his right hand support, shown by the arm gesture, he ends with his hands supporting the mother's waist.

# Turning (continued)

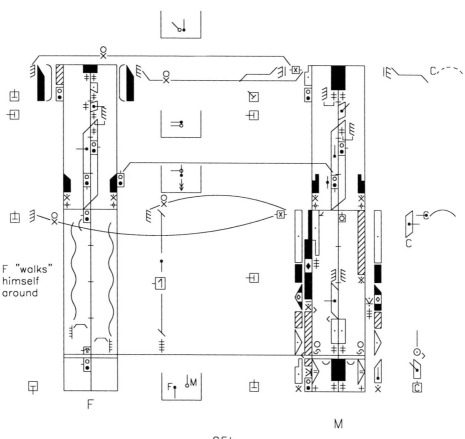

F "walks"
himself
around

F

M

25b

25.3.  Ex. **25c**, again from *3 On a Match*, shows the father (F) rising from
a low foot-kneel and turning on his right knee (around the vertical line of gravity)
before sinking again to a low kneel with the torso tilted forward and twisted to
the right.[98]  From this position F performs 2 $^1/_4$ rolls to the right passing onto
his back and then knees, ending on the left side of his torso.  As he rolls onto his
back his legs spread and then contract before the roll continues on his knees.
The Body Key outside the staff indicates how all gestures are judged.  This key
does not affect the turn sign, it is repeated in the turn sign to indicate rolling
although it is obvious from the starting position and the parts supporting that
rolling is taking place.
    The sequence for the mother also includes a roll.  After a small swivel turn
on a high level kneel, she lowers to roll on her back and then onto her knees,
now in low level.

# Turning (continued)

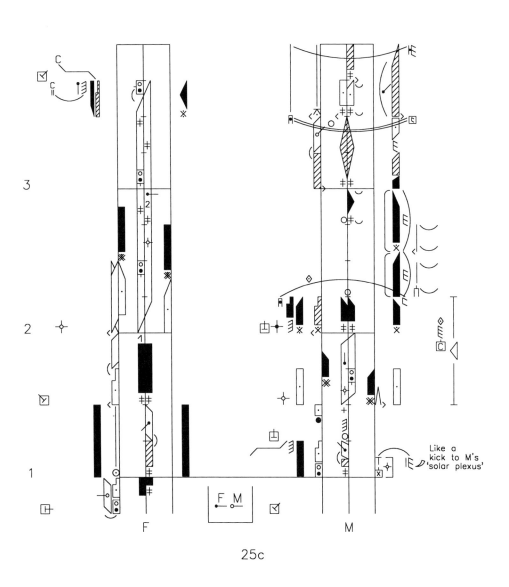

25c

25.4. The phrase **25d**, from *Nun Better* by Pedro Alejandro,[99] shows the dancer lowering from standing to lying on the right side, via support on the right knee and hip. The force of the arm gestures with palms sliding (shown with a slashing effort indication) gives the momentum for the body to roll $^3/_4$ to the left combined with a $^1/_4$ swivel turn so that the body ends on the left knee. Indication of the Standard Cross of Axes inside the second turn sign clarifies this swiveling action. Of interest are the concluding movements. With weight still on the left knee, the right foot steps backward on the ball of the foot (as in a backward high step) and the hands slide forward; the angling sign for the right leg states that it is at a 45° angle with the surface of the floor. The hands take weight as the left foot steps just behind the right, the leg having a similar angle to the floor. The torso ends inclined forward low.

25.5. In **25e** from *Piazzolla Caldera* by Paul Taylor,[100] U lowers to lying on the back, arms sliding diagonally backward (location of left leg has not been indicated in this excerpt) before a $^1/_2$ swivel turn to the left while his arms 'hug' his knees. In the second half of the turn he sits up, swiveling on his hips as he prepares the right leg to take a step forward. With his left arm down and leaning to the left, he walks on a counterclockwise circular path around his left hand.

# Turning (continued)

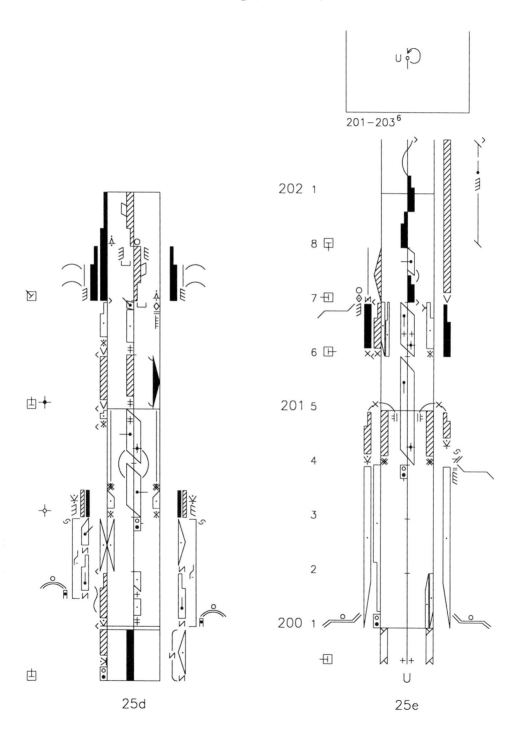

25d                             25e

25.6.  At the start of measure 18 in **25f**, which is from *1492* by Peter
Anastos, performer S takes a low forward step, lowering to the floor before
turning to the right, rolling from left knee to left hip and right hip to right
knee.[101]  This rolling continues, aided by the hands contacting the floor, on a
counterclockwise path.  S's orientation during these rolls refers to the focal point
of the circle.  While S is rolling, T is walking close to him, moving on the same
circular path, his right hand grasping S's right shoulder.  At the start of T's score,
S is indentified as being the focal point for T as he walks along with S.

In measure 19 S takes a step forward and, with his body forward, he kicks
up his legs backward high (very bent) as he hops on his right foot, his hands
taking weight on the floor.  This step is immediately followed by the same knee
to hip rolling during which he completes a full turn to the right.  This springing-
rolling pattern is repeated twice more.  On each of S's hops T swings his left arm
sagittally, bringing his hand near S's bottom as though whipping him up into the
air.  Both S and T continue to travel on the circular path.

After S's third springing-rolling pattern, a quick $\frac{1}{4}$ swivel leads into a $\frac{1}{2}$
roll onto the front of his pelvis, his legs ending backward, his torso forward, all
three held just off the floor, his arms alongside his body.  Another half roll
ending with the legs forward is combined with a $\frac{1}{2}$ swivel turn to the right, the
body coming upright as S ends sitting cross-legged with quick "there you are"
open arm gestures.  Just before this last multiple turning for S, T lets go of S's
right shoulder and, stepping behind S, turns to face front, opening his arms in a
low sideward gesture.

# Turning (continued)

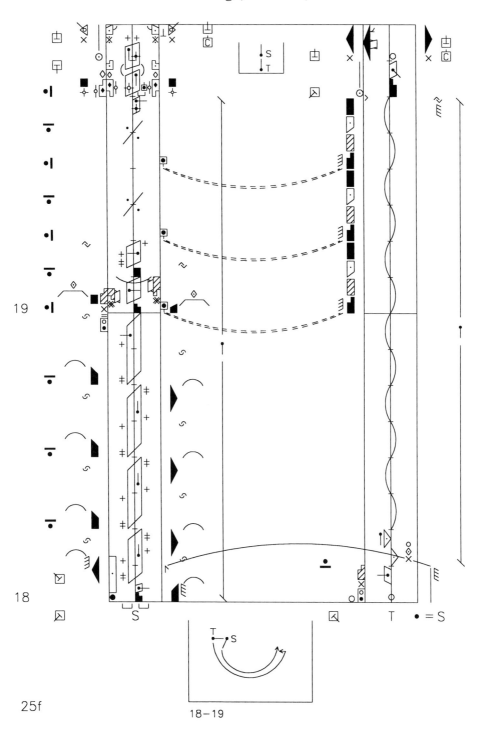

25f

# 26 Somersaults, Log Rolling

26.1. In **26a**, an example from *Fever Swamp* by Bill T. Jones, a handstand occurs, as in **23a** from the same score.[102] Apart from direction symbols, a somersault sign is used here to indicate the handstand. Starting from a torso twist to the right, J's torso untwisting occurs at the start of the $^1/_4$ blind (non-swivel) turn which leads into taking weight on the hands. As soon as J's legs are up, G grabs J's left knee. J then bends his arms, lowering to the floor; rolling down, weight is taken on the back of the head, shoulder area, waist, and then torso. The somersault sign outside the staff conveys the overall movement. G releases his grasp as J is able to control his lowering. The overall action is that of a hand stand forward roll.

26.2. In **26b**, a Pilates-style exercise, the performer starts lying on the front of the body, arms and legs backward, palms of the hands facing up, and the forehead touching the floor.[103] As the performer breathes in (see 23.2), the chest and legs are lifted and the arms taken backward diagonally, causing whole body to contract over the back, weight will now be on the front of the pelvis. From this position small somersaults forward and backward, co-ordinated with breathing out and in, cause the body to rock back and forth over the front of the torso.

## Somersaults

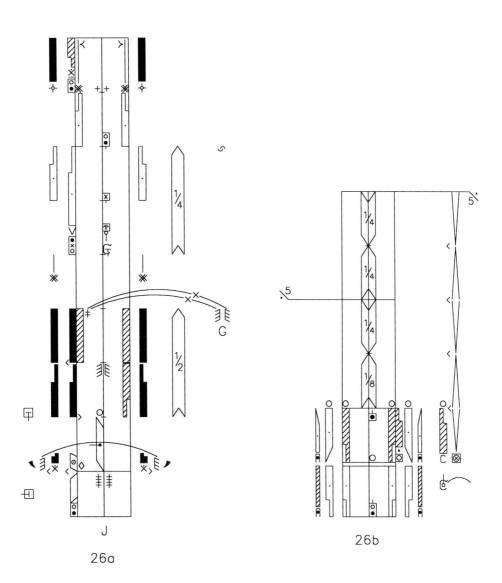

26a

26b

26.3.  At the start of **26c**, which is from *3 on a Match* by Victoria Uris, both F and D perform somewhat similar forward somersault rolls, ending sitting on the floor.[104]  From a squat, M somersaults backward, first putting her hands on the floor to facilitate sitting, then rolling onto the back of the waist, the left shoulder, and the feet, ending on the knees.  Immediately, M rolls to her right, her torso inclining forward toward stage right and retaining that direction during the 'log rolling' traveling downstage through weight being placed on left hip, right hip, right knee and left knee makes a full turn, her hands helping the progression.  D (for Daughter), emulating her mother in the second measure shown here, tucks her right leg under the left to be able to place weight on her right knee as a preparation for a similar hip, hip, knee, knee support sequence rolling $1\frac{1}{2}$ to the left.  During this rolling D also travels downstage.

26.4.  Ex. **26d** shows the second part of D's staff with the turn sign written outside the staff.  This placement is clearer in that the supporting body parts, the indications for Body Cross of Axes and the amount of turn can be seen more easily.

## Somersaults, Log Rolling

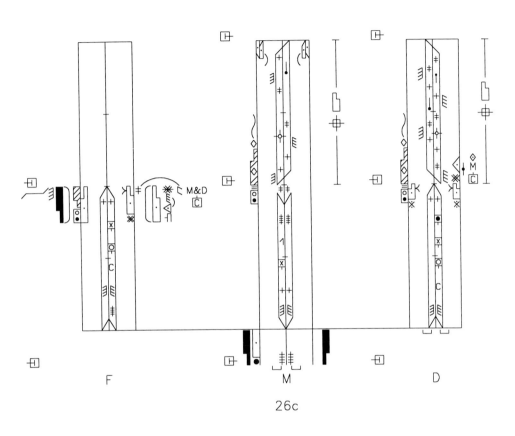

26c

F      M      D

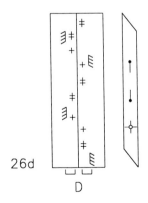

26d

D

26.5. For S, Ex. **26e** shows a somersault action by placing the series of supporting body parts in the support columns and writing the somersault sign outside of the staff to indicate the type of movement.[105] Starting on the left knee, right leg and right arm forward high, S lowers to the left hip and then rolls onto the back of the waist and the back of the chest. The right leg (now grasped at the ankle by the right hand) is backward low, touching the floor, and the left arm is indicated to be downward, judged from the Body Key. After this $^1/_2$ backward somersault, S somersaults forward, rolling onto the left hip and then continuing forward up to a high kneel on the left with the right foot resting on the floor. This sequence is then repeated. As if this was only a preparation to gain momentum for the subsequent movement, S then performs 2 full backward somersaults. In both rolls, S takes support on the left hip with some help from the hands on the floor and then rolls via the back of the waist, back of left shoulder area and onto the left knee. After the second quick roll, S steps backward on the right foot and then rises as the left foot closes next to the right, ending standing in middle level.

T performs the same half somersault rolls backward and forward. After the last one, T steps forward onto the right foot and somersaults forward twice with supporting help from the hands. T then also comes up onto the left knee and right foot and rises up to middle level standing, feet together.

# Somersaults

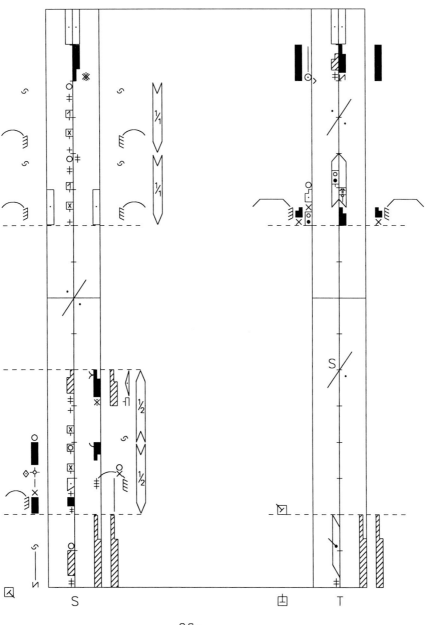

26e

26.6.  Ex. **26f**, from *7 for 8* by Elisa Monte, shows $^1/_4$ somersault in the air, starting from upright to the front of the torso facing the floor.[106]  Performers a, b, c and d run, jump, somersaulting and traveling forward, and land into the right arm of partners A, B, C and D respectively.  The weight of these jumpers propels the partners into a turn to the right.  They pivot around twice, before a, b, c and d put their feet on the floor again and begin to run on a circular path to the right.

Note that a, b, c and d have actually performed another $^1/_4$ somersault (this time backward), when they put their feet on the floor.  However, this movement is not perceived as a somersault; it does not have that character, therefore it is not notated as such.

## Somersaults (continued)

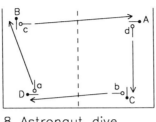

8 Astronaut dive

\* Address partner
(each girl's own
partner with a
matching upper
case letter).

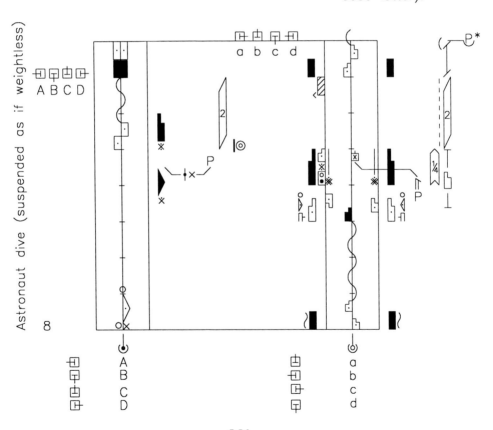

26f

# 27 Cartwheeling

27.1. In **27a**, an excerpt from *1492* by Peter Anastos, T performs a full cartwheel to the right, passing over S's back.[107] At the start S ducks down, holding T's right hand and pulling T to the right in the direction of the cartwheel before releasing. The supports for T's cartwheel are given in the support column, the cartwheel sign being written outside the staff to convey immediately the type of movement.

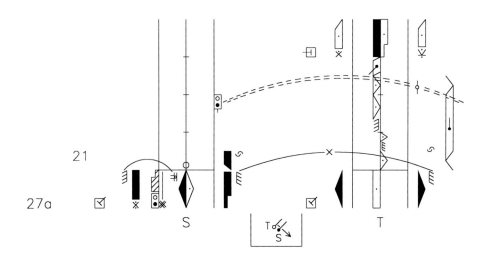

27.2. Paul Taylor's *Piazzolla Caldera* provides the next excerpt.[108] Ex. **27b** shows partnered cartwheels. First A cartwheels to the right onto E, supporting with his hands on E's thighs, while E grabs A by the waist with his arms. A ends with his back touching the front of E's torso. Staying in this relation to each other, the two then 'wheel' on together, so that A lands with his feet on the floor again and E is up-side-down. Note the addition of the resulting torso positions to aid keeping track of the orientations. In the 3rd measure, for example, one can see that E's torso is coming upright after his feet land on the floor. In measure 4, E tilts his torso sideward to help A perform one more $\frac{1}{2}$ cartwheel ending on his feet. After this virtuoso performance, A and E both assume a proud position, hands on the hips (sides of the pelvis), both of them looking at SN.

# Cartwheeling

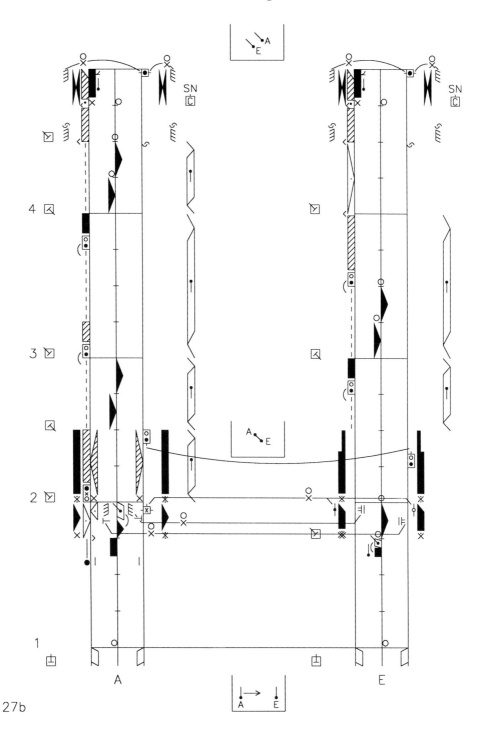

27b

27.3. **Cartwheel on Bar.** The following three examples are given for comparison.[109] The performer in **27c** is hanging from a bar, facing one of the supporting poles. As can be seen from the supporting bows, the left hand is grasping in front of the right. The body then swings in a cartwheel revolution around the bar, the cartwheel sign giving an immediate indication of the movement. For such a cartwheel the legs will begin by swinging to the performer's left. Note use of inverted torso to show fixed end.

This event can also be written showing the directions through which the body unit (wrists to feet) pass, **27d**. For this example the bar is shown to be facing the audience. Note that the Constant Key is used here, so the directions will be toward Constant forward and Constant backward.

Another method of description, **27e**, following Knust's usage, shows the directions in terms of the Standard Key; at the halfway point a half change of Front has occurred (as happens in half a cartwheel) and hence a half change in direction. Note the use here of secret turn signs (for a half change of Front) halfway through the revolution and again at the end as the performer arrives where s/he started.

Some impulse to gain momentum for the revolution is expected.

27.4. **Cartwheel and Turn Combined.** In **27f**, from *Lark Ascending* by Bruce Marks, L is caused passively to perform a cartwheel combined with a turn to the left while being held by T.[110] T starts in a high kneel, facing front and facing L, while L faces stage left with her torso pitched forward low in an exaggerated *arabesque penché* on *pointe* on her left foot, her right leg almost vertically up, her hands taking some weight on the floor. From the left T's left arm grasps her around the waist, while his right hand grasps the middle of her right thigh. She turns around T's left arm, pivoting $1/_4$ to the left and cartwheeling $1/_2$ to the left. She ends facing downstage, her right side being supported on T's left arm. As she comes off the floor, her left leg contracts into a *retiré* position (foot close to the right knee). Note that the legs and arms here are described from the Body Key. For easier reading the two revolution signs are here described according to the Constant Cross, the directions up and down remaining constant for pivoting as well as the left/right directions for cartwheeling. T then sinks to a low kneel and lays L down on her right side on the floor.

The key to indicate that all revolutions are to be read from the Constant Cross is shown in **27g**. This sign uses the basic sign for any form of revolution.

## Cartwheel on Bar

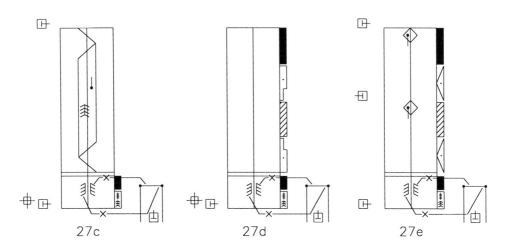

27c          27d          27e

## Cartwheel and Turn Combined

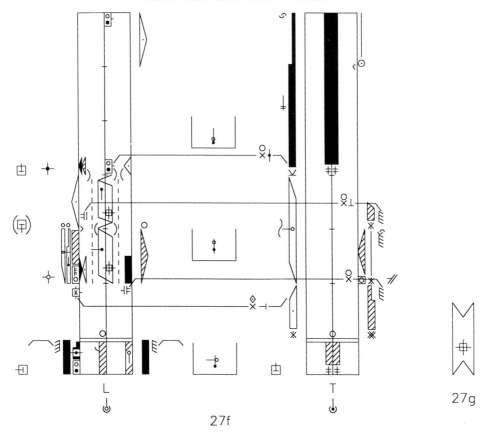

27f

27g

# VI APPENDICES

# A Track Pins

A.1. Track Pins were first presented at the 1975 ICKL Conference and subsequently adopted in 1979. The few questions still left open in 1979 have since been solved.

In Section 19 many usages of track pins have already been discussed, in particular those for the forward tracks (19.6-9). Here other situations, in which track pins are used, are also given.

A.2. **Diagonal Tracks for the Arms.** The diagonal directions for the arms also have the possibility of five tracks, but these are narrower tracks than for the forward direction. Ex. **Aa** illustrates the diagonal tracks.

Though the appropriate diagonally slanting track pins are pictorial, they are more space consuming. Therefore, the convention has been adopted that the forward pointing sagittal track pins are the standard pins to be applied to all diagonal and lateral directions (see also 19.19). Thus, **Ab** is the correct way of writing the center track for diagonal arm gestures.

Ex. **Ac** shows the arm starting in its normal 'side of the body' track in the diagonal direction, for which no pin is needed. It then swings down and returns to the same direction but each time moving to the next track until it ends finally in the track which is the normal track for the left arm in that diagonal direction.

Which body track is being used is clear from the direction symbol. In **Ab** the diagonal direction symbol automatically dictates that the center track pins refer to that diagonal direction.

A.3. **Diagonal Center Line.** When both arms are next to the same diagonal center line, as in **Ad**, the extremity of each arm (usually the fingertips) is next to the center line, illustrated in **Ae** which shows the thumb edges to be facing up. Ex. **Af** shows the same spatial situation but with the palms facing down so that the thumb edges of the hands are at the center line. Exs. **Ag**, **Ah**, **Ai** show similar examples but with the extremities on the center line.

The degree of arm flexion in **Aj** brings the hands together. The thumb edges are facing up and the tips of the fingers are *at the center line*, **Ak**. In **Al** the extremities are *on the center line*, the left being above the right, illustrated in **Am**. The difference between these two examples is slight but is important.

## Diagonal Tracks for the Arms

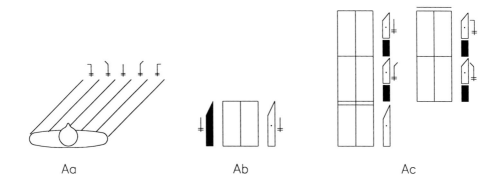

Aa        Ab        Ac

## Diagonal Center Line

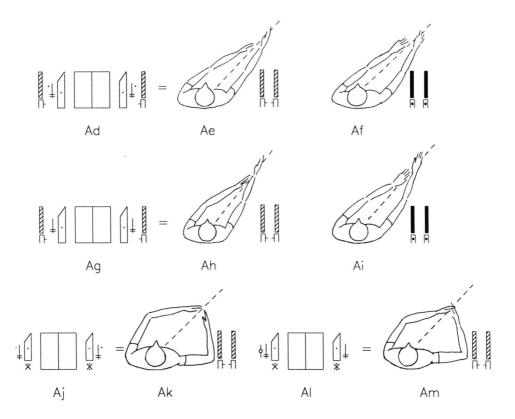

Ad    Ae    Af

Ag    Ah    Ai

Aj    Ak    Al    Am

A.4. **Lateral Tracks for the Arms.** The lateral (sideward) tracks are by nature narrower than the diagonal direction tracks. Ex. **An** illustrates the side tracks.

For arm gestures into the open sideward direction variations from true side are usually shown by intermediate directions. There is usually only a slight sense of relation to the lateral body center line track. For a crossed arm gesture, the placement of the extremity may lie on the outer lateral (sideward) track, on the intermediate track, or on the lateral center track.

Ex. **Ao** illustrates the left arm crossing to the right side, two degrees bent, the extremity falling in the usual, natural sideward track in front of the body. Ex. **Ap** shows the extremity to be in the intermediate body track, while **Aq** shows the extremity to be on the lateral center track, the finger tips directly at the side of the right shoulder.

A.5. Ex. **Ar** and **As** illustrate how these last two examples would be written if lateral pointing track pins were to be used. The sideward pointing pins are visually helpful but unfortunately too space consuming, hence the decision to adopt standardization by using only sagittal track pins. It is often confusing when using lateral track pins (more so than with diagonal track pins), to determine which outer or intermediate track is meant. If in doubt, one can turn the vertical pin $^1/_4$ into the appropriate sideward direction to obtain the visually clearer lateral signs of **An**.

A.6. In **At** the extremities of both arms are on the same line, as shown in **Au**. The arm may to a limited extent make use of the lateral tracks when crossing behind the body. In low and high level there is some range, but not in middle level (the collarbones prevent the needed flexibility). In **Av** the arms are crossed behind the body in the right sideward direction, **Aw**.[111]

## Lateral Tracks for the Arms

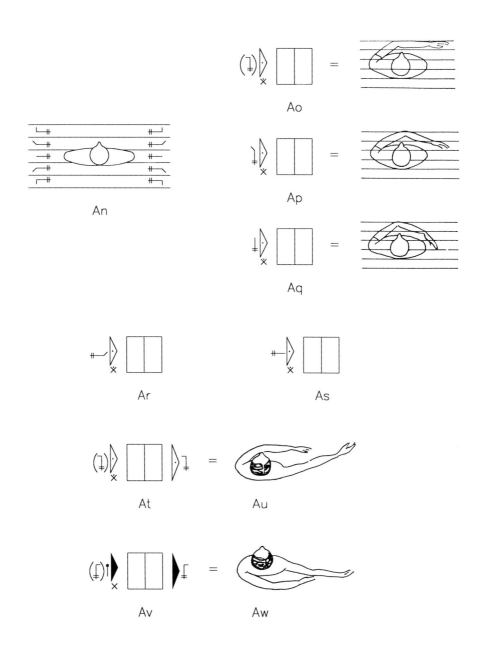

An

Ao

Ap

Aq

Ar      As

At      Au

Av      Aw

A.7.  **Sagittal Tracks for Backward Arm Gestures.**  The range of sagittal tracks also exists behind the body.  Tracks behind the body are shown with backward sagittal track pins, **Ax**.  In **Ay** the arms are down, the extremity of the right arm is on the center line in front, while the left arm is behind on the center line.  In **Az** the arms are backward low with the palms of the hands near the center line, illustrated in **Aaa**.

A.8.  **Vertical Tracks for the Arms.**  The same set of track pins are used for vertical arm gestures.  In the upright standing position the full range exists overhead.  In **Aab** the arms are up, the extremities on the center line.  Because the right arm is slightly bent, its extremity will be below the left arm.  Crossing the arms overhead is shown in **Aac**.  Each hand extremity is above the other shoulder, the right arm being in front of the left.

For the downward place low direction the torso is in the way, hence, if tracks are used, the arms must be either in front or behind the torso.  When the torso is leaning forward, as in **Aad**, all of the tracks are possible for downward gestures.  Here each arm has the extremity next to the center line.

A.9.  **Further Subdivisions of Tracks for Arm Gestures.**  In the chart of **Aae** the tracks which have been discussed so far are illustrated at the bottom.  At the top are shown the additional tracks which on occasion are needed, particularly for gestures in the forward direction.

A.10.   For the balletic arm position of **Aaf**, illustrated in **Aag**, the finger tips (extremities of the arms) are next to the center line and thus almost touching.  In **Aah** they are slightly more apart, having moved halfway to the intermediate forward track.  This position, which is correct for certain schools of classical ballet, is illustrated in **Aai**.  Finger tips separated even more will be in the intermediate forward track, as shown in **Aaj** and **Aak**.  For certain forms of training this distance apart for the arms may be the one desired.

## Sagittal Tracks for Backward Arms Gestures

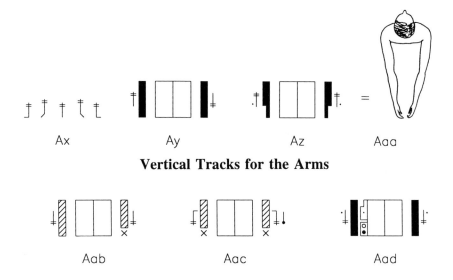

Ax                    Ay                    Az              Aaa

## Vertical Tracks for the Arms

Aab                    Aac                    Aad

## Further Subdivisions of Tracks for Arm Gestures

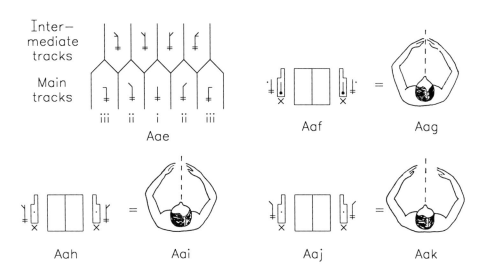

Inter—
mediate
tracks

Main
tracks

iii   ii   i   ii   iii

Aae                    Aaf                    Aag

Aah                    Aai                    Aaj                    Aak

A.11. **Track Pins for Lateral Leg Gestures.** When a leg gesture crosses to the other side, as in **Aal**, it is usual and therefore understood that it crosses in front of the other leg. However, the black relationship pin can be added to provide a specific statement. As a result, the foot will be in the track shown in **Aam**, the lateral sideward-left track. If the leg is flexed there is a greater range for placement of the extremity (the foot) in one or other lateral track. In **Aan** both supporting and gesturing legs are bent and the right foot is placed in the center track to the left. Flexed leg gestures may relate to the lateral tracks in the same way that the crossed arm gesture does in **Ao-Aq**. By this means we can state specific placement of the extremity.

A.12. **Track Pins for Diagonal Leg Gestures.** Ex. **Aao** shows use of the center line in the diagonal direction. While sitting, the extremity of each leg will be on the same diagonal center line, the right higher than the left. For each direction the forward pointing pin always represents the center track of the stated direction. (For track pins applied to vertical and sagittal leg gestures see 19.10-12.)

A.13. **Track Pins for Diagonal Steps.** Track pins can also be applied to diagonal steps with tracks as in **Aap** and **Aaq** for the right and left diagonal directions respectively. The dotted line represents the center line. In **Aar** we see center track pins applied to right diagonal steps, resulting in diagonal 'tightrope' walking. In **Aas**, the pins indicate diagonal walking in the intermediate tracks, for most people the most natural. Walking in same diagonal direction with feet wider apart is shown in **Aat**. Ex. **Aau** shows walking in right diagonal direction with legs crossing; the right foot steps in the lateral track of the left foot, the left foot then steps in the lateral track of the right foot. (For track pins applied to sagittal and lateral step directions see 19.15-19.)

### Track Pins for Lateral Leg Gestures

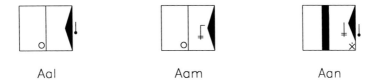

Aal        Aam        Aan

### Track Pins for Diagonal Leg Gestures

Aao

### Track Pins for Diagonal Steps

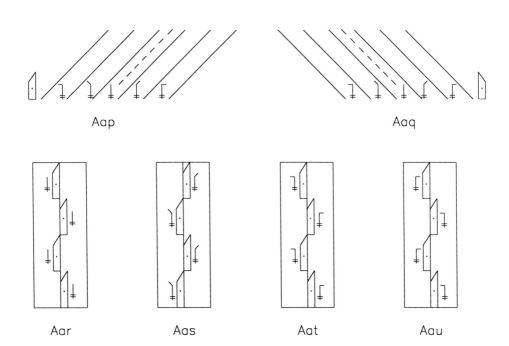

Aap               Aaq

Aar       Aas       Aat       Aau

# B  Pins - when Black, when Track, when Tack?[112]

B.1.  Since the advent of Track Pins, which came into existence because in certain circumstances the track could not be shown in any other way, people have been uncertain about which pin to use for which need.  Notators such as Maria Szentpál had successfully and logically used black pins where now track pins would probably be used.  To understand her longstanding usage we need to start from the beginning to see where usages overlap and where one usage has an advantage over another.  We will start with steps and positions on the feet.

B.2.  **Black Pins.**  In **Ba** the right foot will automatically close at the side of the left foot.  This sideward relationship is specifically stated (i.e. attention drawn to it) in **Bb** through use of the black relationship pin.  In **Bc** the step sideward with the right foot will be in line with the left foot, illustrated in **Bd**.  This sideward relationship can be specifically stated as in **Be**.  Here the pin has the same meaning as in **Bb**; although it is an open step, the side-by-side relationship still exists.  We are familiar with **Bf** in which the forward step for the right foot is on the line in front of the left foot.  It is important to realize that the black pins used in these contexts refer to a *relationship*; their meaning is not one of indicating tracks even if, in application, a track usage emerges.

B.3.  In a 'grapevine' pattern (alternating crossing front and back), as in **Bg**, an overall traveling on a straight path occurs.  In the case of **Bh** which shows traveling sideward with the same foot in front all the time, strictly there will be a gradual veering slightly forward.  However, generally the reader will expect that adhering to the lateral path is intended.  To be more correct such performance should be written as **Bi**.  Here the right foot starts in the 5th position relationship behind the left; as each step is taken the right foot travels sideward in line with this same relationship, thus the 'behind', 'in front' relationships are maintained, illustrated in **Bj**.  In **Bk** sideward steps are all on the lateral central line, the left foot passing first in front as it crosses, then behind, illustrated in **Bl**.  In **Bm** the feet maintain a 3rd position relationship.  The diagonal backward pin for the open sideward step of the right foot results in most of the foot being behind the center line, while about $\frac{1}{4}$ of the foot is in front of the center line.  The same is true for the forward diagonal pin for the left foot, here about $\frac{1}{4}$ of the foot is behind the center line.  This stepping in 3rd position is illustrated in **Bn**.  In all of the above examples a moderate turn out of the feet is assumed; the rotational state should be written in a score.

# Black Pins

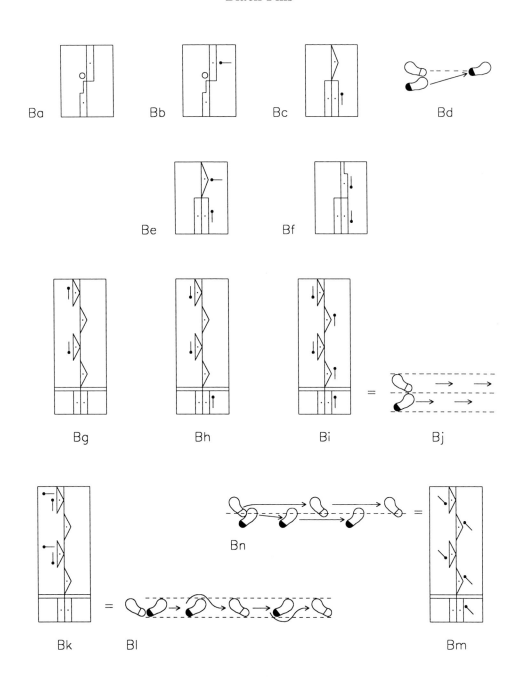

B.4.  **Track Pins.**  Ex. **Bo** shows the same sideward progress of **Bi** using track pins (see also 19.18-19).  Ex. **Bp** illustrates the lateral tracks resulting from the track pins of **Bo**.  The feet do not step on the center sideward line but behind or in front of it.  In this diagram the center line is shown with an arrow.  Ex. **Bq** is the equivalent of **Bm**, but using the intermediate track pin.

B.5.  **Flat Pins, Tacks.**  A 'tack' (flat pin) indicates a slight horizontal displacement from the indicated position.  In the following examples positions with the feet parallel are included; although less familiar to some, they help to make the point regarding the application of 'tacks'.

B.6.  In **Br** the feet are slightly apart; this is illustrated in **Bs** above with the feet parallel and in **Bt** with the feet comfortably turned out.  Slight diagonal displacement is shown in **Bu**, the feet being slightly apart on a diagonal line; shown with parallel feet in **Bv** and somewhat turned out feet in **Bw**.  Ex. **Bx** indicates feet together but with the right foot more forward than the left; illustrated in **By** and **Bz**.  In these examples two pins are used as each foot displaces from the normal place position.

B.7.  Ex. **Baa** shows an ordinary walk, the feet being placed on the natural track forward of the hips.  In **Bab** a slightly wide, 'straddle' walk is shown, the feet being displaced slightly sideward from their normal track.  A diagonal displacement is shown in **Bac**, each step will end slightly wider but also more forward than for an ordinary forward step.  Placement of a tack within the step symbol, as in **Bad**, indicates an intermediate direction; the feet step $^{1}/_{3}$ toward the diagonal direction on each step.  This will produce a wider 'straddle' walk than that of **Bab**.

B.8.  **Combining Black Pins and Tack Pins.**  Variations on 5th position for the feet are shown next, the position being separated in a forward or diagonal direction.  Again, the illustrations show what happens with parallel feet and what happens with a comfortable turn out.  First, 5th position with the right foot in front is given in **Bae**, illustrated in **Baf** and in **Bag**.  As the description here is of the right foot's relationship to the left, only one pin is needed.

B.9.  For ease in grasping the position, read the black pins first for relationship, then the tacks for displacement from the black pin position.  In **Bah** the displacement is forward/backward, illustrated in **Bai** and **Baj**.  Next the opening is on the diagonal, **Bak**, illustrated in **Bal** and **Bam**.  A sideward displacement is shown in **Ban**, illustrated in **Bao** and **Bap**.  Indications such as these may be just what is needed for dances where precise footwork is important for capturing the style.

## Track Pins

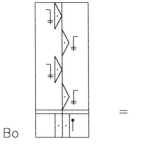  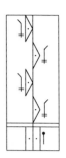

Bo = Bp Bq

## Flat Pins, Tacks

Br Bu Bx

 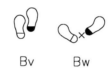 

Bs Bt Bv Bw By Bz

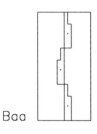 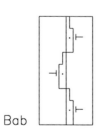 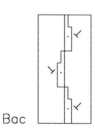 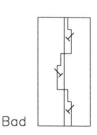

Baa Bab Bac Bad

## Combining Black Pins and Tack Pins

  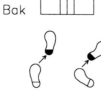 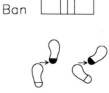

Bae Bah Bak Ban

Baf Bag Bai Baj Bal Bam Bao Bap

B.10. **Pins for All Fours Situations.** When on 'all fours' (hands and feet, or hands and knees), usually the meanings of track pins and black pins no longer coincide. A simple example is given here. In the position of **Baq** the knees are almost together and the hands are placed the normal shoulder width apart. If the track for the hands were to be added without changing the meaning of this notation, it would be that of **Bar**. Ex. **Bas** illustrates the position seen from above.

B.11. In **Bat** the hands are on either side of the center line, illustrated in **Bau**. Hands on the center line with the left hand in front of the right is shown in **Bav**, illustrated in **Baw**.

B.12. In **Bax** the left hand is in its own track and the right hand is in this same track (the left shoulder track) but in front of the left hand. This is illustrated in **Bay**. Here can be seen clearly that the black pin refers to the relationship of the two hands and not to any track. In more complex situations the need for such distinctions occurs. The black pin for 'in front' in **Baz**, could be enough as it is understood to refer to the other hand. However, the extra information given by the track pin in **Bax**, or by use of a DBP direction as in **Bba** makes for clarity and hence faster reading.

B.13. In **Bbb**, which is basically the same as **Bav**, the tack pins indicate that the knees and hands are separated sagittally; the left hand is not only in front of the right on the center line but also slightly ahead of it, **Bbc**.

## Pins for All Fours Situations.

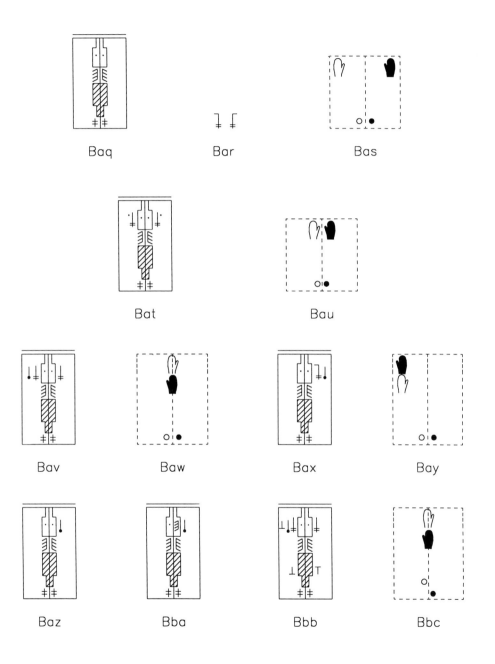

# C Table of Contents from *Kneeling, Sitting, Lying*

Introduction to the Series                                                          xiii

Preface                                                                             xvii

Acknowledgements                                                                    xix

Key to Illustrations and Terminology                                               xxi

I.      KNEELING POSITIONS                                                           2

1       Paired Kneeling - The Five Positions                                        2
           Distance (2)

2       Level in Kneeling                                                           4

3       Foot-Kneel Positions                                                        6
           Distance (6)

4       Mixed Kneeling                                                              8

5       Leg Rotation in Kneeling                                                   10

6       Placement of Lower Legs and Feet                                          12
           Lower leg placement (12); Foot placement (12)

7       Angling                                                                    14
           Analysis and symbology (14); Systems of reference (16);
           Examples (16)

8       Direction-from-Body-Part                                                  18
           Way of Writing (18); DBP for Gestures (18)

II.    SITTING AND LYING POSITIONS                                      20

9      Sitting Positions                                               20
       Using hip signs (20); Using signs for parts of the pelvis (22);
       Level (22)

10     Basic Facts about Lying                                         24

11     The Surfaces of the Torso Used in Lying                         25
       Way of Writing (25); Placement (26)

12     Orientation in Lying                                            26
       Torso direction in relation to lying (26); Facing for body
       surfaces when lying (26); Relationship of torso surfaces to
       room directions (28)

13     Use of Body Sections (Units)                                    30

14     Level in Lying                                                  30

15     Lying on the back (Supine)                                      32
       Degree of involvement of the back in lying (34); Lying on the
       back: variations (34)

16     Lying on the Front (Prone)                                      36
       Regions of body surfaces (38)

17     Lying on the Side                                               40


III.   TRANSFERENCE OF WEIGHT                                          42

18     Kneeling Down, Rising from Kneeling                             42
       Rule 1 (42); Other examples (43); Rule 2 (44); Other examples
       (46)

19     Walking on the Knees                                            46
       Distance (48)

20     Sliding on the Knees                                           50

21   Sitting Down, Rising from Sitting                                           52

      Distance (52); Resultant position (53); Sitting down from
      kneeling (54); Rising to a kneel after sitting (54); Standing up
      after sitting (56)

22   Lying Down, Rising from Lying                                                56
      Lying down from sitting; Sitting up from lying (58); Lying
      down from kneeling (58); Rising to the knees from lying (60)

23   Sliding and Inching on Parts of the Torso                                    62
      Traveling by sliding (62); Traveling by inching (64); Validity
      of support indications (66); Use of columns (67)


IV.   REVOLUTIONS OF THE BODY

25   Introduction                                                                 70
      Pivoting (70); Rolling (70); Wheeling (72); Circling (72); Turn
      signs outside the notation staff (72)

26   Pivoting on the Knees                                                        72

27   Rolling                                                                      74
      Analysis (74); Orthography (76); Change of Front (76);
      Traveling (76); Change in body configuration (78); Other
      examples (78); Relationship between change of Front and
      change of supporting surface (82); Somersault rolls (84)

28   Wheeling and Circling                                                        84
      Change of Front (86); Circling (86)

29   Combined Rolling and Wheeling                                                86
      Wheeling without change of Front (88)

30   Rolling and Wheeling in Sections                                            90
      Rolling in sections (90); Lifting vs. supporting in rotations
      (90); Wheeling in sections (92)

31 The Standard Key in Rolling and Wheeling 92
Front after wheeling and rolling - 'divided Front' (94); 'Secret turn' (95); Stance Key (95); Front and torso tilts (96); Torso directions in wheeling (96); Torso directions in rolling (98); Torso tilts before or during rolling (98)

32 Directions for Limbs While Turning 100
Body hold, space hold (100); Body Key (102); Standard Retention (102); Validity of hold signs (102); Use of keys and diamonds (104); Paths for gestures (104)

V. CLARIFICATIONS 106

33 Systems of Reference 106
Standard Key (106); Other keys (107); Body Key (107); Constant Key (108); Front (108); Standard Key - divided Front (108); Stance Key (109); Standard Key - displacement of attached parts (110); Standard Key - paths for gestures during turns (110)

34 Timing 112
Unit timing (112); Unit timing - gestures as preparation for supports (112); Exact timing (114); Duration lines in the support column (114); Exact timing - placement of symbols (114); Use of Unit and exact timing (118)

35 Distance - Fundamentals 118
Unspecified distance (118); Specified distance (119); Relative statement of distance (119)

36 Exact Distance Measurement 120
Sideward steps (120); Track (120); Statement of exact distance (122); Examples (123); Other supporting parts (124); Point of measurement (124); DBP (126); Leg rotation (126); Other examples(126); Other scales and units. Distance sign (128)

37 Movement Writing and Position Writing 130
Spot holds (130)

38    Carets                                                              132
          Caret for 'remaining' (132); Caret for 'same body part' (136);
          Caret for forward reference (136); Caret for continuation on
          next staff (136); 'Z-Carets' (136)

39    Resultant Movement or Position                                      138
          Timing (138); Retained contact (140); Resultant rolling through
          parts of the foot (140)

40    Floor Contact; Sliding and Pushing in Gestures                      142
          Sliding for limbs (142); Auxiliary hand and elbow contact
          (144); Sliding hand supports (144); Head resting (146);
          Pushing (146)

41    Exact Placement on the Floor                                        148
          DBP (148)

42    Compensatory and Accommodating Movement                             150
          Torso inclusion (150)

43    Weight Distribution                                                 151


44    Reading Examples                                                    154

Notes                                                                     160

References                                                                181

Index                                                                     182

# D Historical Background on Labanotation Textbooks

The authoritative textbook *Labanotation - The System of Analyzing and Recording Movement*, was first published in 1954. The revised and expanded version, published in 1970 (reprinted in 1977) drew attention to a number of topics which were to be dealt with in greater detail in a subsequent publication, referred to as "Part Two". The need for such statements was high-lighted by the reaction of a group in Japan, who, when studying the 1954 Labanotation textbook, assumed that it presented the whole system. Since no handling of long sleeves was included, they decided that the system did not meet their needs. It was therefore important to make clear that much more existed. Labanotation did indeed have the capacity of meeting their needs, and in a wider context it was necessary to draw attention to the fact that the system was applicable across the whole spectrum of human movement.

Detailed information on advanced Labanotation usage has not been generally available. Three volumes on advanced topics were published in 1991 and the present series continues the detailed and more advanced material along the same lines.

### *Labanotation* and *Kinetography Laban*, *Motif Description* and *Structured Description*

The above terms may need some clarification. The specific subject of this book is *Labanotation*, the name given in the United States to the system of movement notation originated by Rudolf Laban and first published in 1928. Most European notators and dance scholars refer to the system as *Kinetography Laban*. There are some differences between Labanotation and Kinetography in notation usages, and occasionally in symbols and rules, and since 1959 the International Council of Kinetography Laban (ICKL) has provided a successful platform for discussions between practitioners on unification and further applications of the system. Differences are now small so that mutual understanding of scores is ensured. Kinetography Laban rules and usages are catalogued in Albrecht Knust's 1979 Dictionary (see Bibliography).

The aim of the present series of texts is to provide a guide to the *Structured Description* of movement, the fully-fledged notation offering a determinate description of the movement progression by detailing choreographed (or otherwise set) actions.  A different and complementary approach is provided by *Motif Description (Motif Writing)*, which uses symbols to represent movement ideas and concepts and to provide a general statement concerning the theme or motivation of a movement.

The term Labanotation is used in this book to refer to the notation system in general and not to mark an opposition with Kinetography Laban or Motif Writing, except where specifcally stated.

## Source materials

Advanced Labanotation contains, whenever possible, systematic discussion of other usages and, where appropriate, comments on the history of symbols and rules and the reason for their inclusion in the Labanotation system.  The material presented is based on all available textbooks, on earlier writings of Knust and Maria Szentpál, as well as on personal discussions and correspondence with specialists such as Sigurd Leeder, Valerie Preston-Dunlop and members of the Dance Notation Bureau in New York and the Dance Notation Bureau Extension at Ohio State University.  Another major source of information are the proceedings of twenty ICKL Conferences.

Much use is made of the comprehensive theoretical account of the system by Knust, summarized in his *Dictionary of Kinetography Laban/Labanotation* (1979), and his earlier publications including his eight-volume encyclopedia of 1946-50 entitled *Handbuch der Kinetographie Laban*.  The textbook *Dance Notation, Kinetography Laban* by Szentpál, published in Hungarian between 1969 and 1976, is unfortunately not readily accessible to readers outside Hungary, but Szentpál generously provided an English translation for her many colleague.

In many cases, writing an advanced text of this kind has meant breaking new ground: the intricacies of writing mixed support situations, revolutions of the body on the floor and acrobatics, for instance, were not adequately covered, and some not included at all, in the 1979 Knust Dictionary.  Some recent developments in the system such as 'DBP' (Direction in relation to the location of Body Part), track pins and symbols for 'design drawing' came too late to be included in Knust's 1979 Dictionary.

The Advanced Labanotation series offers the latest research on the Labanotation system and hence is completely up-to-date as at the date of publication.

**Research Involved**

A major concern in the research for this book has been the comparison of one rule against another to check applicability in all contexts. Often this has led to discoveries producing new arguments for or against a certain way of writing.

Labanotation is rapidly developing and is accepted as a tool in recording, research and in education. Each of these fields has specific requirements. There is a call for maximum flexibility in the notation system, so that it can provide general and simple statements for particular purposes and at the same time be very precise where such specificity is required. In dance research the need for precision has increased to the point where we are obliged to consider questions about the system that only ten years ago did not seem important, let alone when the fundamentals of the system were devised. In this new text we have tried to take these different needs into account while respecting the system as it has been handed down and is now used by people all over the world.

# Notes

These annotations are mainly of three kinds. Firstly, they identify other major
*rules and usages*. Secondly, they mark symbols and rules that have been *recently
introduced* or *not described in other sources*, the origins of these being given.
And finally, they give the *references for particular notation excerpts*.

On important or controversial issues, a short discussion of rationale is
included. Sometimes, old ways of writing are briefly mentioned.

Research of other usages systematically involved *Táncjelírás, Laban
Kinetográfia* by Szentpál and the *Dictionary of Kinetography Laban
(Labanotation)* by Knust (see Bibliography). Where needed, other sources were
also used.

Numbers in parentheses at the end of each note indicate where the note is
in the text. The following abbreviations identify sources, for full bibliographic
information see Bibliography.

## References

| | |
|---|---|
| H70 | Hutchinson 1970 |
| H91 | Hutchinson 1991, Vol. 1, Part 3, *Kneeling, Sitting, Lying.* |
| ICKL | International Council of Kinetography Laban |
| K79 | Knust 1979 |
| LNTR | *The Labanotator* |
| S76 | Szentpál 1969-76 |
| | |
| AHG | Ann Hutchinson Guest |
| AK | Albrecht Knust |
| KIN | Kinetography Laban |
| LN | Labanotation |

1. In acro-balancing, a form related to gymnastics, the spine is *not* supposed to
be arched over the back surface in handstands. This form involves the use of
balance and counterbalance in positions using any number of people. (1.3)

2. Hand positions showing 'personal' grips, a contracted hand, such as those
used by some Chinese acrobats, can be written in detail when necessary or given
in the glossary at the start of a score and an abbreviation used in the score itself.
(1.13)

3. Supporting in high level on the hands can also be written by indicating the palm surface of the finger area as shown below (see the <u>Advanced Labanotation</u> issue on hands and fingers). (1.13)

4. In contrast, according to K79, the finger signs used as support symbols mean supporting on "... the whole length of the fingers and the palm with the exception of the base (heel) of the hand ..." (477b). (1.14)

5. In a blind turn the performer turns without swiveling, i.e. without any sliding friction on the supporting surface. To achieve this the rotation takes place in the arm, above the wrist. (2.1)

6. Ex. **2d** in the past was written with a circular path sign, but since no traveling occurs, hence no path, the turn sign is more appropriate. (2.2)

7. In a 'blended turn' overlap of the step and turning action is shown by the vertical bow connecting the support sign to the turn sign, as in **2f**. The degree of overlap is indicated by the length of this bow. In contrast, **2g** shows no overlap. (2.3)

8. The equations as shown in **3f** and **3h** are modified versions of K79: 473. (3.4)

9. This example is taken from K79: 504a and modified. AK uses a retention sign for the head support. (3.8)

10. The use of a body part sign in the support column together with a direction for the limb above that part, as in **4l**, does not mean a partial support. In the example below, the direction symbol in the support column for the left leg, shown at the same time as a direction symbol for the left leg gesture, is a longstanding way of writing a half support (division of weight). However, it should be noted that in Method C only the body part is placed in the support column, thus the symbol in the arm column provides the missing information

about direction.  This applies here for the knees as well as the hands.  (4.6)

11.  The Split Body Method was originated by Maria Szentpál.  It was presented and discussed at the 1975 ICKL conference (Technical Report, pp. 18-19, Paper C).  The first Split Body Key proposed was based on the Body Key, a), and was drawn as in b).  However, the prevalent use of the Standard System of Reference led to the idea that the sign should be based on the Standard Key, c), and therefore should be drawn as in d).  For usage with the Body Key, the symbol is drawn as in b).  (4.8)

a)  ╬     b)  ╪     c)  ╈     d)  ╪

12.  Method A, its usage and established rules, was the contribution of AK who painstakingly analyzed directions and distances for a range of such positions and movements.  (5.1)

13.  If directions for the hands were truly taken from place (the body center), an intermediate direction should be used showing the arms in **5a** to be more toward the diagonal direction.  However, the convention is that for the place symbol the hands are placed beneath the shoulders.  (5.3)

14.  In H91 it was established that a statement such as **5a** can be an unqualified (expected) position on hands and feet; any measurement signs (as in **5f**) are related to the distance covered by the individual's natural step in comfortable performance.  (5.6)

15.  The centered placement of the distance signs on the staff is standard LN; in KIN they are always written individually as in **5j**.  (5.6)

16.  In H91 the *standard step-length* is defined as being twice the length of the foot (from the heel to toe), thus, when stepping forward with parallel legs, there will be a gap of one foot-length between the heel of the stepping foot and the toe of the other (36.3).  It was stated that for supporting and transferring weight onto parts of the torso, exact distance measurement is related to *body-length* rather

than step-length, thus making use of the same length for measurement as AK does for 'on all fours' situations. To avoid confusion it is necessary to bear in mind that AK uses 'step-length' as a generic term, which at times may mean torso-length. (5.7)

17. At ICKL 1983 it was decided that for gestures the direction and level for the whole arm are generally determined by the relationship of the bulk of the hand to the shoulder (Technical Report I:7). In this issue of <u>Advanced Labanotation</u> this rule does not apply to 'on all fours' situations. (5.8)

18. Exs. **5m** and **5n** have been taken from K79: 486c, d. (5.10)

19. For extension signs for large steps, see H70, p. 163. (5.11)

20. It was these disadvantages, the difficulty of determining direction and distance in AK's established method, that led to the development and trial of alternate ways of analyzing and pin-pointing what was taking place. (5.12)

21. Ways of writing such as **5r** often lead to a problem of space on paper and specific indication of timing. The end position does not represent movement, but the arrival position (the movement is the turn). The symbols, which represent the arrival position, must take some space vertically. When very precise timing is not needed, this fact poses no problem. For indication of very accurate timing of arrival, the Time Dot can be added. The Time Dot sign was adopted at the 1991 ICKL conference (Technical Report I:1). A similar example is **22v** (see 22.13). (5.13)

22. Before he adopted the whole torso sign, AK used the hip and shoulder signs for writing lying down. (5.15)

23. The Time Sign for speed was officially adopted at the 1991 ICKL conference (Technical Report I:1). (7.8)

24. This section is in accordance with the ICKL 1985 decisions on DBP (Technical Report I:3). (Section 8)

25. DBP for non-touching gestures was discussed at ICKL 1987 but deferred for further exploration (Technical Report IV:16). (8.1)

26. *Position Writing.* The term 'position writing' is used for indications which show the end result rather than the movement used to achieve that end result. In ordinary supports on the feet, position writing is used for starting positions, but

may also be appropriate in the course of a movement sequence. In writing such positions, standard direction signs refer not to motion of the body but to the destination, the achieved position of supporting parts relative to each other. Carets are used to indicate exactly how the position is achieved, i.e. which support does not move, or to which spot the new support is related. (8.18)

27. This example was taken from ICKL 1985 Technical Report, Appendix B. (8.21)

28. The common term 'a jump' is used in this discussion for paired hands and paired knees as well as paired feet. To be technically correct, the term 'a jump' is a spring from two feet landing on two feet. (8.28)

29. In **8ac** the drawing of the elongated zed-caret visually refers back to the previous right hand symbol. This contrasts with the drawing of an elongated zed-caret established by S76, Part 3, Section D: 113b (repeated below), in which the caret refers to the new situation of the right hand. (8.29)

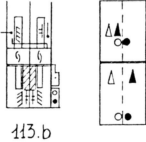

113.b

30. The word 'Front' is written with a capital when it refers to the main orientation of the performer and is not used as in 'in front', 'front surface', front of the person, etc. (8.34)

31. Path signs are not used for gestures of torso or limbs in K79. (8.34)

32. To distinguish SB from AK's standard usage, Maria Szentpál proposed the use of blank direction signs to alert the reader to the fact that a different analysis was being used. Level of the supports was specified through flexion and extension signs in the appropriate gesture columns.

This use of blank direction symbols is illustrated in the positions given here. Ex. a) is the same as **9c**; b) the same as **9f**; c) as **9i**. The movement sequences of d) and e) relate to **9r** and **9s**. (9.5)

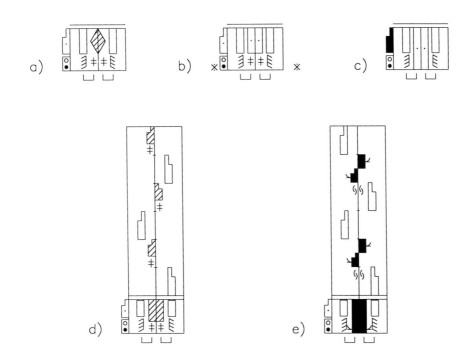

33. When Maria Szentpál introduced the SB system at the ICKL conference in 1975, the Split Body key was not part of her proposal. The need for the key, however, was discussed then. The key, logically based on the Body Key, was subsequently devised by AHG. (9.6)

34. In logrolling, as in a somersault roll, the actual rotation is around a moving axis. This can be compared to the wheel of a car. The surface which contacts the ground keeps changing as the wheel revolves but the axis remains in the center of the wheel. Because the torso is not a perfect cylinder, one is more aware of the change in location of the axis as the body rolls from a front or back surface to a side surface. These changes do not affect the basic action. For additional information on rolling see H91, Section 27. (11.3)

35. The release weight sign was first introduced at the 1973 ICKL conference by AHG and was listed on Ilene Fox's Unfinished List (No. 48); no decision was made at that time on this sign. However it appears in S76, Part 3, Section B: 47a-c and also was re-presented at the 1987 ICKL conference and deferred for further exploration (Technical Report IV:17). (11.16)

36. The decrease sign is understood to mean 'no longer in effect', which is not the same as back to normal. In KIN this decrease sign, understood as the equivalent of back to normal, is used with directions, flexions and extensions. (11.18)

37. Path signs for torso wheeling are not given in K79. (11.22)

38. Direction for somersaults can be related to the Constant Key when other rotations occur at the same time (see **15v-y, 15ac-ad**). (12.2)

39. From K79: 501d. (12.7)

40. AK states that the performer remains on the object until a release sign in the object column indicates that the object is no longer supporting (K79: 586). He gives the example shown here. The release sign shows that the performer jumps *off* the veil. AHG supports AK's standpoint. When the jump is *on* the object, no release sign is given, showing that the performer remains on the object. However, if the jump is not on the spot, as in **12v**, restating the supporting bow can indicate clearly which surface supports.

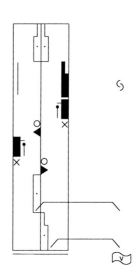

The validity rules for horizontal bows decided at ICKL 1989 (Technical Report I:3A) probably did not take into account the situation where the full body supports on an object. According to this rule, presumably, the bow in **12u** would have to be restated for each landing on the trampoline. (12.19)

41. Former usage from K79: 938. AK wrote "Before the introduction of the release sign, the release of an object was expressed by an isolated sketch of the object.", giving the example repeated here. (12.19)

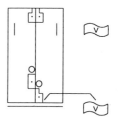

42. This example is based on K79: 501e. (12.21)

43. Illustration from *Terminologie Gerätturnen* by Buchmann, G. et al., p.172. (12.22)

44. This example is a slightly adapted version of K79: 501f. (12.23)

45. The design of the cartwheel sign recognises the lateral revolution within which is 'hidden' a 'pivot' turn. A standard cartwheel (foot-hand-hand-foot) can be likened to revolving a full turn on a straight path with four ordinary walking steps. AK's original cartwheel sign reflected this fact (K79: 933a-b). (13.3)

46. See S76, Part 3, Section E, p.73. (13.4)

47. In K79 and Maria Szentpál's usage, when a cartwheel sign is placed within the staff between support symbols, a phrasing bow linking all these indications, as in a) (from K79: 497a), indicates the unity of the whole, i.e. that the cartwheel turn is spread throughout the steps. With such use of a phrasing bow no specific timing breakdown is undertaken. Note that example a) does not break down the cartwheel into two halves, thus the step direction can be shown as continuously into the same direction. The phrasing bow may also be seen outside the staff as in b) (from S76, Part 3, Section E: 39). The brackets to indicate the extra support columns have been added here. (13.11)

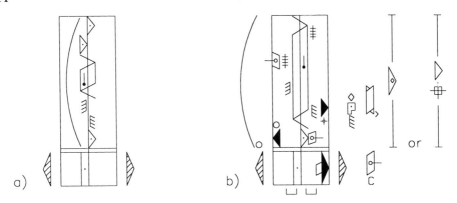

48. Analysis of cartwheeling on a diagonal axis has been mathematically investigated and the results of such progression are set forth. However, practical application of strict turning on a diagonal axis is physically difficult because the performer must contend with the body build and gravity. Rotation on a diagonal axis can be achieved, when the performer is being turned by an outside agent. When performed alone, the performer naturally adjusts in order to accomplish a revolution which has the sense, the feel, of being on the diagonal. (See also 16.2-16.5.) (13.16)

49. Such double statements relating to degree of turn (change of Front), as found in **13s**, are familiar from revolving on a circular path. Turning $^1/_2$ to the left while on a $^1/_4$ circular path to the right will result in $^1/_4$ change of Front to the left. (13.17)

50. Ex. **13ab** not in K79. (13.23)

51. It is planned that acrobatics/gymnastics using apparatus will be dealt with in a later issue of <u>Advanced Labanotation</u>. (14.2)

52. It is planned that details on swimming, being supported by the water, relationship to the surface of the water, etc. will be given in a later <u>Advanced Labanotation</u> issue. (14.9)

53. K79 shows some basic rules on movement in the water and also draws the horizontal bow to show entering the water across the whole staff (K79: 505-8). Here the line extends only from the center line to reduce the visual effect of its looking like a bar line. (14.9)

54. For LN rule see H70, p. 313. In K79 direction for a twisted part is also generally judged from the free end. This is true of the whole torso, the chest, and the shoulder area. It is not true of rotations for the head and pelvis. Direction for the head, when turned, is judged from the free end of the trunk (K79: 335). When a pelvic rotation occurs, direction for a leg gesture is judged from Stance, the forward direction for the supporting foot (K79: 439). (15.7)

55. This analysis, the Stance direction, is standard for AK and, therefore, is automatically applied to **15h** in KIN. See note 54. (15.8)

56. The revolutions of **15o-q** are notated as executed on a trampoline, because it is easier to try out different forms of rotation and their combinations. The examples are kept extremely simple and even artificial, serving only to make a theoretical point. (15.10)

57. LN does not attempt to provide scientific accuracy in describing aerial paths, the indications establish the intended motion with sufficient detail to allow a capable performer to achieve the action. The performer can effect a very slight change in an aerial path; for our purposes it is negligible and does not need to be measured. (15.12)

58. The Standard Key symbol is practical for indicating the Constant Vertical

Axis. It is not applicable within a cartwheel or somersault sign, because in the Standard Key only the up-down axis is a fixed axis. (15.13)

59. 'Twist' is used here as a term in gymnastics, rather than in the technical LN sense. To achieve longitudinal rotation while in the air the arms often move across the body and hence cause a momentary twist in the body. (15.18)

60. As mentioned in Section 13, the body makes small adjustments to make such a revolution possible. (16.2)

61. The diagram of a) shows the orientation of the torso after each $^1/_4$ rotation for **16b** and **16d**. The location of the torso in terms of Constant Cross is easy to determine. At the halfway point the performer is upside down. Less clear are the Front directions for the $^1/_4$ and $^3/_4$ points. The Front makes $^1/_4$ change to the left at the halfway point and then reverts to the starting front. This seemingly odd change of front results from the mixture of somersault action where no change of Front occurs and a cartwheel in which a $^1/_2$ change of Front occurs at the halfway point and then immediately reverts to the original Front. In the action of **16b/16d** the half change of Front is cut down to a quarter. (16.3)

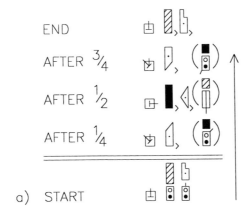

62. These indications for body orientation resulted from discussions between Maria Szentpál and AHG and were presented at ICKL 1971. Examples contributed by Szentpál (S76, Part 3, Section C: 4). (16.7)

63. A blank direction symbol for the torso, as in a), is unusual in structured notation, however it serves a particular purpose. It means that level should be what is appropriate according to the context, i.e. determined by the other indications. Ex. b) states that the torso is more or less forward middle. The ad lib. sign within the forward symbol in c) provides freedom in choice of level. It can be seen that there is a marked difference between each of these. (17.2)

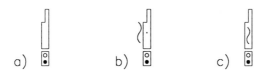

a)          b)          c)

64. At the ICKL 1989 conference concern was expressed that **18a** is a stylistic convention and not natural placement (Technical Report III: 18.6-8). In this Advanced Labanotation textbook we understand that **18a** means both feet under the center of weight, therefore together and touching, but not necessarily parallel (cf. Technical Report III:18.7).

Use of keys can be as follows: for a ballet score the statement of a) below can be used to indicate the specific balletic 1st position of b). Where appropriate, the statement of c) can be made to indicate a slight separation of the feet, as in d). That of e) can be used to show placement directly under each hip, f). These should be given at the start of a score or within discussion material. (18.3)

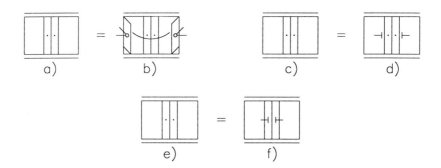

a)          b)          c)          d)

e)          f)

65. K79 defines the difference between **18c** and **18n** as follows (using drawings): each foot is placed in its own track; in **18c** these tracks are adjoining; in **18n** they are separated by a third track lying between them (K79: 136a, 141b). (18.5)

66. Track pins were first presented at the 1975 ICKL conference (Technical Report, pp.15-16, Paper B) and subsequently adopted in 1979 (Technical Report I:2). (Section 19)

67. At ICKL 1983 it was decided that, when stating the relationship of the arm to a body track, the reference is that part of the arm nearest the stated track. The total configuration of the arm in context must be viewed in order to determine the extremity of this closest part (Technical Report I: 7B.13-17). (19.7)

68. In the case of lateral steps, it turns out that use of black pins and that of track pins have the same result, even though each indicates a different analysis. The black pins show a relation to the other foot, whereas the track pins refer to a track in relation to the body. (19.18)

69. For comparison, according to the K79 rules standard directions would be used, diagonal forward for the hands and diagonal backward for the feet (as in the starting position shown). Displacement would be shown by distance measurement. No solution is provided in K79 for the 'walking on a ledge' effect. (19.26)

70. The wording of the ICKL 1981 Technical Report I:4 (restated ICKL 1987 Technical Report I:6.2) is: "Gestural symbols (such as rotation, flexion) and modifiers (such as hooks, pins, dynamic indications, spatial retention signs) that modify either a support or a leg gesture can be written in the ISC (Inner Subsidiary Column) without a body part pre-sign; any direction symbol in the ISC pertaining to a[ny other] gesture, other than an attached symbol, must be preceded by a body part pre-sign. (...)"
    In early scores extra space was created between support and gesture columns simply by drawing the symbols narrower than one column. (20.3)

71. The statement linking the ISC to the support column by use of the horizontal staple can be canceled as in **20h**, in which the ISC is now linked to the gesture column. An alternate possibility is use of the inverted staple as in a), here it signs off the left ISC returning it to gestural status. This usage reflects that already established in Motif Description for 'signing off' the center line indication, as shown in b); the sudden flexion here is for the body as a whole. (20.8)

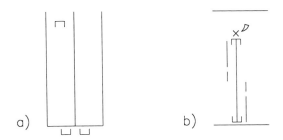

72. The Floorwork Staff, suggested by Maria Szentpál and presented by János Fügedi, was accepted at the ICKL 1989 conference (Technical Report I:5). (20.9)

73. At the 1989 ICKL conference placement and manner of writing count marks ('ticks') was put on two-year trial (Technical Report I:5). "No consensus was reached on the preferred placement and manner of writing time marks." (Technical Report I:5.6) (20.12)

74. Both examples are taken from the 1989 ICKL Technical Report I:5. (20.13)

75. This example is taken from the 1989 ICKL Technical Report I:5. (20.15)

76. Laban's original rule regarding a gap between movement symbols in both support columns, meaning no support, rise into the air, provided a simple way to show 'jumping' (i.e. aerial steps) while supporting only on the feet. Through use of the leg(s) a jumping activity occured. The rule stated in 21.2 and 21.3 follows this established usage. Laban's books do not indicate how he applied, or intended to apply, this rule to supporting on other body parts. As usage of the system developed, the fact that performers can and do spring up from kneeling suggested that this foot-support rule should also be applied to the knees. It was then carried through to other body parts.

A form of 'jumping' can occur from supporting on the shoulders. Other forms of 'jumping' (i.e. a momentary release of weight) can occur from sitting, lying and, by Chinese acrobats, for example, even while standing on the head. To how many of these situations is Laban's original rule for the legs logically applicable? For KIN the decision was to write hold signs for all supports, regardless of movement logic. Application of the rule in 21.4 will not conflict with past LN usage except for springing from the knees. Use of specific indications for releasing contact removes any ambiguity. Discussion on this validity rule has not occurred at an ICKL conference. (21.2)

77. In the past validity for supporting only on the knees has been a questionable case (see H91, Section 24). (21.2)

78. The K79 rule for *all* support indications is that retention of support must be written with a retention sign; release signs are *not* used in support columns except to cancel relationship bows (K79: 603a). (21.4)

79. Ex. a), in which the hold signs are placed directly after each support to be held, is old LN usage. After the two steps shown, these retention signs make it clear that weight is held 'on all fours'. In KIN the statement of retention of supporting parts can be placed at the end of the phrase, as shown in b). In contrast to a) the eye must look back to see which parts are being retained. In both LN and KIN the device in which a retention sign follows a gap is never

used for supporting only on the feet.

An additional rule in KIN is that in a gait on 'all fours' or a like movement, retention signs do not need to be restated at every step; e.g. writing a) as an abbreviation for b) is acceptable (K79: 487a-b). (21.10)

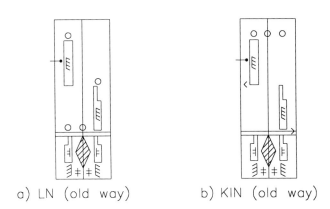

a) LN (old way)          b) KIN (old way)

80. The plain action stroke of a) is used in these contexts to indicate that a gesture occurs, an action appropriate, suitable, related to the context. It does not mean 'any action', a free improvisation. To indicate such freedom an ad lib. sign is placed at the start of the action stroke, as in b). (21.13)

81. Validity of relationships is not discussed fully here. See ICKL 1989 decision on validity of horizontal relationship bows (Technical Report I:3). This rule, based on the established usage for leg gestures touching the floor, has not been found to be conveniently applicable across the board when several contacting, supporting actions occur at the same time. While retention of a supporting or touching relationship is not theoretically required, in practice it has been found helpful. (21.17)

82. The usage of one sign covering more than one column, as in **22e** and **22h**, is not used in K79. (22.2)

83. Originally, complete overlap was shown by a long vertical bow, as in a). Because these long bows, much used by AK, are space consuming and can cut through details which need to be shown, LN adopted the convention of a very small bow having the meaning of complete overlap, as shown in **22t**. (22.11)

a)

84. ICKL 1983 (Technical Report I:6) recommends restatement of the pre-sign because the caret could be ambiguous or hard to read. In our experience, ambiguity of this kind for the caret seems to be limited to instances where it replaces the *knee* symbol. Regarding hand supports in the center columns, in many cases there is room for a caret but not for a hand symbol.

The caret replaced the staple to indicate 'the same support' at the ICKL 1987 conference (Technical Report I:1). (22.14)

85. From *Fever Swamp* by Bill T. Jones (1983), notated by Virginia Doris, 1988 ('Dense Section', p. 123, measure 3). Courtesy of Bill T. Jones. (23.1)

86. From *Icarus* by Lucas Hoving (1964), notated by Ray Cook, 1977, revised 1978, 1979 (measures 26-27). This excerpt shows some modification in timing to adjust to the page length. Other slight modifications and clarifications have been made. Furthermore, the scattering and gathering movements for the arms have been added. Courtesy of Cheryl Yonker. (23.2)

87. From *Return to Life*, a Pilates exercise notated Susan Kaufman, ca. 1958, edited by AHG, as taught by Carola Trier. (23.4)

88. From *Ubungen aus dem Modernunterricht* (Limon-Technique) by Edward Desoto (Frankfurt, 1986), notated by A. Hirvikallio; copyright belongs to Christine Eckerle, 1986. Courtesy of Christine Eckerle. This method of analysis was established by AK. (24.1)

89. From *Bonsai* by Moses Pendleton (1979), notated by Ilene Fox, 1988 (measures 153-155). Courtesy of Moses Pendleton. (24.2)

90. From *Fever Swamp* by Bill T. Jones (1983), notated by Virginia Doris, 1988 (p. 120, measure 1). Courtesy of Bill T. Jones. (24.3)

91. From *3 On a Match* by Victoria Uris (1982), notated by Virginia Doris, 1992 ('on a Match', p. 36, measures 4-5). Courtesy of Victoria Uris. (24.4)

92. From *Fever Swamp* by Bill T. Jones (1983), notated by Virginia Doris, 1988 (p. 122, measure 3). Courtesy of Bill T. Jones. (24.5)

93. From *Bonsai* by Moses Pendleton (1979), notated by Ilene Fox, 1988 (measures 147-151). Courtesy of Moses Pendleton. (24.6)

94. Floorwork exercise, taught by Nina Wiener as guest artist at Ohio State University, 1977. Courtesy of Nina Wiener. (24.7)

95. Exs. **24h-24k** are from exercises in DBP notated by students at Ohio State University and by Lucy Venable, revised in 1991. (24.8)

96. From *Bonsai* by Moses Pendleton (1979), notated by Ilene Fox, 1988 (measures 111-113). Courtesy of Moses Pendleton. (25.1)

97. From *3 On a Match* by Victoria Uris (1982), notated by Virginia Doris, 1992 ('2 Plus 1', p.8, measures 31-32). Courtesy of Victoria Uris. (25.2)

98. From *3 On a Match* by Victoria Uris (1982), notated by Virginia Doris, 1992 ('Detonation', p. 57, measures 1-3). Courtesy of Victoria Uris. (25.3)

99. From *Nun Better* by Pedro Alejandro (1992), notated by Veronica Dittman, 1994 ('B Phrase', p. 16, measures 11-12). Courtesy of Pedro Alejandro. (25.4)

100. From *Piazzolla Caldera* by Paul Taylor (1997), notated by Sîan Ferguson, 1997 ('Concierto para quinteto', p. 127). Courtesy of Paul Taylor. (25.5)

101. From *1492* by Peter Anastos (1992), notated by Leslie Rotman, 1992 ('S's 1st solo', p. 25, measures 18-19). Courtesy of Peter Anastos. (25.6)

102. From *Fever Swamp* by Bill T. Jones (1983), notated by Virginia Doris, 1988 (p. 138, measure 5, counts 1-4). Courtesy of Bill T. Jones. (26.1)

103. From *Return to Life*, a Pilates exercise notated by Susan Kaufman, ca. 1958, edited by AHG, as taught by Carola Trier. (26.2)

104. From *3 on a Match* by Victoria Uris (1982), notated by Virginia Doris, 1992 ('on a Match', p. 40, measure 12). Courtesy of Victoria Uris. (26.3)

105. From *1492* by Peter Anastos (1992), notated by Leslie Rotman, 1992 ('Adagio', p.56, measures 21-22). Courtesy of Peter Anastos. (26.5)

106. From *7 for 8* by Elisa Monte (1985), notated by Virginia Doris, 1985-86 (p. 7, nr. 8). Courtesy of Elisa Monte. (26.6)

107. From *1492* by Peter Anastos (1992), notated by Leslie Rotman, 1992 ('S's 1st solo', p. 26, measure 21). Courtesy of Peter Anastos. (27.1)

108. From *Piazolla Caldera* by Paul Taylor (1997), notated by Sîan Ferguson, 1997 ('Escualo', p. 372, measures 663-666). Courtesy of Paul Taylor. (27.2)

109. These examples are from Maria Szentpál, from correspondence with Ray Cook and AK, Part V: 272a and b, probably from around 1973; a similar example also occurs in S76, Part 3, Section E: 44. (27.3)

110. From *Lark Ascending* by Bruce Marks (1977), notated by Robin Hoffman, 1994 ('First Pas de Deux', measure 33). Courtesy of Bruce Marks. (27.4)

111. Backward pointing track pins could have been used, but for lateral tracks it seems clearer to use the forward pointing track pins. In B.13 backward pointing track pins are conveniently used for backward sagittal arm directions. (A.7)

112. First presented in LNTR No. 71, April 1993. (Appendix B)

# Bibliography

Buchmann, G. et al. *Terminologie Gerätturnen,* Sportverlag Berlin, 1972.

Hutchinson, Ann. Notebooks from Jan. 1936 - July 1938, while at the Jooss-Leeder Dance School.

Hutchinson, Ann. *Labanotation, The System of Analyzing and Recording Movement*, Theatre Arts Books, New York, 1970. (1st published 1954; revised 3rd edition published in 1977)

Hutchinson Guest, Ann. *Your Move, A New Approach to the Study of Movement and Dance*, Gordon and Breach, London, 1983. (3rd reprinting with corrections in 1995)

Hutchinson Guest, Ann and van Haarst, Rob. Advanced Labanotation, Vol. 1, Part 2, *Shape, Design, Trace Patterns*, Harwood Academic Publishers, New York, 1991.

Hutchinson Guest, Ann and van Haarst, Rob. Advanced Labanotation, Vol. 1, Part 3, *Kneeling Sitting, Lying*, Harwood Academic Publishers, New York, 1991.

Hutchinson Guest, Ann. *A History of the Development of the Laban Notation System*, Cervera Press, London, 1995.

Knust, Albrecht. *Handbuch der Kinetographie Laban*, unpublished manuscript (8 vols.), written mainly between 1945 and 1950. Microfilm reprints available from the Dance Notation Bureau, New York.

Knust, Albrecht. *Handbook of Kinetography Laban*, translated by Valerie Preston, unpublished (1 vol.), 1951. Copy at the Language of Dance Centre.

Knust, A. *A Dictionary of Kinetography Laban (Labanotation)* (2 vols.), MacDonald and Evans, Plymouth, England, 1979.

Laban, Rudolf. *Schrifttanz, Methodik, Orthographie, Erläuterungen*, Universal Edition, Wien, Leipzig, 1928.

*The Labanotator*, bulletin, Nos. 1-25 published 1957-65 by the Dance Notation Bureau, New York; Nos. 26-77 published 1978-1994 by the Language of Dance Centre, London.

Preston-Dunlop, Valerie. *An Introduction to Kinetography Laban*, Laban Art of Movement Guild, London, 1963.

Proceedings of the Biennial Conferences of the International Council of Kinetography Laban (ICKL), 1959-1999. Copies at the Language of Dance Centre, the Dance Notation Bureau in New York and the Dance Notation Bureau Extension at Ohio State University.

Szentpál, M. *Táncjelírás. Laban-Kinetográfia* (Dance Notation. Kinetography Laban), Népmüvelési Propaganda Iroda, Budapest, 1969-76 (3 vol., vol. I 2nd. ed., 1st ed. 1964).

# Index

1.3, 5.2 etc. refer to paragraph numbers
**1e**, **6a** etc. refer to example numbers
*S*1, *S*2 etc. refer to section numbers
*n*1, *n*2 etc. refer to endnote numbers
p.1, p.2 etc. refer to page numbers
app.A, app.B etc. refer to appendix numbers

- replaces the entry word(s)

In the longer listings, the more relevant references are placed first, separated from the others by a semi-colon (;).

$^1/_8$ secret turn, 16.3
$^1/_2$ turn, 11.7, 11.9, 11.17, 11.19, 15.18-19, 15.24, 22.12, 25.5-6
  --around spinal axis, 24.9
$^1/_4$ turn, 11.13, 11.23-24, 13.17, 24.2, 24.11, 25.2
$^1/_8$ turn, 13.18, 20.15
  --around the spinal axis, 11.12
  --around the vertical line of gravity, 11.10-11
*1492*, 25.6, 27.1
*3 On a Match*, 24.4, 25.2, 25.3, 26.3
*7 for 8*, 26.6

ad libitum, 6.9
Advanced Labanotation Series, p.xiii
all fours,
- and Related Situations, part II, 19.26, 19.28, 21.14, 22.4, 22.17
- ,Carets, 22.15, 22.17-18
- ,Central Place Method, *S*5
- ,Diagonal Steps on, 19.26-27
- Direction-from-Body-Part Indications method, *S*8
- Direction of limbs to clarify supports method, *S*7
- floorwork staff, 20.9-15
- Isolated Body Part Signs in Support Columns method, *S*6
- ,gait on, 4.5, 5.10, 21.16
- ,jumping on, 13.26-27
- ,lateral steps on, 19.28-29
- ,mixed support situations, *S*4
- ,on, part II
- pins for, 19.20-29, app. B.10-13
- ,positions on, 4.4, 8.3
- reading examples, *S*24
- Split Body method, *S*9, 19.22, 19.24

- ,standing on, 4.1, 5.2, 5.7, 22.4
- ,supporting on, 4.4, 8.25, 9.15, 21.4
- torso directions on, *S*10
- ,track pins for, 19.20-28
- turning on, 11.6-18, 22.9
- ,validity, *S*21, 6.5
  -- of support indications on, 21.4-9
- ,walking on, 5.2, 6.1, 9.9-12
  -- circular path, 6.6-8
Alejandro, Pedro, 25.4
analysis,
- 5 methods for mixed support situations, 4.3
- combined revolutions of the body, 15.6-14
- ,cartwheeling, 13.2-6
- in use of parts of the foot, 22.8
- ,somersault, 12.1-2, 14.8
- somersault and cartwheel paths, 14.8-13
- ,wheeling, 12.10
Anastos, Peter, 25.6, 27.1
arms,
- black pins, 18.6, 19.25
- diagonal center line, app.A.3
- diagonal tracks for the, app.A.2
- elbowstand, 3.1-4
- gesture indications for, *S*7
  -- ,for split body method, *S*9
- in a bridge, 10.7-8
- handstand-level, 1.13
- headstand, 3.7-8
- lateral tracks for the, app.A.4-6
- sagittal center lines, 19.6-9
- sagittal track pin signs, 19.4-5
- sagittal tracks for gestures, app.A.7
- shoulderstand, 3.5-6
- subdivision of tracks, app.A.9-10

arms (cont.)
- vertical tracks for the, app.A.8
augmented
- body sections, 10.9-13, 24.1, 24.8
- torso directions, *S*3
automatic retention, 21.5-9
axis,
- ,body part as, 16.5, 16.11-14
- combined revolutions of the body, *S*15
- diagonal, 13.18
- lateral, somersault, 12.1-2, 14.3-6, 14.10, 14.12
- sagittal, cartwheel, 13.2-3, 14.4, 14.6-7
- somersault and cartwheel paths, *S*14
- ,statement of, 11.4
- ,turning around the spinal, *S*11, 22.9
- ,turning around the vertical, *S*11
axes,
- ,body cross of, 26.4
- ,body part as, 16.5, 16.11-14
- combined revolutions of the body, *S*15
- diagonal, 16.2-5
- of rotation, *S*16
- ,range of pins for, 16.9-10
- ,standard cross of, 25.4
- three dimensional (diagonal), 15.2, 16.2-4
- two dimensional (diametral), 15.2

black pins, app.B
- axes, 16.9
- combined with tack pins, app.B.8-9
- DBP 'place' directions, 8.5
- for lateral tracks, 18.10-13
- for sagittal tracks, 18.6-9
- for tracks, *S*18
- indication of degree of cartwheel, 13.13, 14.7, 16.6
- lateral steps, 19.28
- lateral tracks, 18.10-13
- sagittal tracks, 18.6-9
- sagittal tracks for hands, 18.17
- sagittal tracks for knees, 18.15-16
- tracks, *S*18
'blind turns', 13.11, 13.16
- on the hands, 2.3, 2.7, 13.7
body
- ,combined revolutions of the, *S*15
- orientation, 16.7-8
- part as axes, 16.5, 16.11-14
- ,revolutions of the, *S*12-14
- ,sagittal tracks of the, 19.3
- ,split, *S*9; 4.8-9, 19.22
body orientation, 16.7-8
body sections,
- augmented, 1.2, 10.9-13, 24.1, 24.8
- inverted, 3.2, 10.3, 11.19, 19.22, 23.3, 27.3
- inverted augmented, 1.2

*Bonsai*, 24.2, 24.6, 25.1
'bridge' position, 10.4, 10.6-8

caret(s), 22.14-18
- ,elongated, 8.23, 8.29, 8.31
- ,same part of body, 1.7-8, 20.6, 21.8, 22.14-15
- ,same spot, 8.28, 22.16-18
- ,zed, 8.29, 21.8, 22.18
cartwheel(ing), *S*13
- ,analysis of, 13.2-3, 15.12, 15.14
- and turn, 15.24-25
- basic notation, 13.8-11
- 'blind turns' on the hands, 13.7
- combined revolution of the body, 15.2
- combined with turn, 27.4
- ,degree of, 13.12-13, 16.6
- ,'diagonal', 13.15-18, 16.2-4
- ,'forward', 13.19
- front, 13.4-6
- ,indication of degree of, 13.12-13
- in sitting and lying, 13.20-24
- in the air, 13.25-27
- on bar, 27.3
- on the hands, 13.7
- paths, *S*14
- reading examples, *S*27
- sign, 13.1
- spatial retention, 15.15
- with different step directions, 13.14
center staff line,
- retention signs and pre-signs on, 22.1-3
central 'place', *S*5, 4.3-4
- distance, 5.5, 5.12
  - exact, 5.7-11
  - relative, 5.6
- ,disadvantages of, 5.12-15
- reading examples, 24.1
change of torso direction,
circular path,
- around a focal point, 6.10-12, 21.19
- backward, 14.5
- distance, 14.15
- ,horizonal, 14.2
- 'on all fours', 6.6-7
- ,somersault, 14.15
- turning on the hands, 2.2
- ,walking on a, 15.19, 21.19
clarification(s), part IV
  -- 'crab' versus 'bridge' position, 10.4-8
  -- distance, *S*17
  -- miscellaneous, *S*22
  -- the use of tracks, *S*19
  -- use of black pins for tracks, *S*18
  -- use of columns, *S*20
  -- validity of support indications, *S*21
columns,
- additional support, 4.4, 11.16
- ,'all fours' support, 11.10

columns (cont.)
- ,arm, 1.13, 2.6
- ,arm gesture, 4.6
- carets, 22.14-15
- ,cartwheeling, 13.1, 13.9-10
- ,center support, 22.1-3
- distance measurement signs, 5.6
- inner subsidiary, 4.4
- ,isolated body part signs in support, *S*6; 4.5,
    -- reading examples, 24.2-4
- ,leg gesture, 4.6
- ,object, 12.19
- pre-signs, 22.1-3
- retention signs, 22.1-3
- ,support, *S*20; 1.9, 1.14, 3.2, 4.6, 14.12-13
    -- somersault rolls, 12.3
    -- somersaultng in the air, 12.12-14
    -- turning around the vertical or spinal axis, 11.1-3
- ,torso, 1.2
- ,use of, *S*20
- wheeling, 13.24
combined revolutions of the body, *S*15
combining black pins and tack pins, app. B.8-9
contact retained,
- weight released, 21.18
'crab'position,
- direction of limbs to clarify supports, 7.4-5
- split body system, 4.8, 19.22
- ,turning into, 11.17
- versus 'bridge' position, 10.4-8

definition of track pins, 19.1
degree,
- of bending, 17.5
- of cartwheel, 13.12-13, 14.7
    -- in sitting and lying, 13.22-23
- of leg rotation, 19.17
- of rotation, 14.6, 16.6, 16.13
- of somersault, 12.4-5, 12.7, 12.11
    -- in the air, 12.16
- somersault and cartwheel paths, 14.6-8
diagonal
- axes, 15.2, 16.2-5, 16.14
- cartwheel, 13.15-18
- center line, app.A.3, app.A.12
- pins, 19.11, 19.25
- steps, 19.26-27, app.A.13
- steps on all fours, 19.26-27
- tracks for leg gestures, 19.12, app. A.12
- tracks for the arms, 19.9, app.A.2
direction-from-body-part indications (DBP), *S*8; 1.12, 4.7, 7.6, 17.2, 17.4, 18.4, 19.11, 19.26, 21.16
- diagonal steps on 'all fours', 19.26
- distance, 8.7, 17.4
- divided front, 8.34-35

- examples, 8.8, 24.6-11
- in path signs, 8.15
- level, 8.13-14
- order of reference, 8.16-17
- 'place' directions, 8.5-6
- point of measurement, 8.10-12
- present location, 8.24
    -- of another part, 8.30-33
- previous location, 8.23
    -- of a 'lifted' part, 8.28-29
    -- of the same body part, 8.27
- reading examples, 24.6-11
- reference to,
    -- a static support, 8.25-26
    -- part of the floor, 8.36
- touching gestures, 8.9
- writing of position, 8.18-21
- writing movement, 8.22
direction of limbs to clarify supports, *S*7; 4.6
direction symbols,
- and track pins, 19.1
- ,blank, 9.5
- containing a body part symbol, 8.2
- containing a space hold, 15.15
- to write somersault, 12.23, 26.1
- to write walking on feet, 5.1
- to write walking on hands, 5.1
- to write walking on knees, 5.1
distance, *S*17
- in DBP, 8.7, 8.21
- of central 'place', 5.5-11, 9.1
- of somersault paths, 14.14-15
- measurement signs, 22.3
- split body, 9.4
divided front,
- DBP indications method, 8.34

elbows,
- ,supporting on the, part I, *S*23, 18.1, 21.4, 22.19
elbow stand, 3.1-3
- level, 3.4
explicit statement of retention, 21.10

feet,
- black pins
    -- for lateral tracks, 18.10-13
    -- for sagittal tracks, 18.6-9
- 'bunny hop', 21.15
- distance, 17.2-3
- ,springing only with the, 11.24
- ,supported on hands and, 4.1, 9.7-12, 9.14, 10.4, 10.8, 11.10, 21.15, 24.1-2, 24.6-10
- supporting on the, 11.20, 12.23, 21.2-3
- tracks, 18.2-5
    -- for supports on the feet, 19.15-17, app.A.13, app.B.4
*Fever Swamp*, 23.1, 24.3, 24.5, 26.1
fingers,
- ,supporting on the, 1.13-14, 9.12

flat pins, 16.1-5, 18.4-5
-    tacks, app.B.5-9
floorwork staff, 20.9-15
foot-knee,
-    supporting on the, 8.20, 8.28, 20.15,
     21.2-3, 25.3
foot,
-    end of the body, 16.7-8
-    part contacting in
     -- DBP indications method, 8.9-11
     -- mixed support situations, 22.4,
     22.8
-    positions in
     -- central 'place' method, 5.1-3, 5.6,
     5.8
     -- DBP indications method, 8.20-21,
     8.26, 8.28, 8.31-33, 24.7-9
     -- split body method, 4.8, 9.4, 9.7-8
-    supports in cartwheeling, 13.9-10,
     13.15-16, 13.19, 15.14
'forward cartwheel', 13.19
further subdivisions of tracks for arm
     gestures, app.A.9-10

gesture indications for arms in split body
     body method, 9.13-15

half-turn, 2.3, 11.7, 11.9, 11.17, 11.19,
     13.7, 15.18-20, 22.12
hand(s),
-    and head supporting, 3.7-8
-    ,blind turn on the, 13.7
-    bridge position, 10.7-8
-    crab position, 10.4
-    distance, 17.2-3
-    in DBP indications, S8
     -- reading examples, 24.6-11
-    in direction of limbs to clarify
     supports method, S7
-    in support columns, S6
     -- reading examples, 24.2-4
-    mixed support situations, 21.15, 22.4
-    momentary auxillary support, 22.19-
     20
-    ,non-swivel turn on the, 13.7
-    positions and walking in
     -- central place method, S5; 4.4
     -- reading examples, 24.1
     -- isolated body part signs, S6; 4.5
-    ,positions in split body method, S9;
     4.8
-    reading examples, 23.1
-    sagittal center lines, 19.6-9
-    ,sagittal tracks for, 18.17
-    ,supporting on the, part I, S1
-    supports in cartwheel, 13.8-10,
     13.15-19, 15.14
-    supports in somersault, 14.13, 15.18
-    ,track pins for supporting on the,
     19.13-14
-    ,track pins for all fours, 19.20-25,
     app.B.10-13
-    ,turning on the, S2

-    ,walking on the, 1.7-12
handstand(s), S1
-    into bridge, 10.6
     -- and standing up, 12.23
-    ,jumping from a, 15.18
-    level, 1.13
-    reading examples, 23.1, 26.1
-    ,springing into a, 12.21
-    turning, S2
-    ,walking in a, 21.9
head
-    axis, 15.7
-    stand, 3.7-8
-    ,supporting on the, 3.7-8
-    to foot axis, 15.18, 15.21, 15.23-4
headstand, 3.7-8
Hoving, Lucas, 23.2

*Icarus*, 23.2
ICKL, app.A.1
indication(s),
-    ,angling, 5.13
-    ,direction-from-body-part, S8; 4.7,
     17.4, 19.26
-    ,distance, 17.2
-    for arm geatures, 9.13-15
-    for body orientation, 16.7-8
-    of degree of cartwheel, 13.12-13,
     14.7, 16.6
-    of degree of somersault, 12.11
-    of level in handstands, 1.13
-    of timing, 20.12-14
-    of trampoline, 12.19
-    ,pre-staff, 20.5
-    ,torso directional, 10.2
-    ,validity of support, S21
intermediate tracks for arm gestures,
     19.4-5, 19.14, app.A.4-5, app.A.10
inverted
-    body sections, S10; 1.2, 1.4, 3.2-3,
     11.19, 21.10
-    torso directions, 10.5-6, 10.11, 19.22,
     23.3, 27.3
isolated body part signs in support
     columns, S6; 4.5
-    ad libitum, 6.9
-    circular path, 6.6-8
     -- around a focal point, 6.10-12
-    reading examples, 24.2-4
-    straight path, 6.1-4
-    validity, 6.5

Jones, Bill T., 23.1, 24.5, 26.1

key,
-    ,body, 11.14, 12.2, 13.2, 15.4, 22.6,
     25.3, 26.5, 27.4
-    ,constant, 13.10-11, 13.15-16, 15.18,
     16.4, 27.3
-    ,split body, 4.8, 9.6, 9.8, 9.13, 24.2
-    ,stance, 15.9
-    ,standard, 19.29, 27.3
*Kneeling, Sitting, Lying*, 1.7, 4.1, 5.6,

*Kneeling, Sitting, Lying* (cont.)
    5.8, 8.10, 8.15, 11.4, 11.9, 11.14,
    11.17, 11.20, 11.22-23, 12.2, 12.10,
    13.4, 13.11, 15.4, 16.13, 17.1, 22.19
knees,
-  ,sagittal tracks for, 18.14-16
-  ,supporting on the, 11.2, 21.2-3
Knust, Albrecht, 4.3, 5.2, 5.7, 5.10, 27.3

*Labanotation*, 4.2-3, 13.4, 15.1, 15.7,
    18.1, 21.2
*Lark Ascending*, 27.4
lateral,
-  leg gestures, app.A.11
-  steps, 19.18-19, app.A.13, app.B.3
    -- on all fours, 19.28
    -- on - center line, app.B.3
-  tracks, 18.10-13, app.B.4
    -- for the arms, app.A.4-6
layout, 20.1, 22.5-13
level
-  in DBP, 8.13-14
-  of elbow stand, 3.4
-  of handstands, 1.13
limbs,
-  body part as axis, 16.11, 16.13
-  ,direction of - to clarify supports, *S*7;
    4.6, 9.16
-  placement on center line, 19.6-7
-  statement of - direction, 24.5
Limón technique, 24.1
log rolling, *S*26; 11.7, 11.12, 12.20,
    15.4, 22.12
-  reading examples, 26.3
lying,
-  ,cartwheeling in, 13.20-24

Marks, Bruce, 27.4
miscellaneous, *S*22
'mixed support',
-  use of columns, 20.1, 20.4
mixed support situations, *S*4
-  central 'place', *S*5; 4.4
-  direction-from-body-part indications
    (DBP), *S*8; 4.7
-  direction of limbs to clarify supports,
    *S*7; 4.6
-  isolated body part signs in support
    columns, *S*6; 4.5
-  ,part of foot contacting in, 22.4
-  statement of limb direction, 24.5
-  split body system, *S*9; 4.8
-  use of columns, 20.1, 20.4
momentary auxilary support, 22.19-20
Monte, Elisa, 26.6

*Nun Better*, 25.4

'on all fours', 19.26-28, 21.14, 22.4,
    22.17
-  and related situations, part II
-  ,diagonal steps, 19.26-27

-  ,jumping, 13.26-27
-  ,lateral steps, 19.28-29
-  pins, app.B.10-13
-  reading examples, *S*24
-  ,turning, 11.6-9
-  ,supporting, 20.10, 21.4, 21.6
order of reference in DBP, 8.16
overlap of actions,
-  combined revolutions of the body,
    15.23

part of foot contacting in mixed support
    situations, 22.4
path(s),
-  ,cartwheel, *S*14
    -- ,aerial, 15.12
    -- with a turn, 15.24-25
-  ,circular, 6.6, 21.19, 22.7, 25.5-6
    -- around a fixed point, 6.10-12
-  ,performer's, 18.11
-  ,resultant, 16.12
-  ,somersault, *S*14
    -- ,aerial, 15.12
    -- ,with a turn, 15.18-22
-  ,spatial retention for, 15.15-17
-  ,straight, 6.1-4, 24.3, app.B.3
path signs,
-  in DBP, 8.15
-  , somersault and cartwheel, 14.1-3,
    14.13
Pendleton, Moses, 24.2, 24.6, 25.1
*Piazzolla Caldera*, 25.5, 27.2
Pilates, 23.4, 26.2
pins, app.B
-  ,black, 8.5, 8.9, 12.9, 12.11, 13.13,
    16.6, app.B.2-3
    -- for lateral tracks, 18.10-13
    -- for tracks, *S*18
    -- for sagittal tracks, 18.6-9
-  combining black pins and tack pins,
    app.B.8-9
-  ,flat, 5.14, 18.4, app.B.5-7
-  for all-fours situations, app.B.10-13
-  for axes, 16.4, 16.9-10
-  ,tack, app.B.5-7
-  ,track, *S*19; 1.5-6, app.A, app.B.4
    -- for all fours, 19.20-5
    -- for diagonal leg gestures, app.A.12
    -- for diagonal steps, app.A.13
    -- for lateral steps, 19.18-19
    -- for lateral leg gestures, app.A.11
    -- for leg gestures, 19.10
    -- for the arms, app.A.2, app.A.4-10
    -- for sagittal leg gestures, 19.12
    -- for supporting on the hands, 19.13-
    14
    -- for vertical leg gestures, 19.11
    -- sagittal, 19.4-5
point of measurement,
-  central place method, 5.8
-  direction-from-body-part indications
    (DBP), 8.10-12
positions of the arm, app.A.10

preferred usage of split body method,
    9.16
present location in DBP, 8.24
-    of another part, 8.30
pre-signs, 22.1-3, 22.12, 22.14
-    on center staff line, 22.1-3
previous location in DBP, 8.23
-    of a 'lifted' part, 8.28-29
-    of same body part, 8.27

range of pins for axes, 16.9-10
reading examples, *S*23-27
-    cartwheel and turn combined, 27.4
-    cartwheeling,27.1-2
-    cartwheeling on bar, 27.3
-    central 'place', 24.1
-    direction from body part, 24.6-11
-    isolated body part signs in support
     columns, 24.2-4
-    log-rolling, *S*26
-    on 'all fours', *S*24
-    somersaults, *S*26
-    statement of limb direction, 24.5
-    supporting on the hands, 23.1
-    supporting on the hands and
     shoulders, *S*23
-    supporting on the shoulders and
other body parts, 23.2-4
-    turning, *S*25
reference to,
-    a static support in DBP, 8.25-26
-    part of the floor in DBP, 8.36
release,
-    by indication of
     - action strokes, 21.13-15
     - gesture, 21.11-12
     - release signs, 21.16-17
-    of contact, 19.25, 21.5, 21.18, 22.6,
     24.2, 25.2, 26.1
retention,
-    ,automatic, 21.6-9
-    ,explicit statement of, 21.10
-    of weight, 21.10, 21.19
-    signs, 12.15, 12.18, 21.2, 22.1
revolutions of the body, part III, *S*15;
     14.1
-    $\frac{1}{2}$ turn, 11.17, 14.12, 15.20, 15.24
-    $\frac{1}{4}$ turn, 11.13, 11.23, 13.17, 24.11,
     25.2
-    $\frac{1}{8}$ turn around the spinal axis, 11.12
-    $\frac{1}{8}$ turn around the vertical line of
     gravity, 11.10-11
-    change of torso direction, 11.19-24
-    ,combined, *S*15
-    overlap of actions, 15.23
-    spatial retention for revolution or
     path, 15.15-17
-    statement of axis, 11.4-6
-    somersaulting, *S*12; 13.4, 13.25
     -- in the air, 12.12-19, 12.21-23, 26.6
-    turning around the vertical line of
     gravity, 11.10-11

-    turning around the vertical or spinal
     axis, *S*11
-    turning on all fours, 11.6-9
-    turn with somersault, 15.18-22
rolls,
-    ,somersault, 12.3-10, 13.8, 26.3, 26.5
rotation,
-    ,degree of, 14.6, 16.6
-    ,other axes of, *S*16

sagittal,
-    axis, 13.2, 13.18
-    center lines, 19.6-9
-    leg gestures, 19.12
-    track pins, 19.4-5, 19.19, app.A.2,
     app.A.5, app.A.7
-    tracks, 18.6-9, 18.14-17, 19.3-5, app.
     A.7
     - for backward arm gestures, app.A.7
     - for hands, 18.17
     - for knees, 18.14-16, 18.17
same spot caret, 22.16-18
shoulder stand, 3.5-6, 12.7, 23.4
sitting,
-    ,cartwheeling in, 13.20-24
somersault, *S*12, *S*14
-    analysis, 12.1-2
-    axis, 12.2, 12.9, 13.2
-    distance, 14.8, 14.14-15
-    double, 12.21-22, 14.12
-    front, 14.6-7
-    ,indication of degree of, 12.4-5,
     12.11, 12.16
-    paths, *S*14
-    placement of sign, 12.12-14, 12.22
-    reading examples, 26.1-3, 26.5-6
-    ,release sign within, 12.15-16
-    rolls, 12.1, 12.3-10, 12.14, 12.20,
     13.8, 16.14, 26.3
-    symbols, 12.1
-    traveling, 12.20-22
-    written with direction symbols, 12.23
somersaulting, *S*12
-    backward, 12.1
-    direction, 14.5
-    indication of a trampoline, 12.19
-    in the air, 12.1, 12.12-18, 12.20-21
-    forward, 12.1, 12.22-23, 26.6
-    ,simultaneous - and pivoting actions,
     15.10
spatial retention for revolution or path,
     15.15-17
split body, *S*9; 4.8, 19.22
-    foot and hand positions, 9.4, 9.7, 9.14
-    key, 4.8, 9.6, 9.8, 9.13, 24.2
-    prefered usage, 9.16,
-    walking patterns, 9.9-12
-    with gesture indications for the arms,
     9.13-15
spinal axis,
-    ,turning around the, *S*11, 22.9
'spot hold' for retention of weight, 6.10,
     8.8

statement of limb direction,
- reading examples, 24.5
straight path, 2.5, 6.1-6.4, 6.6, 14.15,
15.15, 15.25, 24.3, app.B.3
support,
- ,momentary auxilary, 22.19-20
Supporting
- on all fours, 21.4-5
- on other body parts, 21.4-5
- on the elbows, S3
- on the fingers, 1.14
- on the hands, S1, S23; 1.1-1.9, 19.9,
  19.13-14
- on the shoulders, S23; 21.12
- reading examples, S23
- ,track pins for, 19.13-17
- track pins for - on the feet, 19.15-17
Szentpál, Maria, 9.2, 9.4-5, 18.11,
  app.B.1

tack pins,
- combined with black pins, app.B.8-9
Taylor, Paul, 25.5, 27.2
time sign, 7.8, 20.15
timing,
- ,indication of, 20.12-14
touching gestures, 8.9
torso directional indication, 10.2
- options, 10.2
torso directions,
- ,change of, 11.19-24
- augmented body sections, 10.9-13,
  24.8
- inverted body sections, 10.3
track pins, S19
- definition, 19.1
- for all fours, 19.20-29
- for arm gestures, app.A.9-10
- for diagonal leg gestures, app.A.12
- for diagonal steps, 19.26-27,
  app.A.13
- for lateral leg gestures, 19.18,
  app.A.11
- for leg gestures, 19.10-12
- for sagittal leg gestures, 19.12
- for supporting on the hands, 1.5-6,
  19.13-14
- for supports on the feet, 19.11
- lateral steps, 19.18-19
  - on all fours, 19.20-25, 19.28-29
- ,sign for sagittal, 19.4
- ,use of, S19, app.A
tracks,
- black pins for lateral tracks, 18.10-13
- black pins for sagittal tracks,18.6-9
- diagonal tracks for the arms,
  app.A.2-3
- ,intermediate, 19.4, 19.14, 19.18,
  19.20, app.A.4-5, app.A.13, app.B.4
- lateral tracks for the arms, app.A.4-6
- ,normal, 19.2
- ,sagittal, 19.3
- sagittal - for the arms, app.A.7

- use of black pins, S18
- vertical tracks for the arms,
  app.A.8
trampoline, 13.13, 13.25, 13.27, 14.8,
  14.14, 15.3, 15.18, 15.20
- ,indication of, 12.19
traveling,
- somersault, 12.5, 12.20, 12.22
- cartwheel, 13.10, 13.15-17
turn,
- and cartwheel, 15.24-25
- areial, 12.13-15, 15.5
- blind, 2.1, 2.3, 2.7, 11.21, 13.7,
  13.11, 13.16
- log rolling, S26; 11.7, 11.12, 12.20,
  15.4, 22.12
- pivot, 11.2, 11.4, 11.6, 11.20-21,
  12.9, 13.4, 15.2, 15.10, 26.6, 27.4
- secret, 11.22, 16.13-14, 27.3
- with somersault, 15.18-22
turning,
- around the vertical or spinal axis,
  S11
- on all fours, 11.6-10
- on the hands, S2
- on the spot, 19.28

Uris, Victoria, 24.4, 25.2, 26.3
use of
- black pins for tracks, S18; 19.19
- columns, S20
- track pins, S19

validity, S21; 6.5
- of support indications, S21
vertical,
- axis, 11.2, 11.4, 11.11, 11.21, 12.9-
  10, 13.23, 13.26, 15.2, 15.4, 15.8,
  15.13, 16.12, 22.6
- leg gestures, 19.11
- line of gravity, 11.1-2, 11.4, 11.10,
  25.3
- tracks for the arms, app.A.8

Walking
- on the hands, 1.7-12
weight released, 21.18
- sign, 21.5
Wiener, Nina, 24.7

zed caret, 8.29, 21.8, 22.18

# Useful Contact Information

Language of Dance Centre
17 Holland Park
London W11 3TD
United Kingdom
Tel: +44 (0) 20 7229 3780
Fax: +44 (0) 20 7792 1794
email: info@lodc.org
www.lodc.org

Dance Notation Bureau Extension
The Ohio State University
Department of Dance
1813 N. High Street
Columbus OH 43210-1307
USA
Tel: +1 614 292 7977
Fax: +1 614 292 0939
web: http://www.dance.ohio-state.edu
e-mail: marion.8@osu.edu

Language of Dance Center
1972 Swan Pointe Drive
Traverse City
MI 49686
USA
Tel: +1 231 995 0998
Fax: +1 231 995 0998
email: Tinalodc@aol.com

The Labanotation Institute
The University of Surrey
Guildford
Surrey GU2 5XH
United Kingdom
Tel: +44 (0)1483 259 351
Fax: +44 (0)1483 300 803
e-mail: J.Johnson-
Jones@Surrey.ac.uk

Dance Notation Bureau
151 West 30th Street, Suite 202
New York NY 10001
USA
Tel: +1 212 564 0985
Fax: +1 212 904 1426
web: http://www.dancenotation.org/
e-mail: notation@mindspring.com

Andy Adamson
Department of Drama and Theatre
Arts
University of Birmingham
P.O. Box 363
Birmingham B15 2TT
United Kingdom
e-mail: a.j.adamson@bham.ac.uk